FEEDING THE MEDIA BEAST

FEEDING THE MEDIA BEAST

An Easy Recipe for Great Publicity

Mark Mathis

Purdue University Press
West Lafayette, Indiana

Printed in the United States of America

Library of Congress Cataloging-in-Publication Data

Mathis, Mark, 1961–
  Feeding the media beast : an easy recipe for great
publicity / Mark Mathis.
     p. cm.
  ISBN 1-55753-247-8
 1. Publicity. I. Title.
  HM1226 .M38 2002
  659.2—dc21

                       2002004478

For Dianne, my grace

CONTENTS

Acknowledgments

Thank you to the following people
who helped birth this book.

For their inspiration
Jack Trout, Steve McKee, Albert Baca

For their editorial sweat
Bruce Carpenter, Margaret Hunt,
Steve Lawrence, Renée Jones

For their patience
Dianne, Weston, Waverly, and Doc

◆ ◆ ◆

Publicity Simplified

The author who benefits you most is not the one who tells you something you did not know before, but the one who gives expression to the truth that has been dumbly struggling in you for utterance.

—Oswald Chambers

Complexity is the enemy. Fundamental truth is our friend. But you already knew that—even though you didn't read it in a headline. Prepare to be surprised by how much you know. Prepare to be shocked that you didn't know you knew it.

You want positive, high-impact—and not to mention free— publicity that drives success in our media-crazed culture. Who doesn't? But how do you get it, keep it coming, and in the process not get burned? Countless public relations professionals and media gurus promise they have the answers to these questions, and some of them do. The problem is, they have more answers than anyone outside the PR business would ever want to know. They've got advice and tips and strategies and dos and don'ts for every conceivable situation. It's a dizzying mess that's best left to experienced, high-priced experts, right? WRONG. Getting great publicity is not nearly as complicated as it seems or as tricky as some PR gurus would like you to believe.

The premise of this book is simple. To win the publicity game you must play by the Media Rules. There are only a dozen, and they are as plain as the nose on your face. These Rules are not my Rules. They are the Rules of the game that were established by the Media Beast—the all-encompassing term for the press. The Beast follows these 12 Rules religiously, which makes him extremely predictable. When you know what the Beast needs, you've got a practical, logical system for getting what you want—publicity. It's not complicated. It's fundamental truth—most of which is already in your head.

A Fresh Look at Publicity

As you can already tell, this book is written from the contrarian point of view. The "experts" claim that consistently winning news exposure is a sophisticated art form. In fact, some like to call it "the art of spin." Specialists in the field are referred to as "spinmeisters" or "spin-doctors." They belong to an elite club that charges high prices for its services. One such expert wrote a book about his spinning exploits, and in the preface he warned his readers that it takes "years of studying, more years of understanding, and still more time to refine your own style and skills." He claimed that it's a "business of subtleties—and it is one's ability to appreciate those subtleties that often makes the difference between winning and losing in the court of public opinion." To that I respectfully say, "HOGWASH!"

Please don't misunderstand me. I am not calling this gentleman a liar. He truly believes that effectively utilizing the power of the press demands the skill of a high-wire performer. That's because he has spent a lot of time working through his own intricate, subtle, highly complex way of managing all the minutiae of the PR business. Through the years, he has developed a fine, *intuitive* sense of how to get the most out of news reporters. It works for him, but then again, his entire life is devoted to "spinning." You, however, do not have the time, the resources, or the patience to learn how to become a *publicity artist*. But more importantly, it's completely unnecessary. Forget complexity, and forget paying high-priced spin doctors, while you're at it. You don't need them.

What you do need is a *systematic* understanding of how all publicity works. You need something easy to learn, easy to remember, and easy to apply. You need the Media Rules methodology, fundamental truth that will enable you quickly to work your way through virtually any publicity situation.

Why the Media Rules Work

Think about the activities of life in their most basic terms. So much of what we do is centered on acquiring knowledge and then using it to make our lives better. Put another way: learn it, use it, and get good at it. Oh, if it were only that easy. Wouldn't you like to "know" everything you ever "learned"? How much material from that biology class do you remember? How about those geometry formulas? The fact of the matter is most of us have lost far more knowledge than we have retained. Learning isn't the problem—it's keeping the learning that's so difficult.

It is estimated that 90 percent of people who take short-term seminars never apply what they learn. The same is true for those who read self-help books. The roots of this problem are obvious. First, attempting to absorb a massive amount of new information in a short period of time doesn't work. It's like the college student who crams all night. He passes the test, but within a week his short-term memory has dumped the information, and 98 percent of it is gone forever. Second, a significant majority of books and seminars offer up a lot of new information that is delivered in the form of long lists of dos, don'ts, tips, and strategies. There are no reference points for this new knowledge—no skeleton upon which to attach the information. And because this "learning" is not connected in a systematic, logical fashion, bits and pieces begin to float away. They are quickly booted out of your brain space by other, more immediate concerns. It's a downward spiral from there. Because the information fragments so quickly, there is little opportunity to actually put the theory into practice. You don't use it, so you lose it.

The Media Rules methodology avoids these problems because it does not require you to learn a lot of new, disconnected information. This is stuff you already know. You just need a little help in looking at publicity from a different angle. Once you witness how the Rules work, you will wonder how you could have missed seeing what now appears to be so obvious. Best of all, the Media Rules do not stand alone. They are part of a network. Each Rule reinforces all the others, making them easier to remember. And that's the key. Because you retain the Rules, you use the Rules. The more you apply the system, the more it becomes ingrained in the way you think. Ultimately, you won't have to think about the Rules much at all because you will view all publicity opportunities through this framework. The big payoff is that your systematic knowledge will be more powerful and effective than the intuition of all those so-called "spin doctors."

The Belly of the Beast

There are four vulnerabilities common to all news outlets. These are the forces that drive the wants, needs, and desires of the News Beast.

As you will see in chapter 1, the Beast is Handicapped, Harried, Hungry, and Human. These key weaknesses—the soft underbelly of an industry that doesn't want you to know how vulnerable it really is—have a tremendous impact on how journalists do their jobs.

Once you have a good understanding of the Beast's instinctual drive, you will have no difficulty recognizing and using the Rules to feed this fascinating creature. Even though few journalists consciously recognize the Media Rules, they obediently follow them nonetheless. It's kind of like having a diagram of the Beast's hot buttons. Push this one to get a reporter's undivided attention. Push that one to become his friend. Avoid that one at all costs because it will bring down his wrath.

The Media Rules fit into four categories: Seducers, Enablers, Aggressors, and Hazards. The Seducers are the three basic elements that attract all journalists. Yes, there are *only* three. The Enablers are the three rules that must be followed to put the Seducers to work. Remember, the system is *active*. The Aggressors are the three principles that any publicity seeker needs to follow *consistently* to generate free exposure. That's the value of having a system —it can be used over and over again. Finally, the Hazards are the three troubleshooters that will help you evade *bad* publicity. In those cases where it cannot be avoided, a good grasp of the Hazards will greatly minimize the damage. As an added bonus, the same Rules that get you great publicity also show you how to deliver excellent soundbites and quotes.

How about it? What do you say we meet the Beast? Don't worry. All that roaring you hear is the product of myth, mystery, and misconception.

CHAPTER 1

◆ ◆ ◆

The Nature of the Beast

So here he is—napkin on the lap, a fresh glass of water, clean silver-ware, and a menu of absolutely delectable publicity items. The TV-Bone Steak sounds too juicy to pass up, but the Baby-back of the front-page ribs are pretty tempting as well. What kind of salad should he get—an Internet Caesar or a tossed magazine? And look at those deserts!—rhubarb radio pie, newsprint pudding, and feature story cheesecake. Who could possibly have just one? Better order all three and have a sound-bite of each. Boy, this guy looks pretty hungry. Where is that waiter anyway?

I've got news for our publicity-starved diner. The waiter isn't coming. In fact, the News Café doesn't employ any waiters, nor does it serve any food. In this odd media restaurant, the proprietors are the ones who devour the grub while the *customers* toil in the kitchen and scurry among the tables.

There is a fundamental problem in the way many people perceive the publicity game. As they ponder what sort of news coverage they want, their attention is focused in the wrong direction—on themselves. They're thinking, "What kind of tasty cuisine can the news media serve me?" That's the wrong question. What any publicity seeker should understand is that you must give in order to receive. The Media Beast is eager to grant you the most powerful form of marketing known to man. However, in order to receive this gift, you must serve up a storyline that the Beast cannot resist.

Of course, there is a problem that must be addressed. Feeding the Beast isn't as straightforward as it might sound. You need to know how to handle this customer because he's a little quirky. (Get used to it—*he's* the customer, not you.) There are times when he can't be bothered, and other times when he is starved for attention. The Beast hates mayonnaise and cooked spinach, but he will eat tuna fish sandwiches and spinach salad. He gorges on meat and potatoes and desserts but wouldn't touch a beet for all the Angus in Texas. And, never, ever attempt to hold onto any food that he has demanded. The Beast will not hesitate to bite your hand off—or worse.

In order to get the quantity and quality publicity you want, you need two things. First, you must know your customer better than he knows himself. That's the material we will cover in this chapter. As you will soon see, the news media are not nearly so mysterious as they seem. Once you understand the handicaps and motivations of the Beast, you will then need to play by the Media Rules—12 requirements that are consistent among all media. The Rules are amazingly simple. You already know most of them; you just don't know that you know them.

Are you ready to put on an apron, grill some steak, toss some salad, and be really nice to a highly irritable glutton? It may sound like hard duty, and sometimes it can be, but wonderful rewards await those who learn that before you get your publicity pie, you must first serve the Beast.

The "Corporatization" of the Media

Journalists are not the enemy. In spite of what you have been led to believe, news people are not dangerous vipers. To the contrary, the vast majority of folks who work in the business are passionate professionals who want to make the world a better place. They tend to be idealists, but that's a good thing. Our democracy would not work without them. Journalists are not the enemy, but the corporations they work for, well . . . let's just say that many of them could use a good flogging.

In this book I will repeatedly refer to the "Beast," which is an all-encompassing term for the system that pushes the news gathering process. Therefore, the Beast is the newsroom—not the editor, the corporate ownership—not the news director, the medium—not the reporter. It's an important distinction to make, because those who form successful partnerships with the Media Beast are accepting of how offensively blunt the *system* can often be. While you may disdain the weaknesses of the institution, you should have great empathy for those who toil within. These people are your ticket to winning great publicity.

Journalism has never been an easy business. It has always demanded its people labor long hours for minimal pay. The work environment is messy, loud, and contentious. Reporters must ask nice people hard questions. They must reduce complex issues to a manageable form—which tends to upset those closest to the story. It's difficult (albeit highly rewarding) work. Only the hardy need apply. I remember when I was still relatively new to the business I was given a plaque from the California Conservation Corps that contained the CCC's motto: Hard work, low pay, miserable conditions, and much, much more. I set it on my desk, where it stayed for a few hours, until my boss noticed it. He told me to make the sign disappear. Guess the message hit a little too close to home.

As hard as it was to be a reporter then (1986), it's a lot harder now. In the past decade, the media landscape has undergone sweeping changes that have all but eviscerated the profession. In a word, the news business has become "corporatized." Journalists Robert Kunkel and Gene Roberts thoroughly document the problem in their book *Leaving Readers Behind: The Age of Corporate Journalism* (2001, University of Arkansas Press). As Kunkel and Roberts demonstrate, "Relentless corporatization is now culminating in a furious, unprecedented blitz of buying, selling, and consolidating of newspapers, from the mightiest dailies to the humblest weeklies." As of this writing, three massive conglomerates (Gannett, Knight-Ridder, Chicago Tribune Co.) own a quarter of all daily newspaper circulation. And it's not just newspapers. These mega-media corporations and others are buying up TV affiliates, radio stations, and magazines at an alarming rate. Fewer and fewer companies are controlling more and more print space and broadcast time.

Why should you care about these changes? Because the corporate bean counters have a strategy—consolidate, streamline, do more with less, and above all else, make lots of money, which they do. Most media outlets are enormously lucrative ventures, where profit margins of 20 to 30 percent are quite common. The price to be paid for this corporatization (aside from greatly degrading the profession—not the subject of this book) is that the stresses of the business have been amplified. The people whose job it is to actually produce the news are being squeezed in a most unhealthy way.

For you, the publicity seeker, this is a bad news/good news situation. The bad news is that the Beast has become far more dangerous. The extreme conditions in most newsrooms—leaner staffs, fewer experienced journalists, more work with less time to do it— mean the chances of getting unfairly burned in the press are greater than ever. But the good news is that there are incredible opportunities for people who know how to use this pressure to their advantage. In order to accomplish this task, we will reduce the Beast's problems to a simple, manageable form.

In the following pages, I will make generalizations for which there will be exceptions. Our goal is to seize upon a small number of consistencies that are true for the vast majority of news providers. I will make a few distinctions where needed, but very few. This simplification makes the task of understanding the Beast easier and more efficient. Now, let's take a closer look at the Beast's four primary weaknesses—limitations that the Media Rules exploit. The Beast is Handicapped, Hungry, Harried, and Human.

The Beast Is Handicapped

Today's news people are ill suited for the job of journalist. Basically, they are *under: under*-educated, *under*-paid, and *under*-appreciated, not to mention *under*-age. (I warned you of the generalizations.) Because of the squeeze being applied by corporate bosses, the job requires more from them than they are capable of delivering. The demands of the news environment have, for the most part, exceeded the capabilities of those who work within it.

Reporting is for the young. Few people in their mid-30s and up are willing to endure the pain, stress, and health-depleting lifestyle of a frontline news gatherer. Therefore, the majority of local reporters, and many on the national level, fall within the age range of 22 to 40, and that category is skewing younger all the time. While reporters have always been the youngest members of the newsgathering profession, the corporatization of the business has made it even less mature. The reason is that reporters with pimples don't cost as much as those with a few gray hairs—not that seasoned journalists have ever been paid much more than blue-collar wages.

When I became a reporter in the mid-80s, journalism school graduates typically started their careers at small town newspapers and small market radio and television stations. They would put in a couple of years and then jump to a bigger city, spend some time there, and then jump again. While this progression of media-hopping is still the norm, the pace has been greatly accelerated. In fact, the most promising journalism students are able to skip the small cities altogether. It used to take ten years to get to places like Los Angeles, New York, Denver, Dallas, Miami, and Washington—and that was if you were good. Now, a journalist can find herself in the big city within a year or two out of college.

The youth movement in American journalism may be good for the scalpel-wielding corporate bosses, but those who had hoped to make news their lifetime profession are not happy. To get an ear full of their discontent just log on to any one of the websites dedicated to airing the businesses' dirty laundry—<TVSpy.com>, <NewsBlues.com>, and the vulgarly named <f___edTelevision.com>. One NewsBlues poster suggested that the call letters of WNGX in Atlanta be changed to WGNX because they now stand for "We've Got No eXperience in this market." An employee at KRON in San Francisco publicly wondered if the station's parent company would "Hire enough staff to cover the additional newscasts? And will that staff possess college diplomas with dry ink?" It's the same story at newspapers, magazines, and radio. People with little newsgathering experience (let alone life experience) are in charge of giving us the news of the day.

Unfortunately, the youth movement in the media only begins at the reporter position. It extends deep into the newsroom as well. You can't cut resources, freeze pay, increase the workload, hire less-experienced staff and expect to keep your best people. More and more seasoned journalists have discovered that they can reduce their stress, increase their salary, and generally improve their lives by simply getting out (yours truly is one case in point). The median age and experience level of editors, producers, news directors, and photographers have dropped precipitously. At one station where I worked in the early 1990s, my life was controlled by three producers in their mid-20s. None of them had ever interviewed anyone, had ever reported on a single story in the field, or had ever stood in front of a live camera. Their lack of understanding of what it took to get the job done made my days extremely difficult. This kind of frustration is the rule rather than the exception.

Andrew Cohen, editor of *Athletic Business*, gives basic tests to people who apply for editorial positions at his publication. Most applicants fail—miserably. This self-described curmudgeon (at the ripe, old age of 39) says you would be astonished at how many would-be editors fail his test in the first sentence of their applications. "One guy, the news editor and chief copy editor of his college paper, misspelled the name of the local newspaper in which we ran the ad," said the frustrated editor. In the end, Cohen and others like him must hire the grammatically challenged and hope to educate them properly (like the applicant who promised "superb grammar, spelling, and *puncuation* skills"). Mind you, we aren't talking about the craft of telling a balanced story, but the simple mechanics of correctly putting words on paper.

The movement toward an even younger journalism workforce presents an interesting and difficult problem for the news industry—and for those of us who wish to seize publicity. The historic mission of the news business has been to gather information relevant to the community, reduce it, refine it, double-check it, and then release a well-processed product. However, intense corporate pressure to produce more news faster has made this goal largely unattainable. The mission has changed. In the 21st century, the Beast is bulimic. The new objective is to absorb as much information as possible and then regurgitate it at lightning speed. Along the way there's little time to actually learn about the topics that are being reported on.

Journalists typically know little about the stories they are covering. In fact, even before the recent trend toward youth, the news business was described as "the craft of explaining to others that which journalists know nothing about." News people don't learn much about business, government, politics, the law, or any other subject in college. What they study is the craft of gathering information and the presentation of that information in a print or broadcast format. After J-school, when graduates *become* journalists, they still acquire little or no real-world experience outside the news envelope. Even those who spend time reporting on a specific "beat" (crime, health, education, etc.) do so from a distant outsider position. As we will soon see, the people who work for the Beast experience the world from a completely different viewpoint from yours. Therefore, their worldview is also different. But first, let's take a closer look at the Beast's voracious appetite.

The Beast is Hungry

As any good publicity hound should know, the way to the Beast's heart is through his stomach. The news animal is hungry. He is always hungry. The Beast is like the man in the movie *Diner* who managed to eat every entrée on the left side of the restaurant's menu and still have room for dessert. Actually, the news animal is much worse. It sits at an all-you-can-eat buffet table 24 hours a day and still complains of hunger pangs.

Do we really need all those network news magazine shows? Of course not, but they are cheap to produce (and people still tune in) so the corporate bosses have packed the airwaves with them. In 1996, NBC, ABC, CBS, CNN, and FOX dedicated 26 hours a month to hour-long newsmagazine shows. By 2001, that number had more than tripled. The networks save hundreds of millions of dollars by *not* producing expensive sitcoms and dramas. Did you know, for example, that in the 2001 season each of the six regulars on NBC's *Friends* made $750,000 per episode? That's $4.5 million a show before a script, a camera, a set, a production staff, and a thousand other expenses! With these kinds of numbers, it's easy to see why the networks are so in love with shows such as "Dateline," "20/20," and "60 Minutes" that cost peanuts to produce.

But that's only the beginning. The networks also save a bundle by double, triple, and even quadruple dipping. Stories produced for the evening news can be altered to fit the newsmagazine format, the morning news, and network specials. No telling how many actors and actresses have had their shot at fame sacrificed on the alter of info-tainment. Network news executives subscribe to the philosophy of Gordon Gecko from the movie *Wall Street:* "Greed is good." Corporate owners of local television affiliates agree with Gecko's good greed philosophy as well.

. . . the way to the Beast's heart is through his stomach. The news animal is . . . always hungry.

Not so long ago, most local stations (except in large markets) were content to produce less than two hours of news a day. Typically, there was a half-hour of news at six P.M. and another 30 minutes at ten or eleven. Five-minute "cut-ins" were wedged into network morning shows. Some stations put on a half-hour of news at noon. That was it. But local stations learned from the networks that increasing news product while simultaneously reducing overhead could fatten the bottom line.

Rather than spend money on costly syndicated programming, local stations began expanding their time allotment for news. In 1994, I worked at a station that produced 12 hours of news a week. Within three years, that station had expanded to nearly 30 hours and has since exceeded 40. In most markets, morning "cut-ins" have been replaced by full-blown newscasts, lasting 90 minutes or more. Hour-long noon newscasts are common. Late afternoon shows have also been added. Even the once sacred Saturday morning cartoons have been dumped or bumped up in favor of news. There is no escaping it. News reporting is everywhere, all the time.

As most local television stations have dramatically increased their news output, they have not correspondingly increased the number of reporters, producers, anchors, videotape editors, etc. Equipment (cameras, editing bays, computers, etc.) has been added but at a much leaner news-to-hardware ratio. The same can be said for the newsroom itself—less space per volume of work completed. Computerization has made journalists more efficient but not nearly enough to compensate for the increased pressure to produce more and do it faster. Many of the medium's advances in technology have actually compounded the workload problem.

In today's newscasts there are a lot more bells and whistles. All those headlines, banners, fancy graphics, animation, and audio enhancements that add energy to a newscast drain time away from the reporters and producers who must create them. Under these conditions, it's easy to see why the accuracy and reliability of the news product has taken a dive.

In November 2001, the Project for Excellence in Journalism (PEJ) published a disturbing report titled *"Gambling with the Future: local newsrooms beset by sponsor interference, budget cuts, layoffs, and added programming."* PEJ surveyed news directors at 118 stations around the country between June and August 2001.

Among the results of the confidential survey: half of all stations had suffered budget cuts in the previous year—a majority of which were unscheduled; two-thirds of the stations added broadcast hours; and 57 percent had to produce the same or more news despite layoffs, budget freezes, and budget cuts. One news director told PEJ, "We added product (newscasts), then three months later reduced staffing through a hiring freeze, and we're still producing the additional newscasts." Another news boss lamented, "The cutbacks have made a lean staff malnourished."

Of course, reporters, producers, and anchors are none too pleased. "Budget cuts have killed staff morale—no raises, a hiring freeze, no overtime," one news director told PEJ. Another grumbled about "a higher level of frustration over high expectations with not enough resources." Unfortunately for the TV news folks, the trend is showing no sign of abating. And, there's not much of a temptation to take their experience and run to a newspaper. Conditions there are just as bad.

As I noted earlier, media conglomerates are in vogue in the news business today. When a mega-media company purchases a newspaper, the staff almost always gets cut, leaving fewer journalists to do the work. The *Asbury Park Press*, New Jersey's second largest newspaper, is a typical example. In 1997, Gannett, the largest newspaper company on the planet, purchased the *Press*. Within one year, the staff was slashed from 240 people to 185.

A secondary impact of fewer corporations owning large numbers of media outlets is that competition is reduced or eliminated. With little or no pressure to compete for readers, viewers, or listeners, it's easy to "streamline" through the fat, past the muscle, and into the bone—such as in underpaying, overworking, and generally mistreating already frazzled journalists. I think you can see the Beast's next big problem coming.

The Beast is Harried

In the hit film *Top Gun*, Maverick (Tom Cruise) declared: "I feel the need . . . the need for speed." In comparison to those who work in the news media, Maverick was an amateur. Jet pilots have a need for speed only intermittently. News people run at full throttle most of the day.

The primary reason for the frenetic behavior of journalists is that they face continuous, unrelenting deadlines. The six o'clock news comes at six o'clock every day (so does the 5 A.M., Noon, 5 P.M., and 10 or 11 P.M.). The morning newspaper must be printed and delivered to the distribution dock at the appointed hour every morning. News is broadcast via the radio on the hour and half-hour. Of course, this schedule is under the constant threat of being preempted by "breaking news," in which new deadlines are spontaneously added. The journalist's life is chaotic, to say the least.

It was ten minutes before a midday newscast in Las Vegas, Nevada, when my 24-year-old producer raced to my cubicle. She told me that we had dramatic video of a tree trimmer who had tangled with a power line. She gave me a few facts and told me to type up a quick story on this man who had been "electrocuted." I whipped it out and quickly headed to the anchor chair. Moments later I was telling our audience, "A Las Vegas man is dead at this hour, following an accident with a power line . . ." The words had barely left my mouth before the producer began screaming at me through my earpiece that the man was not dead. During the first commercial break I explained to the producer that when people are electrocuted, they stop breathing—permanently. This is the kind of scene that gets played out at news organizations across the country every day. Is it any wonder that the credibility of journalists has greatly suffered because of the abundance of mistakes made under pressure?

And as if the journalist didn't already have enough to worry about, the Internet came along. It has helped to accelerate the pace of news delivery by allowing any news organization with the desire and the resources to update stories, minute by minute, if need be. Could the corporate bosses possibly heap any more pressure on our beleaguered journalists? When Fox ordered 11 more episodes of its critically-acclaimed drama "24" during the fall 2001 season, one newsman posted his concern on <TVSpy.com>: "Although I enjoy the show, I'm not so sure I like the idea, because if the show continues for 11 more episodes/hours, that means our employers might think there are actually 35 hours in a day and make us work more than we already do." To fulfill his duties, the Harried Beast must constantly run. It's enough to exhaust the Energizer Bunny.

If two TV stations cover the same story on the same day, who determines which story is done the best? Which reporter was most fair, accurate, or comprehensive? The fact is few people will watch competing versions of the same story. The audience of one newscast will not know how competing stations covered the same story unless they are actively trying to make a comparison— which isn't often.

So how is the audience to know which news operation is doing the best job? Because standards of accuracy, fairness, thoroughness, and relevancy are ambiguous, impractical measurements, the only marketable item left (aside from awards and ratings) is speed. That's why there is such intense pressure to tell the story first, even if you beat the competition by only a minuscule margin. In the world of broadcast news, being able to say, "as we were the first to report . . . " carries the implied message that "we are the most competent," a powerful marketing tool. (An exclusive story is something truly worth bragging about.)

Newspapers used to enjoy this same spirited race, but because most dailies have no print competition, the need to whisk a story along is not what it once was. Nevertheless, because of understaffing, print organizations are still in a big hurry to finish the day's work.

The craziness of having to be "the first to report" reached unprecedented heights in the presidential election of 2000. As polls closed on election night, the Voters News Service (VNS) made a mistake in projecting Vice President Al Gore as the winner of Florida's 25 electoral votes. (VNS is a consortium funded by the networks to conduct exit polling so winners can be projected long before all the votes are counted.)

VNS was undoubtedly feeling pressure from the networks to quickly make the call in this key state. After returns from heavily Republican districts came in, VNS and the networks were forced to retract the Florida projection and declare the Sunshine State too close to call. A few hours later Fox News declared that Texas governor George W. Bush had won Florida. Apparently believing that Fox knew something they didn't, all the other major networks rushed to declare Bush the victor in Florida as well and, therefore, the next president because the state's 25 electoral votes would have cinched the election.

In the harried panic to name the next president for their viewers, the networks ignored the fact that Fox—*not* VNS—had called Florida for Bush. Of course, they all had egg (or as NBC's Tom Brokaw put it, an omelet) on their faces when less than an hour later the projection had to be recalled a second time.

Accuracy is the first casualty of haste. It's as true for the networks as it is for your local TV station or newspaper. That's why so many people fear the Beast—he makes a lot of mistakes that hurt those who are in the news. But the Beast's youthful haste is not something you will fear, once you use the Rules to turn the media's vulnerabilities to your advantage.

The Beast is Human

You now know a lot more about the frustrating lives that today's journalists are leading. There's no need to belabor that point any further. However, we do need to take a closer look at the kind of person who works in the belly of the Beast. Even if you set their frantic, aggravated existence aside, you will see that those who bring you the news from the outside world are not likely to be part of the culture that you live in. This is an important point. Because journalists are Human, they see the world the way *they* see it, and that has a direct impact on how stories are told—or not told.

In general, news people consider themselves to be part of the cultural elite. Whether or not they admit it to themselves, journalists tend to think they are smarter, more worldly, and, in general, more enlightened than the rest of us. But don't take my word for it. Consider the results of an eye-opening study conducted by *Orlando Sentinel* newspaper editor Peter Brown.

In 1994, Brown and a professional pollster surveyed journalists and ordinary people in five medium-sized cities around the United States and in one large metropolitan area. One hundred news people and 100 residents were polled in the cities of Dayton, Ohio; Roanoke, Virginia; Syracuse, New York; Tulsa, Oklahoma; and Chico/Redding, California. In Dallas/Fort Worth 300 journalists and residents were queried. Brown's study also analyzed the residential data of 3,400 news people. Using a system that classifies neighborhoods on a census block basis (a much smaller unit than a zip code), the study looked at how journalists live in contrast with others in the community. As any pollster will tell you, where you live says a lot about how you live. The results were interesting, to say the least.

According to the study, journalists are more likely than the average person to live in neighborhoods where residents are most likely to trade stocks, but less likely to go to church or do volunteer work. Brown found that journalists were over represented in neighborhoods where people are especially fond of foreign movies, fine wine, and espresso. As you might expect, these people are also much more likely to express disdain for the suburbs and rural areas. Brown concludes, "Journalists simply do not share political, religious, or monetary values with the general population."

Similar studies conducted by the Media Research Center <mrc.org> and other organizations confirm that journalists are also much more likely to support liberal positions such as abortion rights and gun control, while strongly identifying with people who claim to be society's victims. Conservative syndicated columnist John Leo occasionally writes about this social disconnect. Leo writes, "Reporters tend to be part of a broadly defined social and cultural elite, so their work tends to reflect the conventional values of this elite. The astonishing distrust of the news media by readers at large isn't rooted in inaccuracy or poor reportorial skills, but in the daily clash of worldviews between reporters and their readers." William McGowan, author of *Coloring the News,* echoes Leo's sentiment. In his book, McGowan documents how the Beast's love of left-wing political correctness has driven a wedge between the press and mainstream America. According to McGowan, "Much of the American public has the sense that news organizations have a view of reality at odds with their own and that reporting and commentary come from some kind of parallel universe."

Many Americans don't need a study to confirm what they already believe to be true: The media lean to the left. And why wouldn't they? The news professions attract liberal-minded people in the same way that businesses attract the conservative-minded. Those who want to make money flock to careers that are financially rewarding. They become bankers, entrepreneurs, lawyers, stockbrokers, and orthodontists. People curious about the physical world become geologists, biologists, astronomers, and physicists. Likewise, those who want to right the wrongs of the world—and achieve a measure of fame along the way—are drawn toward the news media.

Where do journalists come from? They are manufactured in America's universities in a liberal arts curriculum. Journalism schools teach students that they are "the voice of the people." Reporters are to stick up for the poor, the downtrodden, and the disadvantaged, in our sometimes-oppressive capitalist system. It is their job—so they are taught—to "comfort the afflicted and to afflict the comfortable." It's a noble and necessary calling, but there is a problem here. Chances are quite good that you will be classified as "comfortable," regardless of whether you are or not (much more on this in chapters 12 and 13, the Rules of Balance and Ambush). The point is that journalists are disconnected from the general population—and for more reasons than their politics or philosophical bent.

There is a motto in the news business: In order to move up, you must move around—a lot. The career ladder of the journalist will typically lead her through multiple cities and/or newsrooms in a short period of time. Unlike careers in the corporate world, the news business does not frown upon those who bounce from job to job. It is expected that a talented reporter, editor, producer, or photographer will serve two years or less in a given position before moving on to a larger city. Or, perhaps, the journalist will take a lateral or downward move to a better position. For example, the goal of a television reporter in Oklahoma City is to move up to Dallas or Kansas City. If he wants to be an anchor, he might move down to a smaller market such as Colorado Springs. In either case, the reporter assumes more status and/or salary. People who gather news for small newspapers aspire to do the same thing for larger newspapers. Some make their climb from within the walls of the same organization, but these folks are more the exception than the rule.

This excessive moving by those who gather the news of America's communities makes the Beast far more dangerous than it would otherwise be. How can a reporter be counted on to deliver accurate, relevant, and meaningful news when she is a relative new-comer and has little desire to be a long-timer? (Remember, I am generalizing. There are exceptions to the move-around-a-lot trend of young reporters.) "Just passing through," is a comment I heard, and even made, while working my way through New Mexico, Califor-nia, South Carolina, Nevada, and back to New Mexico. One friend and co-worker in California never unpacked his personal posses-sions in the year he was waiting to move on to a better job. He slept on a mattress on the floor and stored his clothes in open moving boxes. Would your life be much different if *you* were a journalist? Don't count on it. You're a human, too.

If you're not going to stay, there are other great disincentives to becoming part of a community—like getting married, buying a home, having children, establishing friendships outside the news business, etc. Therefore, many journalists live in an insular envi-ronment that is disconnected from yours—physically and socially. An industry truism is, "News is hard on mortgages and marriages, so wise journalists avoid them." In doing so, they sacrifice their connection to the community. It's not good for the profession, but as you will see, this gap between news gatherer and the outside world is your opening to powerful publicity opportunities.

A 4-H Rodeo

Throughout this book, I will keep reminding you of the news me-dia's four primary problems. The Beast is Handicapped because the people who work for him are *under—under*-educated, *under*-paid, *under*-appreciated, and *under* great stress. The industry that drives these poor souls is constantly *under*fed and *under* the gun to produce more with less. Therefore, the Beast is also Hungry and Harried. Finally, the Media Beast is Human. The difficult news environment shapes the behavior, attitudes, and lifestyle of journalists. And, because they are mere mortals, they have a difficult time setting aside, or even recognizing, their biases. It's a dark view, I know. But it's accurate—a quality that any journalist can appreciate.

There is a terrifically bright side to the dim picture I have painted. The Beast's four great difficulties are the foundation to your publicity success. Insider knowledge of the four H's is the key that unlocks the power of the Media Rules.

So saddle up. It's time to ride the Beast.

THE RULES

Ask just about anyone if he knows what "news" is. His immediate response will be, "Of course, I do." Really? Ask him to define it. Watch the confused reaction. Listen to the rambling, disjointed reply. Or, as in some cases, examine the vacuous stare that is the countenance of someone truly stumped.

Do you know what "news" is? Really?

It doesn't matter how long you've been a marketing director, a public relations specialist, an advertising executive, or even a journalist. No matter how many newspapers you've read or newscasts you've seen, I'm willing to bet you don't "know" what news is—not at its most basic level. Feel challenged? Then take the test.

Define it.

Pinpoint news in a single word.

Of course, you know the definition of news. You just don't know that you know it.

◆ ◆ ◆

CHAPTER 2

The Rule of Difference

~ importance is not important ~

What was your word? If you're like most people, you settled on a term like "information," "importance," "happenings," or "sensational." While all these words play a part in news, they are either too broad or too narrow. Most of them, however, point to an underlying assumption that news is something that bears a measure of relevance to our lives. It is in someway significant to the community.

This assumption is false. While news can be important, it very often is not. Seen, read, or heard any in-depth stories lately on radon contamination or deteriorating public infrastructure? Has your local newspaper explained how the crushing burden of taxes is strangling small business? How about all of the tax dollars that your city is paying to various public servants who have retired after only 20 years on the job? You've seen precious little of these kinds of stories because the news media are, for the most part, not compelled by the importance of the stories they cover or generate.

News is information that journalists believe people *want* to see, hear, or read. It is only occasionally—contrary to popular myth—information that people *need*. And what is it that people desire? They want what people have always wanted from those who have brought information from the outside world—something new. News is NEWs. To put a finer point on it, news is what's different.

Don't be overly concerned about your failure to immediately nail down the definition of "news." I've yet to meet anyone in marketing, advertising, public relations, or even in the news business who could quickly answer this seemingly obvious question. The truth is, I struggled greatly with the question, even with a degree in journalism, nearly a decade of reporting, and many years as a media consultant.

Grandma Bites Bowzer

Identify something different, and you have pegged a potential news story. The same cannot be said for the serious issues of life. To the news media, *importance is not important* unless it is also different.

For the Beast, importance is only one small measure for determining value. And it ranks relatively low on the list if you exclude clear and present danger. Other more treasured measurements are drama, scandal, tragedy, oddity, and comedy. What's the common denominator that runs through all of these? Difference.

The value of a news item is determined by how much it deviates from the norm. Therefore, "Dog Bites Man" is not a worthy story. Such incidents are all too common. "Man Bites Dog" isn't a whole lot better. How many times have you heard this example used to describe news as something out of the ordinary? Reporters are looking for something much more extraordinary, like, maybe an old man biting a dog—better yet, an old woman. Here's a headline for you: "Woman, 73, bites pit bull's neck to snatch own Scottie from jaws." Now, that's news! It also happens to be a real headline from a true story.

In June 2001, Tallahassee, Florida, resident Margaret Hargrove took her 9-month-old Scottish terrier out for a walk. Along the way a neighbor's pit bull pounced on the puppy, locking its powerful jaws on the dog's head. Grandma Hargrove tried to pull the pit bull's jaws apart but couldn't do it. So, she leaned over and chomped down on the dog's neck—twice. The pit bull yelped, let the Scottie go, and then attacked Hargrove, dragging her down the street by the arm. That's when 13-year-old Bradley Strawbridge ended it all by whacking the pit bull on the head with a bat. The *St. Petersburg Times* was the first to pick up the story. Then came NBC's "Today Show," followed by newspaper, TV, and radio reports that extended all the way to Canada, Australia, England, and who knows where else. Was Hargrove's story important? No, but it sure was different.

Of course, some of the news that reaches us through TV, radio, magazines, newspapers, and the Internet is important. The media will always cover wars, racial strife, natural disasters, major political debates, and other big picture news. (The Rule of Difference, by the way, is a big part of truly important news as well.) But the point I wish to make is that, for the most part, the Beast is addicted to the unique. The news media's level of interest for *any* story is connected directly to its difference.

When a man is critically injured after being run down by a car, it's a weak news item at best. If the victim is 86-years old, the story gets a little more interesting, but not much. If the old timer, George Dudley, of Medusa, New York, is sitting in a lawn chair in his front yard at the time of the accident, you've now got the attention of a few reporters. The story gets better—actually worse—when it's discovered that the "driver" was a 2-year-old child who wiggled herself out of her car seat and hit the gear lever of the idling minivan, while her mother was mailing some letters. Now you've got a story that gets widespread attention.

In many cases, it's not the news item itself that draws the

attention of journalists. It's the context surrounding the item that makes it interesting.

Do reporters think it's newsworthy when a utility trailer is stolen from the parking lot of a home improvement store? Not even on a really slow news day. Two trailers? Yawn. What if the thief swipes three trailers from the same store on the same morning? Getting warmer, but this is the kind of story that gets buried on the crime page. As you might have suspected, there's more.

On a bright spring day, an ambitious criminal stole a trailer from a Home Depot, but the trailer came off when he took a curve too fast during the getaway. Instead of reattaching his ill-gotten gain, the bandit went back for a second but also lost this one on the same curve. On the burglar's third attempt, he kept the trailer in tow but encountered a new problem. He clipped the cruiser of a police officer who was trying to figure out why two brand new but slightly damaged trailers were abandoned along the roadside. Our robber made the front page of a major daily newspaper with a large photo.

On July 23, 2001, Quixall Crossett, a 16-year-old gelding, failed to finish the Ropewalk Chambers Maiden Chase. Who cares? Horses are a lot like baseball players—they fail a majority of the time. That's true, but few horses have managed to fail quite so successfully as Quixall Crossett. On that summer day, the British horse lost its 100th consecutive race.

Pick up any newspaper. Watch any newscast. Listen to any radio report. Get online with any news website. All that you will see and hear is what's different outside your front door. Have you ever seen the headline, "Municipal Water System Still Going Strong After 70 Years"? Or how about a television anchor proclaiming, "No problems in the county jail this month"? What about this sports report: "A healthy week of practice for the Tigers"?

Common and important everyday occurrences do not qualify as news—unless for some reason they are different. If municipal water systems typically fail after a few decades, a strong run of 70 years could be a worthy headline. If the county jail has been beset by chronic inmate violence, a month of calm is news. A week of injury-free practice is an appropriate story for a team that's been beaten up all season. Normalcy almost never qualifies as news, except when it is not normal.

Difference is Everywhere

You can be sure that the Rule of Difference is true for news, because it is true for everything related to human perception. People are most enamored by those things that are least common.

Why does the fashion industry constantly change hemlines, tie width, texture, color, and a multitude of other clothing standards? Designers know that a new style is only desirable so long as it is perceived as being fresh. When the new style becomes the standard, staleness quickly follows, prompting a desire for change.

Toy fads work the same way. One year it's Beanie Babies, the next year it's Tickle Me Elmo, and the next year it's Pokémon. Humans get bored easily. They crave things that are different.

Smart advertisers seek out difference in their message. Apple tells consumers to "Think Different." Dodge says it plain and clear: "Dodge, Different." Coors beer markets itself as "Original" Coors. Corona beer proclaims that its taste is "Miles away from ordinary." Pepsi solicits the "new" generation. Samsung urges electronics buyers to "Defy the ordinary." 3M tells us to "See the difference."

"New and improved" is the most common phrase in advertising. But the most effective ads push a lot harder on difference than they do on quality. That's why Heinz now makes "Blastin' Green" and "Funky Purple" ketchup.

People misunderstand the motivating factors of the news media because they discount the media's humanity. All people are drawn to the unusual, including reporters, who are anxious to give the public what it wants.

Champions of Difference

Is Muhammad Ali the greatest boxer of all time? Not even close. Rocky Marciano never lost. Henry Armstrong simultaneously held three weight class championships. Archie Moore knocked out more than three times the opponents that Ali did. Marvin Hagler won more fights than Ali and lost fewer. Julio Cesar Chavez lost just one fight and knocked out 74 of his 89 opponents.

So why is Ali regarded by most as "The Greatest" when he wasn't even the best heavyweight? He used the news media as his own P.R. and advertising machine. He did this by intuitively following the top Media Rule—the Rule of Difference.

Ali set himself far apart from all other men who dared to be a pugilist champion. No boxer had ever shouted at the world with such confidence. Yes, he had great boxing skills. But there have been, and are, thousands with great skills. Ali showcased his talent with an intelligent bravado that was never seen before. A smart, good-looking, articulate, entertaining, and strangely likable heavyweight boxer who spoke in catch phrases? That was different! That was news.

Ali wasn't just a champion of the Rule of Difference; he employed nearly all of the Media Rules during his career. That's why many polls crown him "Athlete of the Century" when it's quite a stretch to even call him "Boxer of His Weight Class." Ali wasn't the greatest boxer, but, as a total package, he was the greatest boxing champion.

While Muhammad Ali is an excellent example of how to use the Rule of Difference to achieve greatness, there is another heavyweight who achieved significant notoriety with less talent. George Foreman was just another boxer until he discovered the power inherent in not being like everyone else.

After retiring umpteen times, Foreman finally found a niche in the elder-hood of his career. He became the lovable, bald, over-the-hill bruiser who hit the hamburger stand as hard as he hit mostly second-rate opponents. Foreman joked and ate his way to a title fight, television commercials, a sitcom, and millions of dollars. He also stole a piece of boxing immortality because, like Ali, Foreman was different. Who else would have the audacity to name all five of his boys George? Consequently, the media and the public came to love him almost as much as Ali. It's too bad Foreman didn't discover his wonderful personality sooner. Can you imagine what would have happened if Ali and Foreman had hit their peak at the same time? That would likely have been the greatest sports rivalry of all time—mostly because it would have been the most different.

Making Difference Work for You

So, you're not a politician or a professional athlete, and you don't have a big idea, service, or product, but you still want to attract media attention. How do you do it? Pay attention to what everyone else is doing and do something else. For added punch, make it visual, timely, interesting, dramatic, humorous, shocking, or outrageous. Search for any difference you can think of and then play to that strength.

Take a lesson from the Polar Bear Club. Everybody else swims in the summer. The Polar Bear Club swims in icy waters from New York to Wisconsin to Colorado on the first day of January. Are its members insane? Perhaps. Do they get a tremendous amount of media attention around the world every year? Absolutely.

How many hotels do you think there are in Hollywood, California? There must be hundreds. And yet, the Standard Hotel manages to get the attention of the national press when all of the others do not (that is, if they even thought about trying). How did the Standard do it? By being different, of course. You see, behind the front desk is something highly unusual—a glass box. It looks a lot like a fish tank; only the objects on display are mammals—young women, to be exact. While guests check in, a "model" reclines in the box. She might read a book, talk on her cell phone, write in a journal, or even just take a snooze. It doesn't matter, so long as she appears interesting to the peepers . . . uh, I mean, guests.

Did you know that more than 60,000 books are published annually? The authors of every one of those books want desperately to get coverage in the mainstream press, but only a small fraction does. And once a book has been out for a while, the prospects for becoming the subject of a news story shrink to pitiful proportions. But don't tell that to Nicholas Boothman, author of *How To Make People Like You in 90 Seconds or Less*. Even though Boothman's book is in its sixth printing, he still attracts the Beast wherever he goes. His strategy isn't complicated—it's just different. Boothman simply tells news organizations that he can demonstrate the effectiveness of his method right in front of their disbelieving eyes. He dares reporters to take him to places where people are known to be grumpy (bus stations, airports, government offices), and he works his science. For added effect, Boothman wears red shoes, which, of course, become part of the story. Every little bit of difference helps.

> Journalists cannot resist reporting on any enterprise that manages to separate itself from the pack.

You don't have to be as bold as the Polar Bear Club, the Standard Hotel, or Nicholas Boothman to attract the Beast. But you must find a way to separate yourself from your competition, which is what will make you interesting to a reporter—and his audience.

Following the terrorist attacks of September 11, 2001, a handful of savvy marketers figured out ways to make the best of a very bad situation. Within days of the attacks, applications from businesses began flooding into the U.S. Trademark office. Some ideas included "Osama Yo' Mama!" T-shirts, Osama Piñatas, and God-Bless-Our-Firefighters teddy bears (chapter 10, Rule of Timing). In Riviera Beach, Florida, the Tactical Edge gun shop and shooting range took a nice shot at getting publicity—literally. The company began selling Osama targets for ten dollars each. The reputable companies, such as Tactical Edge, didn't profit directly from the sales of their products. They gave their proceeds to charitable organizations helping 9/11 victims. However, they did get some tremendously valuable media exposure that didn't cost them a thing. Even if you don't approve of the tactics of such opportunistic companies, you should admire their attention to the Rule of Difference.

If you're someone who doesn't have his or her eye on national exposure but simply a mention in the local paper or on the evening news, I bring wonderful news. Opportunity abounds. The smaller the audience, the less bold or original you have to be. Want proof? Just survey your local newspaper, and you'll see that many of the people and organizations winning press coverage are being different—but not that different. Conduct the same experiment with local television, radio, and magazines, and you'll get the same result. The harsh reality is there are relatively few people in the world who are both creative and pugnacious enough to aggressively seek media attention. Stand out from the crowd—even just a little—and your publicity prospects will grow.

The Beast Loves a Niche

The next time you're scanning the business page of your local newspaper or flipping through a business magazine, look for stories about people or companies that fill a niche. You'll be surprised at the large percentage of stories that fit into this category. Journalists cannot resist reporting on any enterprise that manages to separate itself from the pack.

Melanie Marchand is a fitness consultant based in Philadelphia. She's good at what she does, but that's not why she received national exposure through Knight Ridder newspapers. The reporter who did the story was sufficiently impressed—not by her biceps, but rather by her marketing savvy. You see, Marchand is an African-American woman who trains only one kind of client—other African-American women. Her company is cleverly named SIS, which stands for Sisters in Shape. By reducing her client base to only "Sisters," Marchand separated herself from all the other fitness gurus who, as good as they may be, lack a compelling niche.

Venture Law Group out of Menlo Park, California, is a big believer in the Rule of Difference. Back in 1993 the firm made a decision to focus exclusively on Internet Start-ups. The strategy worked better than its founding partners could have dreamed. After helping launch such companies as Yahoo!, drugstore.com, and eToys, it has become one of the most profitable law firms in the nation—all the while shunning the most prestigious corporate clients. Not surprisingly, it's also become a magnet for media attention, which generates even more profit-inducing credibility.

Chicago photographer Steven Gross is the best at what he does. How do I know this? I read it in the newspaper, of course. Others have learned about the photography of Steven Gross through magazines and television. What makes this guy stand out among all the hundreds of thousands of photographers out there? Difference. Gross has a great niche. He is a wedding photographer who only shoots black and white film. Not only that, Gross's pictures are candid, not posed. As one reporter put it, "Most weddings are run by the photographer, pose after pose. Ironic that the wedding is centered around the production of a wedding album, and yet such albums are always a disappointment, not quite right, not quite real . . . plastic fruit." Gross's black and white images reveal emotional intensity, not starched discomfort. I'll be calling Gross when my daughter gets married, if I can afford him.

Louis Barajas is an accountant in East Los Angeles. Prior to starting his own company, Barajas worked for the prestigious Kenneth Leventhal accounting firm in the upper-crust town of Newport Beach. When he left, Barajas was handling the reorganization of Donald Trump's finances. It was a great job, but he wanted something different—real different. He went back to his old neighborhood and began marketing his services to a clientele that was greatly in need of an accounting specialist. As Barajas explained to the *Orange County Register*, most Southern California Hispanics are accustomed to hiring jack-of-all-trades accountants who do taxes, divorces, and marriages but lack specific expertise. They now have an expert to call their own, one whose client base is almost entirely Hispanic.

Creating a niche for your business is a great idea because it allows you to establish a unique presence in the mind of the consumer. That same marketing power is also what will make the news media want to tell the world why you are extraordinary.

Think Practical in a Different Way

Corporate America has a true blue method for getting publicity. Every year large and small businesses alike give generously to worthy causes. It's a wonderful thing to do. It's just too bad that more of them don't do it better by being different.

I'm continually amazed at how many organizations squander potential media opportunities by simply not thinking in practical terms. These groups, which want to "make a difference" with their philanthropy, could make a much bigger difference it only they didn't piecemeal their resources. Difference without drama (chapter 3, Rule of Emotion) is dead.

As anyone in corporate marketing knows, CEOs everywhere are bombarded with requests for donations. They come from disease groups (cancer, heart disease, diabetes), environmental groups (reduce water use, save the whales, protect the spotted owl), education groups (early childhood reading, special education funding, scholarship programs), and the list goes on and on. The temptation to appease as many groups as possible with bite size contributions can be overwhelming. Most corporations succumb to the pressure. But what is the payoff? The corporate philanthropist gets a plaque and perhaps a two-line mention in the "corporate giving" section of the newspaper. Big deal.

Please don't misunderstand me. I strongly advocate corporate donations. I just don't advise giving to everyone. Let your competitors embrace low-risk, low-gain conventional wisdom. Don't diversify. There is no power in an unfocused strategy of any kind. Put all your eggs in one basket. Give everything you've got to a small number of organizations (preferably one) and splash that impact (difference) as far, as high, and as wide as possible. Make it something tangible that the press can get its arms—and cameras—around. Now you've captured a moment that enhances your reputation and also attracts notoriety to the charitable organization—which in some cases can be even more powerful than the gift itself.

I once consulted with a client who was putting together a charity ball. In early discussions some people wanted to give the proceeds to several organizations. I lobbied hard against such a plan, and, fortunately, a majority of the group agreed that it would be best to focus our attention on one target. We chose a Boys and Girls club and raised close to $40,000. So what did we do with the booty? Did we just throw the money into the general fund and let the Club spend the cash on things like salaries and administrative costs? Are you kidding? After the ball, the club went out and purchased basketball goals, balls, computers, and all sorts of equipment—stuff that made for good pictures and videotape. When the unveiling of the ball's proceeds came, the community, through the news media, got a real good look at the good that had been done.

Most companies spread out their charitable giving as thin as a pancake, and their publicity impact flops just like a flapjack, too. Don't act like everybody else when it comes to your philanthropy—or any of your other publicity efforts. Make a big impact. Be different.

An Intel-Inside Case Study

In the mid-1990s I worked with computer chip manufacturer Intel Corporation, which was seeking approval for the largest industrial revenue bond (IRB) in world history— $8 billion. The proposition was a tough sell because the sales and property tax forgiveness for Intel over the life of the bond was nearly a half billion dollars. As part of the media plan, we explained to the people through the press that this bond was a big win for the community and the state of New Mexico. The project would bring thousands of high-paying jobs, thousands of spin-off service-sector jobs, more tax revenue (Intel pays a significant amount in corporate and other miscellaneous taxes), and increased opportunities for local residents. But we knew all of this was not enough to stave off accusations of "corporate welfare" from a handful of powerful anti-Intel activists (chapter 12, Rule of Balance).

The solution to this dilemma was not found in a shower of corporate giving to the community (I should mention that Intel *does* give generously to a multitude of causes, but that philanthropy was of little help to us in this enormous project. Also, Intel has the resources to spread a lot of money around. The vast majority of us do not.) Intel won approval for its IRB with one bold stroke of difference.

The massive Intel plant sits adjacent to the small but growing city of Rio Rancho, with a population at the time of just over 40,000. The region (Albuquerque metro area) had a big problem in that Rio Rancho had no high school. Residents were forced to bus their kids to Albuquerque and two other school districts. Worse yet, state leaders said they didn't have the money to begin building Rio Rancho a high school for at least five years. So what did Intel do? You guessed it. The manufacturer of fast computer chips put its brainpower toward constructing a $30 million high school. And, of course, it was built in record time. That's difference.

Not long after Intel built Rio Rancho's high school, the city became a finalist for the "All American City" award, given out by National Civic League. It's no coincidence that Intel's big splash attracted enough national attention to put the relatively young town on the radar screen for such an honor. That's what publicity does. It draws attention to things and in turn creates opportunity for even more attention, sales, name recognition, profit, etc.

The Interview Done with Difference

Nowhere is the Rule of Difference more critical than in the reporter interview. How many talking heads have appeared on television in the past decade? How many actualities (radio's term for soundbite) have been broadcast across AM and FM frequencies? How many quotes have been printed in newspapers, newsmagazines, newsletters, trade journals, and on the Internet? If each one were worth a buck, we could pay off the national debt and throw a lavish party for everyone.

Now, how many quotes from the past week do you remember? Chances are, not a single one. The sheer volume of media is the primary reason for our lack of recall. But there is another contributing factor. Most of what is said is not worth remembering. It's not even worth taking notice of the first time it is spoken. Why? It's boring, bland, overly technical, or uninspiring. In short, the person speaking or being quoted has failed to set him- or herself apart from the monotony of the medium.

Even famous, often-quoted people who should know better typically say unremarkable things when they are interviewed. Is it because they don't think creatively? Is it because they are extremely busy and don't give the interview a thought until the reporter arrives or calls? Is it because they have big egos and inflated confidence in their ad-libbing ability? Is it because they don't understand the power of difference? Yes.

There are many trappings among the cultural elite. Their attention is on other things. They are already admired for the thing that sets them apart from others. Why would it occur to them to be even more special among the special? When a reporter asks a question, something always comes to mind, doesn't it? Yes, and usually it's the same thing that others have heard and repeated countless times before. I call it "mental auto pilot aboard the cliché express." The Rule of Difference is continually violated.

Cliché Kings

What does John Elway say in 1998 after the Denver Broncos win 12 games in a row? The quarterback says something to the effect of: "We're just going to play one game at a time." Isn't that pretty much what Bob Griese said in 1972 when the Miami Dolphins achieved the same dozen-win accomplishment? Didn't Joe Theisman repeat that phrase when the Washington Redskins bagged the first dozen in 1983? Isn't that what all high school, college, and professional athletes say when their teams have won or lost a few games in succession?

If Theisman and Elway had prepared in advance by thinking differently, they would have come up with something a lot more memorable, enhancing their persona with the news media and their fans.

Theisman could have said, "On opening day, I forgot to brush my teeth. After we won our second game I realized I had forgotten to brush that morning as well. So I've given up on oral hygiene on game day. Want to smell my breath?" That's a quote that would have been played over and over again.

People love their heroes to have a sense of humor and humility in the midst of their triumphs and defeats. Nobody wants to hear, "We're just taking them one game at a time." Elway should have said, "Anyone can win 12 in a row. It's knocking down number 13 that's so hard." When the Broncos lost the 13th game that season, Elway could have quipped, "I'm just glad to get number 13 out of the way. Now we can start winning football games again." His sense of perspective would have won him endearing favor with the fans.

Think for a minute and you can name a good number of sports clichés. "I don't care what my role is so long as the team wins." "I'm just happy to be here." "Don't let our opponent's record fool you, this is a good test for our team." "We still haven't played four good quarters of ball." "It's not over 'til the fat lady sings." "The ball just didn't bounce our way today." "We had too many mental mistakes." "We gave this one away." "This is a rebuilding year for us." "When the going gets tough, the tough get going." And then there is the greatest sports cliché of all time: "Our backs are against the wall." Ugggh.

While athletes and coaches are the worst violators of the Rule of Difference, they are by no means alone. What mayor, CEO, general, or other leader hasn't said, "We've accomplished our goal, but there are many challenges ahead?" Or perhaps it's, "The chips are down, but we're not going to give up."

There is a cliché for every career and every profession. The policeman says, "The suspect was taken into custody without incident." The lawyer says, "We will not try this case in the media." The crusader says, "If this helps just one person it will all be worth it." The hero says, "I just did what anybody else would have done." The fallen and repentant preacher says, "I have sinned against you."

If you don't think of a unique answer to the obvious question in advance (chapter 5, Rule of Preparation), your brain will have no choice but to search its archives for whatever pops up first. And what will that be? But, of course, it will be that answer that has been used so many times before that it's already a cliché. You know, the phrase that's "tried and true." There's a quip for everyone on the cliché express.

Difference is King

In order to take advantage of the media spotlight, you must be different from those around you. Do not be duped by the assumption of "importance." Whether it's the story or the quote within the story, the news media—and its consumers—do not lust after what is important. They are seduced by what is different.

◆ ◆ ◆

CHAPTER 3

The Rule of Emotion

~ you are the condiment ~

In the 1950s TV series *Dragnet*, Sergeant Friday often said during an interview, "Just the facts, ma'am." He wasn't interested in what the woman thought about the facts or how the facts made her feel. Friday just wanted the essential details and nothing more. That's how many people view the news media. They believe that the biggest and best facts are what get reported. They're wrong.

On January 31, 2001, the United States Commission on National Security/21st Century released its final report. This was a heavy-duty commission made up of high-ranking military officers, prominent intellectuals, former Cabinet secretaries, and members of Congress. The commissioners spent two years and $10 million analyzing the nation's security—or lack thereof. The report announced that the United States was not prepared to deal with terrorism, and it recommended wholesale changes in our national security policy. This report was chock-full of some seriously disturbing facts. One of its conclusions: "Americans will likely die on

American soil, possibly in large numbers." So what was the media's response? There were only a few stories in the nation's leading newspapers. NBC and ABC ignored the report, while CBS produced one piece.

How could such a thing happen? The *American Journalism Review* went searching for answers in its November 2001 issue. National reporters told *AJR* that the report was "DBA"—dull but important. That's right, not enough emotion (even with dire predictions), not much interest. Commission executive director, Gen. Charles G. Boyd, and former Colorado Senator Gary Hart visited with the editorial boards of the *New York Times*, the *Washington Post*, and the *Wall Street Journal*. Boyd told *AJR* that during those meetings, "We got some serious yawns, and that was about it." That all changed on September 11, 2001, when terrorists released more emotional news than this nation had seen since December 7, 1941.

Pain versus Brain—A Mismatch

Chemistry is driven by facts. The same is true of physics and aerodynamics. Annual reports are based upon facts (or at least they're supposed to be). The drama of human interaction, however, is a different story. People do not live their lives along straight, logical, factual lines. We are emotional creatures who make most of our decisions based not on accurate information but on how we *feel*.

Because the news of the day is generated by humans, reported by humans, and consumed by humans, it is inevitable that news is driven by human emotion. If you want news people to pay attention to what you are doing, don't try to make them think—make them care. Forget about convincing their minds. Focus on seducing their hearts.

Don't get me wrong. Reporters do value relevant facts. But that value is nearly always determined by the emotive circumstances surrounding the facts. Consider, for example, the news media's fixation on America's drug problem. Over the past 20 years, there's no telling how many thousands of stories have been done on lives lost to heroin and cocaine addiction. Indeed, the stats are discouraging. The FDA estimates that these two illegal drugs kill four Americans every day, or nearly 1500 a year. However, that statistic pales by comparison to America's legal drug of choice—nicotine. A whopping 400,000 people die annually for the love of smoking, dipping, and chewing. That's nearly 1,100 people each and every day! To put a finer point on it, more people die from nicotine every 31 hours than die from heroin and cocaine in a year.

Here are two more shockers. The Centers for Disease Control estimate that 300,000 Americans die every year because they refuse to get off the couch. That's right, inactivity stops the breath of 822 people every day. The CDC says that another 5000 people croak on an annual basis (nearly 14 daily) as the result of food poisoning. We don't hear much about the death toll from nicotine, laziness, or bad food because the pictures and circumstances surrounding these quiet killers don't make for emotive news coverage.

Journalists are just like the rest of us; they love drama and hate boredom. Therefore, the preponderance of what they do is focused not on stories that will strain the brain but on those that will make you feel the pain (or any other emotion).

The Beast Loves a Soap Opera

People vanish in this country every single day. Most are gone forever and receive little or no mention in the press. But throw in a congressman and an illicit affair, and now you've got the emotional juice that can fuel a mega-story.

In the spring of 2001 not too many people outside of northern California or the Washington, D.C., beltway had ever heard of Congressman Gary Condit. By summer, it would have been difficult to find someone who didn't have an opinion about the man's character. The media went absolutely overboard when rumors circulated that the married representative had been romantically involved with Chandra Levy, a congressional intern who had suddenly disappeared. As weeks passed, Levy had not been located, and Condit continued to insist that he and the 24-year-old woman were only friends. The media applied enormous pressure on Condit, culminating in a one-on-one face-off with ABC correspondent Connie Chung. (We'll talk more about Condit's huge mistake in chapter 13, the Rule of Ambush). Condit finally admitted to the affair but claimed he knew nothing of Levy's disappearance.

Step back, and look at the facts. Gary Condit was only one representative in a House of 435 members; Chandra Levy, one missing person out of thousands that vanish every year. Considering her probable death (Levy is still missing as of this writing) and the fact that the two were intimately involved, this was a legitimate story. However, it was a thousand times larger than the facts would dictate. But facts don't drive news stories. Emotions do.

The so-called "Trial of the Century" was an excellent example of the Rule of Emotion. The accused murderer, O.J. Simpson, is a Hall of Fame football player, media figure, and actor. His ex-wife was a gorgeous blonde with a supermodel's figure. They lived in the wealthy Los Angeles suburb of Brentwood. The murder scene was horrific; Simpson's alibi, implausible. Ron Goldman, the second victim, was caught in the wrong place at the worst possible time. There was an exhaustive list of intriguing details: the low-speed freeway pursuit; overwhelming DNA evidence against Simpson; a highly suspect prosecution strategy; racist police investigators; an incompetent judge; a high-priced, Hollywood-style defense team; a stunningly quick acquittal; and on and on. It's difficult to imagine a murder case with more emotional intensity.

So what did the news media do? It covered every conceivable aspect of the case to a level of reprehensible absurdity. In fact, the scorching spotlight put on the trial no doubt changed the way in which it was litigated. It may have even changed the verdict. Did the lawyers for the defense attempt to use the media to achieve its purpose? Undoubtedly.

But what were the facts? A man *allegedly* murdered his ex-wife and her companion in a jealous rage. Is this anything unusual? No, horrific crimes of passion are committed in this country all the time. If celebrity, race, and wealth were not part of the story, this case would never have attained its emotional appeal. If it had happened on an Iowa farm, the people of Kansas would never have heard of it, much less the rest of the world. The identities of the players involved in this common crime made it the most publicized murder trial in world history. The Rule of Emotion is a very powerful thing.

The death of Princess Diana is yet another extreme example of the Rule of Emotion. She was a young, beautiful mother of two who had been jilted by a cold royal family. Moments after her death in a high-speed car crash, the news media began blanket coverage of the story. The passing of the pretty princess was a non-stop media obsession for weeks.

Again, what were the facts? A woman dies in a car crash with her boyfriend and an intoxicated driver. The car was traveling at an unacceptably high rate of speed. Is this type of incident something unusual? No. Unfortunately, it's a tragic reality that repeats itself on a daily basis.

Was the death of Princess Di a valid news story? Absolutely. Was it worthy of being treated as an event of great planetary significance? Hardly. However, the news media is far less concerned with the significance of the facts than it is with the emotional appeal of the story.

Drowning in Emotion

Perhaps more than any other recent high profile story, the case of Elián Gonzales gives us compelling testimony to the Rule of

Emotion's power over the Beast. You no doubt remember that Gonzales was the Cuban boy plucked from the ocean during an illegal Thanksgiving holiday voyage to the United States. His mother drowned. Elián's Miami relatives wanted to give him a home. The boy's father said he already had one in Cuba. Additionally, Elián's mother had taken him without his dad's consent.

The news media turned the custody battle and subsequent seizure of the boy by federal agents into a mega-story. The *Miami Herald* won a Pulitzer Prize for its reporting of the Elián saga. *Associated Press* photographer Alan Diaz also won a Pulitzer for his memorable photo of a government agent poised to take the boy from a relative, machine gun in hand. But how important was the fight over the young Cuban to anyone outside the family? On the "importance" scale of 1 to 100, this story would have been difficult to measure even in fractions. However, on the emotion scale, it ranked in the high 90s.

"Sounds reasonable," you say, "but can you prove it?" As a matter of fact, I can. Have you heard of five-year-old Jonathon Colombini? I'm willing to bet you haven't. Colombini's mother, Arletis Blanco Perez, illegally took her son to Cuba without his American father's consent. Jon Colombini then asked the U.S. government to help him retrieve the child. In a factual sense, this is the Elián Gonzales story, only in reverse. Logically, the Colombini case should trigger even more media interest because this time the boy is an American being held illegally in a Communist country. But you haven't heard of Jonathon Colombini because there's very little emotion surrounding the facts. The only reason this custody battle got the tiny bit of media attention it did is because it so closely mirrored that of Elián Gonzales.

I've used high profile examples to illustrate my point, but the Rule of Emotion holds true for every level of news product. If you want a mention in a small weekly newspaper, find some emotion (and difference) and let a reporter know about it. Want a story in

Newsweek, the *Wall Street Journal*, on *ABC News,* or *CNN?* The same Rule of Emotion applies. Obviously, the larger the news outlet, the stronger the competition, therefore, the more emotive—and universal in its appeal—the story must be. However, for most local press coverage, even a little emotion will give you a fighting chance.

Want Publicity? Make Reporters *Feel*

As any marketing professional knows, people don't buy the steak—they buy the sizzle. The same is true for news. It's not enough to have a good steak (facts). You've got to have the alluring, aromatic, and tantalizing presentation (emotion) to go along with it.

Let's consider three generic stories that would seem to have no chance of getting a reporter's attention. First, the activity inside a cooking school; second, a company trying to sell posters; and third, an Internet start-up selling used merchandise. As is, these *stories* just lie there like a worn-out rug. Add some sizzle and reporters come running.

Why would any journalist want to do a story on the frustration going on inside a cooking school? Isn't frustration part of the educational process? True, but what if the *irritation* was the focus of the learning, not the food? Now you've got my interest—and that of the *Wall Street Journal.*

The Viking Culinary Arts Center in Franklin, Tennessee, found itself in the national limelight because of its specialty in teaching executives how to get along. In the newest fad in corporate "team building," management consultants have discovered the tension that quickly builds inside a kitchen produces an excellent learning environment. Corporations are paying up to $9,000 a day to teach their executives how to make a good Spanish omelet and, more importantly, in the process, how to get along with one another. Now, that's a story a reporter can get her fork into.

Posters are as common as walls. It would be difficult to drive two city blocks without passing a store that sells them. So why would the *Dallas Morning News* be interested in telling its readers about a two-year-old company that sells posters? It's because the corporation, Despair Inc., hangs irony and humor instead of inspiration and happiness. In a world of cheery images urging us to reach for achievement, growth, and fulfillment, Despair Inc. is cashing in on our secret desire to lower the bar. Their mantra is: "Lower your expectations and break the chain of pain." One print in Despair's "Demotivators 2000" series was a picture of a gorgeous sunset. In the foreground is a sinking ship. The caption beneath reads, "Mistakes: It could be that the purpose of your life is only to serve as a warning to others." Anytime accepted standards are violated in a humorous, shocking, saddening, enraging, or inspirational way, news people want to tell everyone about it.

A new company comes up with an idea to sell used merchandise over the Internet. So what? In the new economy Internet start-ups are as common as the products and services they hope to sell. What this company, <Half.com>, needed—and found—was a way to distinguish itself from the crowd. The national news media took a brief, but intense, interest in the new company when it persuaded a small Oregon town called Halfway to rename itself after the website. It was unusual (Rule of Difference), surprising, and kind of funny. To quote Devin Gordon of *Newsweek*, "The media ate it up (can you blame us?); so did venture capitalists (can you blame them?)." Anyone who can find humor (or any other emotion) in the boring world of business and commerce is going to be successful in attracting high-value publicity.

The Emotive Interview

While the Rule of Emotion is important to winning free publicity, it is absolutely critical to maximizing the impact of exposure once you get it. The most compelling part of any good news item is the expressed human emotion within the story—the quotes or soundbites. If the interviews are not compelling, the story won't be either. That's why a high premium is placed on getting emotive words to go along with dramatic pictures.

The shocking video of Rodney King being beaten by Los Angeles police officers was repulsively riveting. However, King's comments made in the wake of it all were even more powerful—seizing the attention of the American people. "Why can't we all just get along?" is now etched into our public consciousness.

Jesse Ventura became a compelling figure in American politics because of his size, demeanor, and frankness. However, such novelty quickly loses cachet among members of the news media who have an attention span comparable to that of a third-grader with ADD. What keeps Ventura in the spotlight is what he says, not what he looks like.

Shortly after being elected governor of Minnesota, Ventura told *Newsweek*, "My brain is operating at such a level that I don't want to put my foot in it." The words that come out of the former professional wrestler's mouth are so shocking, funny, or non-politically correct that reporters can't get enough of him. They even have a name for his free-flowing quips—"Jesseisms."

Professional athletes retire and then un-retire all the time. It's a boring cliché, unless, that is, the sports star has something compelling to say upon his return. When John Riggins un-retired from the Washington Redskins in 1981 after a one-year absence, he had something emotive to tell reporters: "I'm bored, I'm broke, and I'm back." The amusing statement made such an impression on *Dallas Morning News* Reporter Frank Luska that he used it in a story about un-retiring athletes some 20 years later.

But emotive comments need not be laugh-out-loud funny or outrageous to be highly quotable. When 38-year-old Michael Jordan un-retired for the second time in 2001, his fans wanted to know one thing: Could he still make the game's best players look like dorks? Jordan smartly shot well below the hype. He modestly assured them, "Most of you guys probably wanted to see if I can still dunk—I can still dunk." Followers of "his Airness" no doubt chuckled as they dreamed of the gravity-defying jams to come. Former NBA star Clyde Drexler, who is one year older than Jordan, quipped, "I think it's great for Michael. For myself, when I think about doing it, my toes hurt."

Bland facts in an interview won't arouse anyone's interest, least of all a reporter's. What they—we—all want is something distinctly human, like broke superstars, aching toes, and the possibility of future glory.

Facts Are Not Your Friend

There are two kinds of soundbites or quotes—those that convey facts and those that reveal an emotive response to the facts. A robot can be programmed to deliver data, but it takes a face, a voice, and a countenance to provide context to the information. In spite of this reality, many newsmakers sound more like a cold machine than a warm body.

Reporters always prefer the emotive to the factual. Always. In the rare instance when a factual statement is a good quote ("Everyone in the house is dead" or "The crowd fell completely silent"), the emotional impact behind the fact is more powerful than the statement itself.

In any good news story, the reporter presents specific information, and the people being interviewed provide the emotive framing of the subject at hand. When the interviewee makes bland, factual statements, the story will have little, if any, appeal. It will be boring, as will the interview subject. From a ratings or circulation standpoint, blandness is equated to leprosy. From a marketing standpoint, a blah interview will do nothing to enhance your image. In fact, it may damage it.

"Wait a minute," you say. "I hear and see bland, boring comments all the time in the news media." Yes, you do. In spite of what should be glaringly obvious—facts tell, emotions sell—most newsmakers refuse to let go of the factual axiom. As hard as reporters try to drag feeling words out of their interview subjects, they don't get a lot of cooperation.

Why do so many people refuse to give the reporter what he wants and make themselves look good in the process? Quite simply, they are nervous. And why wouldn't they be? It's well documented that the number one human fear is that of public speaking because of the danger of appearing stupid, silly, or incompetent. When speaking to a news reporter, it's possible to sound idiotic to a much wider audience. You could also be misquoted (more on that in a moment). So the natural reaction is to make conservative, boring, safe statements.

> Reporters always prefer the emotive to the factual. Always.

We can see ample evidence of the fear of appearing stupid trumping the desire to sound insightful in our pop culture. In the movie *Apollo 13*, reporters come rushing up to the wives of astronauts Fred Hays and Jim Lovell, following the launch of the spacecraft. Mrs. Lovell, a four-time veteran of spousal space launches, whispers to the newcomer, "Remember, you're proud, happy, and thrilled." Mrs. Hays dutifully tells the throng of reporters, "We're very proud, and very happy, and we're thrilled."

In the baseball movie *Bull Durham*, veteran catcher Crash Davis has some words of wisdom for wild rookie pitcher Nuke LaLoosh. "You're going to have to learn your clichés," Crash tells

Nuke. "They're your friends: 'We've got to play 'em one game at a time.'" Nuke complains that Crash's clichés are boring, to which his mentor says, "Of course. That's the point." Like most news-makers, Crash Davis looks at a reporter and sees danger instead of opportunity. That's what happens when you don't know the Media Rules and *crash* too many times.

The goal of all interviews is (or should be) to capture emotion. Newspaper reporters want to print the ten most emotion-provoking words that come out of a person's mouth. Broadcasters want ten emotive seconds, or less. And this makes complete sense. A news story with boring, factual quotes is like a pizza with no pepperoni or sausage, a stew with no salt or pepper, a sundae with no choco-late syrup or whipped cream. As a person being interviewed, *you are the condiment*, not the entree. Precious few realize this seem-ingly obvious fact. They know it. They just don't know that they know it. You, however, are no longer one of "them."

Boring Blows It

Basketball coach Darrell Walker apparently went to the Crash Davis and Sergeant Friday school of quotes and soundbites. After then Washington Wizards President Michael Jordan named Walker as in-terim coach of his team, Walker told the media, "I'm just happy to be here." He followed up that oft-said phrase with, "It's a dream come true." Walker capped it off: "I just want us to go out, be com-petitive, get after people, play defense, and have some fun." In one interview the Wizards new coach managed to knock off three of the greatest clichés in professional sports. What should Walker have said? How about, "Right now I feel like the Wizard of Oz." He could have followed up that quote by humbly saying, "I just hope Toto stays away from that big curtain."

The ironic thing about playing it conservative is that interview subjects often commit the sin they are trying to avoid. In the days after the U.S. electorate voted for a president in November 2000 (and still didn't know if it would be George W. Bush or Al Gore), former Senate Majority Leader George Mitchell appeared on CNN to provide expert analysis. You would think that someone with Mitchell's media experience would be prepped and ready for the occasion. He wasn't.

In her first question to Mitchell, anchor Judy Woodruff asked him about the hand recount going on in Florida. If the state's supreme court ruled against allowing the hand recounts into the vote, Woodruff queried, would that prove to be a "mortal blow" to Al Gore's bid for the presidency? Mitchell's response: "Any adverse decision would not be helpful." Duh. In Mitchell's attempt to not overstate his position, he stated the obvious—and didn't do his "expert" image any favors. If Mitchell understood the Rule of Emotion, he could have responded, "A mortal blow . . . probably not. A blinding headache . . . you bet."

Publicity loses much of its value if you fail to make an impression, and the place to do that is in the interview. What good is it to win a publicity hit only to have your message lost in the ocean of news generated every day?

A reporter can only use what he or she is given. Because so many people are on their guard when they are interviewed, the great quote or soundbite is relatively rare. Compounding this problem is the fact that there is a shortage of reporters who know how to coax great quotes out of their nervous subjects.

When being interviewed, the best defense against saying something stupid is also the best offense for saying something brilliant: be prepared. It's not as tricky as you might think. Full details on that subject are disclosed in chapter 5, the Rule of Preparation.

"I was Misquoted!"

A lack of emotion in an interview doesn't just guarantee a forgettable quote. It also increases the chances that the quote used will be taken "out of context."

Remember, a reporter's goal in the interview is to give the facts of the story meaning by framing them in an emotive context. When the interview subject doesn't give the reporter what he wants, he will be tempted to stretch the little bit of feeling that he does get with a paraphrase here and an edit there. Often times during this process, the words will be accurate, but the intent of the person who spoke them is utterly lost. While the complaint of being misquoted may be valid, the responsibility lies as much with the interview subject as with the reporter. By the way, there is a lot of complaining going on.

In a 1998 study conducted by the American Society of Newspaper Editors, 73 percent of the people surveyed said they had become more skeptical about news accuracy. The report stated that those most critical of newspaper coverage were people who had first-hand knowledge of a story. A journalist had interviewed thirty-one percent of the sample. Of those, 24 percent said they had been misquoted. In one out of four encounters with a reporter, people believe they have been wronged! If more people understood their role in the interview process, much of this angst could be avoided.

Journalists don't have the luxury of printing or broadcasting the boring stuff that surrounds the spicy tidbits of an interview. In any good story the bland gets edited out, and subsequently some context may be lost. Your choice is to whine about the unfairness of the process or to adjust the way you deal with it. I strongly suggest the latter.

The simple solution to the problem is to make brief, stand-alone statements that capture a degree of emotion. Sounds easy, doesn't it? It's not, unless you are committed to the craft. To be good at giving quotes, a person must think creatively, concisely, futuristically, and emotively.

Positively Planned

The Rule of Emotion also applies to news conferences, public statements, and speeches. Imagine a fictional company called Dystag, which has announced a decision to downsize. What quote or soundbite would you use from the following public statement?

"The harsh reality of business is that we are all beholden to the bottom line. As a result of lagging profits in the third and fourth quarters, the board of directors of Dystag has made a decision to downsize the workforce over the next year by ten percent, which will affect approximately 500 people. We will be assisting some of these employees through the opportunity of transferring to other facilities. Some positions will be eliminated through attrition and early retirement incentive packages, and some employees will be reassigned to other departments within this facility."

In such a long, technical, and complex statement, the reporter doesn't have much to choose from. The only line with any kind of emotional punch is the first one. But speaking about "harsh realities" and "bottom lines" will make the company appear cold and insensitive. In the end, the spokesperson will cry foul, asking why the reporter didn't use what he said about early retirement packages and attrition. But the mouthpiece can only blame himself for making his most powerful statement a negative one.

Contrast the first statement with the one below.

"Our goal is to make Dystag stronger for its 5,000 dedicated employees and the people of Lewistown. We believe that not one employee will lose a single paycheck through this readjustment phase. Some employees will accept generous retirement packages, others will move on to exciting opportunities within our corporate family. Dystag is strongly committed to its employees and to Lewistown and that philosophy will never change."

In the second version, each sentence stands alone. The dry, technical language has been replaced by words that convey positive emotion. But wait a minute, you say. Doesn't the second statement sound like a public relations whitewash? Perhaps. Does it matter? No. Remember, the reporter is looking for ten good words or ten compelling seconds. Give it to him. The loss of 500 jobs will get reported in the story, regardless. The company's optimistic view of the leaner, meaner strategy will too, but only if it's presented in a quote or soundbite that fits the interview formula.

From the Heart

"It's not what you say, it's how you say it." How many times did you hear that line when you were a child? How often have you said it to your own children? It's great advice that we all need to heed when talking with other people but especially with the Beast. Of course, you know that more than 80 percent of communication is non-verbal. Unfortunately, even though we all know this, few of us actually use this information to our advantage.

For many reasons—usually nervousness—people tend to let go of their humanity when speaking to reporters. They think they have to come across as official, competent, and under control. Instead, they wind up sounding cold, insensitive, and uncaring. In their diligence to perform well, they sacrifice the one thing that is most critical to their message—emotion. Preparing for an interview or a public statement is always a good idea. In fact, most of chapter 5, the Rule of Preparation, is devoted to this topic. However, if I had to choose between a well crafted but stiff statement and a spontaneous eruption of emotion, I would take the latter every day of the week and twice on Sunday. So would the Beast.

One of the most striking examples of excellent, heart-felt communication I've ever seen came from then New York mayor, Rudolph Giuliani, after terrorists flew two planes into the World Trade Center towers. Immediately after the buildings fell, the mayor surged to the forefront of the crisis and stayed there for weeks. In the first few days, Giuliani, even more than President Bush, seemed to carry the sorrow, anger, and pride of a nation. But in demonstrating a remarkable ability to communicate calm and resolve, Giuliani really didn't say anything remarkable. The New York mayor stepped up to the microphone and said such things as, "I know a lot of people are going to be concerned about this, but we are in good hands," and "We are going to rebuild and rebuild stronger." Not poetic, not great prose, but just plain talk.

Giuliani's unscripted but absolutely genuine words won him enormous support within New York, the nation, and certainly the press. Dozens of effusive stories were written about the mayor's ability to lead in a crisis. Jessica McBride of the *Milwaukee Journal Sentinel* wrote, "The mayor appears tired and drawn and looks as if he's aged overnight, but that only makes him seem human." And it was Giuliani's humanity that most impressed the people that McBride interviewed. "He's on top of things, and I admire that he's giving the city hope that we can get through this," said one New Yorker. "He's calming us down. I think he has proved to the city that he cares about us," said another. Notice how the mayor's "caring" is directly connected to him being "on top of things." One man who admitted he didn't vote for Giuliani remarked, "He's coming across as helping people out." *Newsweek*'s Jonathan Alter wrote a glowing column on New York City's top politician. Alter penned, "The city and the country have found that most elusive of all democratic treasures—real leadership." Below a picture of the mayor (with a stoic Senator Hillary Clinton in the background) the caption read: "Sensitive and tough, the mayor took charge." Giuliani's sudden popularity was even featured in cartoons. In a *Newsday* drawing, one terrorist tells another, "He's an inspiration to millions!" The second terrorist responds, "His leadership is unmatched!" An angry Osama bin Laden responds, "Would you two shut up about Giuliani!?" All of this adulation for a man who came under intense fire for parading his girlfriend around city hall while he was still married? That's the power that comes when you speak from the heart.

Where was New York Governor George Pataki during the Giuliani love fest? He was there, usually standing in the background with a blank look on his face. When Pataki spoke, he was coolly official, his humanness well hidden. If Giuliani were a younger, healthier man, he would have a bright political future. Pataki, on the other hand, would be well advised to consider retirement.

Postmaster General John Potter could have learned a lot from watching any one of Giuliani's many news conferences. Unfortunately for him, during his critical moment in the spotlight he came across more like Pataki. At the height of the Anthrax scare, Potter held a news conference to warn the American public of potential danger. Potter was nervous, stiff, and about as reassuring as a powder-filled envelope. The postmaster flatly told the cameras, "We're telling people that this is a threat, and right now the threat is in the mail." The only thing scarier than what he said was how he said it—with no compassion and no reassurance. ABC News was so taken aback by Potter's failure to communicate effectively that the network made the postmaster's mistake the center of a news story that evening. ABC's reporter advised Potter (and the rest of us) not to forget the number one rule when communicating to the public through the news media—speak from the heart. There you have it, straight from the mouth of the Beast.

The Rich Get Richer

Finally, there's one more punishment that awaits those who don't give good interviews. As you recall from chapter 1, the News Beast is in a big hurry. Reporters have a lot of work to do and not much time to do it. They are not happy when they must spend extra time trying to extract something useful out of a boring interview. They get downright grumpy when their precious time is squandered further by having to contort their copy to fit poor quotes. Such journalistic gymnastics are a time-consuming drain. Therefore, those whose quotes state "nothing but the facts" will not get called back for future interviews, if the reporter has another option. And, of course, the opposite is also true: Good, tight, emotive quotes get you called back again and again and again. You'll become one of the fortunate few whom the unskilled come to envy.

The reporter doesn't want the facts in your quote. He wants your human response to the facts. Supply all the necessary information in a press release. But come interview time, stick to the Rule of Emotion.

One Thing to Remember

In your quest to win high-value publicity, remember Sergeant Friday and Crash Davis and don't be like them. Good news stories are not about the facts, nor are the interviews.

◆ ◆ ◆

CHAPTER 4

The Rule of Simplicity

~ simplify to amplify ~

Have you heard the one about Moses and the TV reporter? With the prophet still speaking in the background, the reporter looks into the live camera and says, "Moses has just come down from Mt. Sinai with God's Ten Commandments. Here are the top three . . . "

News reporters have one primary function—to simplify. A reporter can be brilliant. He can be a proficient grammarian and a dogged investigator. He can be a master of eloquence and wit. But if he cannot simplify, he might as well become a veterinarian.

A reporter's job is extremely basic. He gathers information. He keeps what he believes is most essential to the story. He discards the rest. That's it. While this job may sound easy, it isn't. The volume of relevant information to any story almost always dwarfs the news hole it has been given. (Additionally, the mass of *irrelevant* information towers over what is germane.) The journalist's plight is further compounded by the fact that he has little time to complete his task of information sifting.

For a news person, every day is a little like being a kid on an Easter egg hunt. He searches a wide area, quickly grabbing what he can. When he's out of time, he immediately sits down to size it all up. The hardboiled eggs (irrelevant material) are tossed. The plastic eggs with prizes are set aside (relevant, but not critical). Only the eggs with the candy (key elements) become the center of attention. Now, throw in a hailstorm (extreme time constraints) and a rabid dog (inherent complexity of most stories), and you've got a pretty good feel for the plight of the journalist.

Simple Seduction

Albert Einstein said, "Everything should be made as simple as possible, but not simpler." Follow his advice, and you will do quite well with the news media.

Every day millions of people try to attract the attention of news organizations. Most of them—including no small number of P.R. professionals—fail miserably. They fail because they violate the Rule of Simplicity. Hold out a watermelon and ask a reporter to take a bite, and she will turn up her nose. Offer her a juicy, scarlet-red slice, and you will have her eating out of your hand. A reporter hasn't the inclination or the time to reduce your story to a manageable form. Therefore, do it for her (chapter 6, Rule of Easy).

A stay-at-home mom used the Media Rules to get coverage for an annual Christmas ballet. The challenge, she knew, was to separate her event from all the rest. That was a good plan, except for the fact that this ballet wasn't all that different from the dozens of other shows held during the Christmas season. So she applied the Rule of Simplicity. Instead of pitching the ballet, she pitched a dancer. One girl in the show suffered from scoliosis, which required that she wear a back brace 23 hours a day. In her one hour of freedom, she danced. Bingo.

It's no coincidence that when the housewife simplified her story, it became much more emotive and attractively different. The result was a two-minute feature that ran twice on a local television station and another story that ran in a large daily newspaper. The reporter was drawn to the dancer's compelling situation; the public was drawn to the dance to watch the girl.

Simplicity, like all the Seducers and most of the Media Rules, works on every level of news coverage. Take politics, for example. In February 1999, the New Hampshire presidential primary effectively ended the campaigns of Republicans Steve Forbes, Alan Keyes, and Gary Bauer. Four candidates were left: Republicans George W. Bush and John McCain, and Democrats Al Gore and Bill Bradley. In the primary's aftermath, *Newsday*'s James Pinkerton astutely noted, "The media now have a dramatic format they can work with; two two-man races." Again, notice that the emotive quality of the story takes a big jump once simplicity enters the picture.

What do you know about NBA great Wilt "The Stilt" Chamberlain? If you're a sports fan, you probably recall that he's the guy who scored 100 points in a single game. Chamberlain was annoyed by the fact that people tended to think of him just in the context of that one shining moment within a long, brilliant career. Chamberlain lamented, "People don't talk about the 50-point average, the 69-13 Lakers championship team I played for. They talk about the night I scored 100." What Chamberlain should have realized is that one spectacular (simple) moment is a much stronger draw than the complexity of a career. Just ask those who have known Bob Beamon, John F. Kennedy, or Neil Armstrong.

As a side note to the life of Wilt Chamberlain, it's a good bet that he would have wanted his 100-point game notoriety back at the time of his death. In the minds of many people, that great moment was replaced by his dubious, impudent claim that he had had sex with 20,000 women—a boast with more simple, emotive, and different impact than the feat of 100 points.

How does a reporter spell ignore? Just like his editor or producer does—c-o-m-p-l-e-x-i-t-y. Large, unwieldy stories not only contain too much information, they also tend to dilute any different or emotive appeal the story may have. The key is not to expect too much. Chop off a piece of the story that in turn is a reflection of the whole. Now you're offering something that can tempt a reporter.

By now you may have noticed the interrelated nature of difference, emotion, and simplicity inherent in news coverage. Every great news story has a healthy dose of all three. Good news stories have an ample supply of at least two. You will almost never see a news item that has only one. But don't be confused by this seemingly symbiotic relationship. While difference, emotion, and simplicity are the key ingredients of all news coverage, they are not equal partners. Without simplicity, difference and emotion lose their impact.

Like a magnifying glass, simplicity intensifies the power of difference and emotion. For example, consider the broad category of education. You'll not see a generic story on the subject. Where would a reporter begin? Now, narrow it down a bit to the objective of improving education. That's better, but it's still too big for a journalist to get his mind around. Reduce it further to a proposal of offering vouchers to parents fed up with a poor public education system, and now you've got a story.

Consider the subject of medical incompetence killing nearly 100,000 Americans a year, as reported by the Institute of Medicine. That's a different kind of story—doctors killing patients. Accidental death is certainly a highly emotive issue. But without a way of simplifying the topic, the news media will have little to do with it. Now, focus on a core piece of the problem and watch what happens. Thousands of people die every year because of bad handwriting by doctors. The poor penmanship leads to mistakes made by pharmacists so people wind up taking drugs that ultimately kill them.

Simplifying any subject automatically amplifies difference and emotion. The key to winning publicity is to identify what you have that is different and/or emotive. Then magnify its power by cutting it down to size. *Simplify to amplify.*

Promote Your Simplicity

If you want the news media to give your product or service some of that high-octane publicity, take a lesson from corporate success stories that pop up every day in magazines and newspapers. The vast majority of them have the same thing in common—simplicity. Don't think big; think small. Don't be general; be specific. Don't add to the story; subtract from it. It's the simplest and most tangible benefit of what you're selling that has the highest probability of capturing the Beast's attention.

PlumpJack Winery received national exposure when it announced a unique feature on its 1997 Reserve Cabernet Sauvignon. The $135 bottle of wine has no cork. Instead, it sports a new twist-off cap. That's right. The thing that wine connoisseurs once looked down their aristocratic noses at turns out to have more longevity than the old-fashioned topper-stopper. Vintners have historically lost as much as ten-percent of their best wines because of corks that crack or shrink over time, causing the wine inside the bottle to spoil. The screw top is virtually impervious to shrinking and cracking.

The news media is always enamored by a new twist on the familiar. Marketers at H.J. Heinz Co. know all about this fact. First they sold their ketchup in an octagonal glass bottle. Then came the plastic squeezable bottle, then the recyclable plastic squeeze bottle. But most recently the news media raved about what could be the best improvement yet—the trap cap. It's a new top that solves the age-old condiment conundrum of how to get to the ketchup without enduring the initial rush of watery yuck. Heinz didn't spend 18 months developing the improvement just for a great media hit. But the ketchup king did know the press would be first in line to launch its marketing campaign.

How about a new "spin" on the familiar? The Tropicana Casino Resort in Atlantic City was first to roll out a new product called Pedal 'n Play. It's a recumbent bicycle connected to a slot machine. The contraption allows gamblers to get a workout without ever touching the one-armed-bandit; the bet and spin controls are on the handlebars. While the gimmick may be ridiculous (and short-lived), the point is still valid: reporters were drawn to the product's novel simplicity.

It's estimated that big-city residents are bombarded with nearly 3,000 advertisements in a single day. What are the chances then of getting the mainstream news media to notice *your* specialized advertising technique? Pretty slim, unless, that is, your method is incredibly simple, emotive, and different, like that of Beach and Billboard. The company invented a machine that's dragged behind the trucks used to clean beaches each morning. After the trucks have created a freshly swept canvas, Beach and Billboard's machine stamps a marketing message into the sand. While many of us will never have the pleasure of erasing the ads with our own bare feet, the news media wanted to make sure we all knew they were there.

Simple ideas and simple solutions—if you've got one, tell a reporter. She'll then tell a whole lot of people who will want a sampling of what you have to offer.

Yikes! It's a Number

A primary goal of any would-be news seducer should be to extract all unnecessary complexity out of the story you're pitching. The first place to start is with numbers. Search your story for a number, any number, and you will almost always find complexity that can be avoided or reduced.

John Carver, head of the federal agency that supervises accused felons released from jail and awaiting trial, learned this lesson the hard way after an encounter with the *Washington Post*. In February 1999, Carver met with a *Post* reporter following a story that ran the previous month. During his meeting with the reporter, Carver gave her a 37-page spreadsheet that detailed the escapee statistics from the Washington, D.C., area over a three-month period. (Can you see trouble coming?) Armed with that information, the reporter produced another story that highlighted what appeared to be an alarming problem; out of 226 escapes, 83 of the felons were later charged with new crimes. What the reporter apparently didn't realize was that 63 of the 83 charges were for the crime of escaping from a halfway house. The *Post* followed up that story with an editorial characterizing the city's halfway house program as "a serious threat to public safety."

When dealing with the news media, all numbers should be reduced to the simplest form that provides the most clarity. If you don't do it, the reporter (who knows a lot less about your subject than you do) will assume the task. Is that a risk you want to take?

Journalists prefer stories that have few—if any—numbers. Why? For people who make their living peddling words, numbers can be scary. That's part of the reason they got into the word business in the first place. It is an interesting human truth that, in general, people who love words hate numbers. The reverse is also true. Do you know any eloquent CPA's or witty nuclear physicists? How about any novelists, actors, or singers who don't need CPA's to protect them from their agents?

In an August 30, 2000, piece in the *Wall Street Journal*, Massachusetts Institute of Technology professor Arnold Barnett attempted to tackle this common problem of reporters bungling number stories. Barnett addressed three issues that have received considerable press attention. In each case (executions of innocent people, accusations of racial profiling by New York City traffic cops, and the claim that capital punishment had driven down the murder rate), the press had greatly exaggerated the numbers. Bartlett concluded that, "We should not overreact to such frightful statistical 'analyses.' Some of them might reflect not deliberate distortion but rather innocent intellectual disorder." In other words, the numbers confused the reporters, and their stories reflected that confusion.

Barnett's story itself presented an ironic validation of the Rule of Simplicity. After multiple readings of his op-ed piece, I found myself utterly incapable of deciphering his mathematical line of thought. For example, on the issue of press reports that inflated the number of innocent people being executed, Barnett wrote, "The 1-to-7 ratio, however, represents neither of these rates but rather a confused amalgam of their components. It divides the number of known innocents freed from death row by the number of executions. In other words, it divides the numerator of the error rate for capital-sentencing by the denominator of the rate for executions." What? To Barnett's credit, he later tried to clarify his position with an analogy, "[I]t is akin to computing an earnings-per-share statistic by dividing the earnings of one company by the number of shares of a completely different one." Like other word people who read this piece, I said to myself, "Now I get it . . . I think."

Remember the big Y2K scare? It was a complex story that the news media was forced to take on because experts believed that there was a great potential for significant or even catastrophic consequences. It is estimated that a whopping $300 billion was spent on "fixing" the Y2K problem, $100 billion in the United States alone. The term "Y2K compliant" became common vernacular as millions of people focused their energies on the mission of preventing a disaster of biblical proportions. Then January 1, 2000, arrived, and everything still worked. So what happened? Did we spend all that money on a problem that didn't even exist? Apparently so, but that's not the point. In the aftermath of the great Y2K scare, I didn't see or read a single story that even attempted to address the subject. Did you? There were a week's worth of stories that stated what we all knew, that nothing serious had happened. By February, the mainstream press had abandoned the story. What about all the hype, the money, the panic? By its conspicuous silence, the news media said, "Too many numbers, too much complexity, too confusing, we've tired of the whole thing."

The interesting part of the Y2K debacle for media critics was that, for the most part, the mainstream press really didn't take a hard look at the issue. The complexity of all those nasty numbers and technical data was too intimidating. So instead of doing the hard work of analyzing facts, news managers instead focused on emotions. Remember all the stories on people who were stockpiling food and water at secluded mountain retreats? How was that kind of story going to help us survive the impending technological apocalypse? While the press tried to get us to *feel* the story, a determined, straight-shooting preacher picked apart all the disinformation. Hank Hanegraaff published *The Millennium Bug Debugged*, which clearly explained why fears of a technical meltdown were greatly exaggerated. A few national media outlets, such as *The Wall Street Journal*, gave small mention to Hanegraaff's well-reasoned book. They did so because *Debugged* presented a simplified analysis of the problem (his thesis was also *different* than what most "experts" were saying). However, because Hanegraaff was attempting to lower the irrational pitch surrounding Y2K (violating the Rule of Emotion), his book never rose above the flood of other stories that assaulted us for months before nothing happened. Following the big non-event, the mainstream press could have gone back through the mess in an attempt to explain why so many people spent so much money chasing a problem that was so not there. But that would have been complicated, not to mention, a royal pain in the butt (chapter 6, Rule of Easy).

Numbers are Numbing

Experience has shown that making things too simple for a reporter is rarely a problem. Making things too complex, on the other hand, is a daily hazard for every newsroom on the planet. If you want a story told correctly—or even told at all—complexity (especially the numerical kind) is not a luxury you can afford.

I once trained the administrative staff of an entire school district that had been having problems with reporter errors. On the district's first big test, the superintendent was quizzed about the attrition rate for teachers. This intelligent administrator followed The Rule of Simplicity well—but not well enough. She provided all the statistics that the reporter would need and even categorized them. Unfortunately, she failed to follow Einstein's advice in that she did not simplify enough. She did not boil the numbers down to a level the reporter could easily grasp—a percentage. Left to his own and lacking computational skills, the reporter determined that fully one-third of the school's teachers were leaving, and that's what the front page headline said—"Turnover Rate Hits 33%." The actual figure was 12 percent. If the superintendent had reduced her number to a percentage, the reporter would have been compelled to double-check his own calculations, or, at a minimum, question the administration's arithmetic. Either way, the Rule of Simplicity would have stopped the headline from even being written.

In another school district, a barrage of summer rains created a number problem for the news media and district officials. A reporter asked why there were so many leaks in the schools—a total of 80. The maintenance director responded, "We've got 11.5 million square feet of roof in the district. Having 80 leaks isn't really that bad." Really? Who can tell with a number that big?

Let's apply the Rule of Simplicity to this problem and see what happens. If we divide the number of leaks into the total square footage of roof space in the district we come up with only one leak per 143,750 square feet. But that number is still way too large to visualize. So how about dividing the number of square feet per leak into the average size of a home in the city (1,800 square feet). Now we've got a number people can relate to—one leak for every 80 homes. After going through this process of simplification the maintenance director could have said, "We had the equivalent of only one school leak for 80 homes, that's an entire subdivision! When you consider how old these buildings are and the small number of people we have maintaining them, I'd say we're doing an excellent job." The Rule of Simplicity can turn a bad news story into a good news story.

To "word" people—and that's most of us—numbers are numbing. The use of numbers in a news story will typically complicate the text, not simplify it. Can you comprehend the magnitude of $2.86 billion? I can't, not without a word picture, anyway. And yet, such large numbers are thrown about every day on television, radio, and newspapers, as if the general public actually knew what they meant. If I tell you that one billion dollars is the equivalent of a stack of $100 bills as high as the Washington Monument, now you have a much better (albeit still inadequate) comprehension of the number. Words and images give numbers meaning.

Perhaps the primary reason that reporters have problems simplifying numbers is that doing so requires time-consuming mental dexterity. A journalist's time is always in short supply. Don't take away the newsperson's most precious resource. Instead, do yourself and her a favor by first reducing complexity and then giving the numbers context and meaning through words and images.

Staging Simplicity

The Rule of Simplicity also applies to press releases and the staging of media events. Even if there are several interesting facets to the item you're pushing, don't sell it all. Sacrifice. Pick your *best* bullet. The industry is hardwired to avoid complexity. It's a strategic mistake to attempt to be the exception to the rule.

Let's say community leaders are excited about a regional transportation plan. Can they get meaningful news coverage to gain public support? Without simplifying the plan, it's a crapshoot. Now, what if one of the roads in the regional plan would cross through a neighborhood, an ancient burial ground, or require the cutting down of an old tree? Will there be coverage now? You bet there will. News people don't want the whole story, just the most compelling piece of it.

For any complex issue to be a successful media seducer, it must be boiled down to its simplest terms. And sometimes that's not even enough. Want to fix an abominable tax code? Join the club. Virtually no one will defend U.S. tax law as being good public policy, but every plan to reinvent it has failed. It doesn't matter that much simpler tax plans have been proposed. Even the most basic, common sense approaches involve more complexity than the news media (or the political establishment) will tolerate. Without extensive coverage by the news media (and perhaps an economic collapse), no new tax plan has a chance.

Interview Simplicity

As I explained in the early part of this chapter, there is a somewhat symbiotic relationship between difference, emotion, and simplicity. In a compelling news story, these elements line up like peas in a pod, with simplicity being first. It's as true for the interview as it is for the story itself.

Great quotes—that is, those which are most potent because of their difference and emotion—are predictably the most simple. As C. W. Ceram succinctly put it, "Genius is the ability to reduce the complicated to the simple." E. F. Schumacher couldn't have agreed more; "Any intelligent fool can make things bigger, more complex and more violent. It takes a touch of genius—and a lot of courage—to move in the opposite direction."

Reporters, like the rest of humanity, always like the simplest expression of ideas. Nothing is quite so attractive as simple truth—especially when that's all you have room for.

When the great basketball coach and broadcaster Al McGuire died in January 2000, he was praised as a great simplifier. McGuire was the author of many round-ball snippets, such as "tap city," "white knuckler," and "aircraft carrier." As Arnie Stapleton reported for the Associate Press, "In McGuire's argot, a 'thoroughbred' who was 'dynamite' in practice and mediocre at 'curtain time' was a '3 o'clocker.'" CBS announcer Dick Enberg said, "Al was the most unique and incredible person I ever met. He saw life at a different angle than the rest of us. He could cut through all the fat and get to the bone of the matter quicker than anyone I've ever met."

Al McGuire was an entertaining (different) and colorful (emotion) personality who was impossible not to like. He achieved that legacy by expressing his ideas in creative, simple terms.

Legacy in a Line

As unfair as it may seem, an entire presidency is summed up in one simple line. It is the line of legacy. Abraham Lincoln said, "A house divided against itself cannot stand." That one statement captured his position on the Civil War and ultimately defined his presidency. FDR said, "We have nothing to fear but fear itself." Roosevelt's appeal to American courage became his contribution to presidential folklore.

Every American president seeks out the memorable. John F. Kennedy grasped his line only moments after being sworn into office: "Ask not what your country can do for you. Ask what you can do for your country." Ronald Reagan was dubbed "The Great Communicator," and yet the sum of his eight years in Washington is conveniently reduced to a single command, "Mr. Gorbachev, tear down this wall."

... the simplest line that best defines the most provocative moment of a presidency is the one that sticks. For Richard Nixon it was, "I am not a crook."

Years before Bill Clinton's tenure was up as commander-in-chief, we heard countless news reports about the man in "search of his legacy." President Clinton was wasting his time searching, and the news media were wasting our time telling us about it. Mr. Clinton's legacy had already been cemented into the public consciousness: "I did not have sexual relations with that woman, Ms. Lewinski."

The Rule of Simplicity is not partisan. Republicans, Democrats, Independents, and Libertarians should all fear and revere its power. Without exception, the simplest line that best defines the most provocative moment of a presidency is the one that sticks. For Richard Nixon it was, "I am not a crook." For George Bush Sr., it was, "Read my lips, no new taxes."

Reporters and news consumers don't have the time or the patience to decipher complicated prose. They want their quotes served up fast and neat. Veteran broadcaster Jeff Greenfield put it this way: "The niftiest turn of phrase, the most elegant flight of rhetorical fancy, isn't worth beans next to a clear thought clearly expressed."

Simply Speaking Saves Context

There is an added benefit to speaking in clear, simple terms. Ideas that are easier to understand are more difficult to take out of context.

In the previous chapter, I cited the 1998 study conducted by the American Society of Newspaper Editors. As you recall, nearly a quarter of those in the study who had been interviewed by a reporter complained that they had been misquoted. It's a fair assumption that these people were their own worst enemies because they talked too long, gave the reporter too much detail, and did not succinctly express their ideas.

When the Italian magazine *Oggi* published a story quoting Pope John Paul II's doctor as saying that the Pontiff had Parkinson's disease, the doctor complained he was misquoted. Gianfranco Fineschi, who replaced the Pope's hip in 1994, told the Associated Press, "I was asked if the Holy Father had Parkinson's, to which I replied, 'I cannot exclude that he suffers from a Parkinson's-like illness, but it is not my field.'" Anyone who uses a double negative when talking to a reporter is asking for trouble. And if Parkinson's disease isn't his field, why did Fineschi even offer an answer? Using the Rule of Simplicity, the surgeon could have said, "My specialty is hip replacement. Ask me anything about the Pope's hip, and I've got an answer for you."

If you want a reporter accurately to convey your point of view, simplify your point of view. Don't trouble him with lots of unnecessary information. He doesn't have time for it. Instead, do the reporter's simplification work for him. He'll appreciate the effort because you have just made his day's work a lot easier (chapter 6, Rule of Easy). You've given accuracy a better chance. As an added bonus, the reporter will have a clearer understanding of your position. That clarity will often result in a more favorable representation of the facts, as you see them.

So why don't more newsmakers simplify their message? The biggest reason is that they don't know the core message they want to convey (chapter 5, Rule of Preparation). The person being interviewed fails to organize his or her thoughts. When the reporter arrives, the interview subject expects that the journalist will somehow seize the critical mass of the story (a subject he may know little about) and cut right to the heart of it. Predictably, the reporter and the interviewee too often fail to find the mark.

The Rule of Simplicity is also violated because of unrealistic expectations. Many interview subjects painstakingly explain the entire history of the story. They elaborate on a multitude of solutions to the problem. They are exhaustively thorough and are quite pleased with themselves when the reporter leaves. Then, when the story is printed or broadcast, the naïve interviewee is stunned. "What was *that!*" they cry. "After giving that reporter all that information, she chose to use only *that!* She left out everything important!" My question is, what did they expect . . . a mini-documentary . . . a full-page feature? Nevertheless, people who have watched thousands of newscasts and read thousands of newspapers are surprised when their story turns out to be *so short.*

In a January 1999 study done by the Project for Excellence in

Journalism, it was reported that 70 percent of local television news stories are less than one minute and that nearly half of all stories were less than 30 seconds. All that television reporters want from you is one clear, compelling statement that will occupy a small time slot, typically between five and ten seconds. For radio news, the constraints are often tighter.

The Rule of Simplicity is most critical when dealing with broadcast reporters because they have a lot less time between assignment and deadline. Even so, young reporters are notoriously bad at conducting long interviews. They typically roll much more tape than necessary in order to get a multitude of sound bites to choose from. It's the cover-all-bases strategy. The problem with this tactic is that deadlines come fast. Logging tape (looking for a sound bite in a videotape machine), on the other hand, is slow. Under pressure to get the story done before the fast-approaching newscast, the reporter will seize upon the first usable "bite." Will it be your best quote? Maybe you'll get lucky. Probably you won't.

The solution is to edit yourself and your material *before* you dump it on the reporter. By simplifying your message, you offer the newsman his greatest joy—clarity. You also spare his most precious resource—time. He will be grateful. You will reap the reward.

Angle Anglers

Occasionally you may encounter a reporter who doesn't seem to be in a hurry at all. These people are typically freelancers, news magazine writers, or trade journal types. The Rule of Simplicity still applies. In fact, it may even be more important.

Reporters not pressed by a deadline—and a direction—are fishing. They may have a general idea for a story but are not committed to any particular angle. This can be trouble. It's like target shooting without a target. How can you set your sights on the bull's eye when you (and the reporter) don't know where it is?

Talking to a reporter who does not have a clear direction will virtually guarantee that your comments will be taken out of context. A reporter who decides on an angle *after* his first interview is likely to wedge the quote or sound bite into his story—somewhere. Will it be a good fit? Will it convey your central-most thought on his new-found angle? Is that a risk you want to take?

How do you deal with an angle angler? Follow the Rule of Simplicity. Ask him to clearly define his angle so you can comment appropriately. If he can't clearly express one, this is your lucky day. Give him a direction for his story (chapter 6, Rule of Easy; chapter 8, Rule of Resource). Describe in simple terms what you believe is a worthwhile story. Then resist the powerful temptation to explain the details, thereby violating the Rule of Simplicity. End the conversation. If the reporter seizes on your idea, he will call you back. This time, he will have an angle—your angle.

The Rule of Simplicity does not dictate that you dispense with background information. Make sure the reporter clearly understands the relevant framework of the story (chapter 5, Rule of Preparation). Just don't give him background information in the interview. You'll surely regret it.

Decide what your message is. Give the reporter your simple, emotive, different point of view. Give it to him again (chapter 7, Rule of Repetition). Then stop talking.

The Rule of Simplicity may be simple, but it's not easy. Obeying it requires forethought, planning, sacrifice, and determination. I'm convinced that many CEOs, public relations directors, small business owners, politicians, and other newsmakers would be willing to do the work, if only they knew the high price of complexity.

Okay . . . Now What?

By now you're probably sick of hearing my mantra—Difference, Emotion, Simplicity. Prepare to get sicker (just kidding . . . sort of). I have pounded away at these three concepts—and will continue to re-reference them—because they are at the heart of the Media Rules. All news stories begin and end with them.

Recognizing the uncommon, the colorful, and the uncomplicated in any potential news item is your ticket to seizing the powerful marketing force inherent in publicity. But where do you go from here? How do you apply this knowledge that before now has been sitting unused in your head waiting for structure? That's what the next section, the Enablers, is all about. The next three rules will provide you with a simple, practical, systematic way to engage the Beast.

CHAPTER 5

◆ ◆ ◆

The Rule of Preparation

~ frame or be framed ~

Fail to prepare . . . prepare to fail. Why is it that so many leaders hold steadfast to this wise precept in most things, except when dealing with the press? Hordes of otherwise brilliant people seem to believe that collectively the news media are some fickle, omnipotent giants. Sometimes they torture. Sometimes they bless. Their actions are arbitrary and unpredictable. Therefore, preparing for anything other than the basics is not even a consideration. News people, by the way, love this misconception. It's what gives them their power to intimidate. It also acts as a mist of uncertainty that cloaks the industry's true condition—panicked desperation to feed the Beast's insatiable appetite.

You, however, now know the truth—the News Beast is extremely predictable. Reporters, editors, producers, and photographers are all impatiently drawn to the same three seductive forces: difference, emotion, and simplicity (DES). Find a story that has ample doses of DES, and you have a bone that the Beast will chew on. Say something different, emotive, and simple in your interview, and that's the quote the journalist will like best. DES is the three-legged stool of news predictability. Anything predictable can be prepared for.

Planned "Spontaneity"

In June 1999, talk show host Jerry Springer faced the Chicago City Council's Police and Fire Committee. Members of the council had apparently become alarmed that the eight-year-old "Jerry Springer Show" was encouraging violent behavior from its guests and might even have staged some of the violence. (I wonder what tipped them off?) Martha Irvine, one of many reporters who covered the hearing wrote, "All the ingredients were there—cheering fans, hissing opponents and a bank of about 20 TV cameras." In other words, this story had a powerful dose of DES. What reporter could resist such a show?

Springer, a masterful media manipulator, came prepared. When he was questioned about producers allegedly bringing a banned felon into the country to appear on the show, Springer didn't answer the question. As Irvine gleefully reported, "[H]e leaned toward the microphone and sniped, 'I've never been a member of the Communist party.'" Springer supporters howled their approval. With one tight, compelling comment (DES), Springer was able to portray himself as the innocent victim in a lynching that smacked of McCarthyism. The Rule of Preparation is a powerful thing.

Virtually anyone can tempt the Beast to give them the publicity they desire—if they prepare. Remember the 1999 World Cup soccer championship for women? Sure you do. It was the United States against China. The game was tied at the end of regulation and had to be decided by goal kicks. Brandi Chastain booted the winning goal and immediately yanked off her jersey in celebration. Her ecstatic face and exposed sports bra became the front page, magazine cover, and lead story in media outlets across the world. Chastain claims the outrageous act came in a moment of temporary insanity. I'm not convinced.

It seems much more likely that Chastain was prepared to shed her shirt when and if the dramatic opportunity presented itself. Fortunately for her, it came at the absolute best time, the winning goal of the final playoff. The speed with which she pulled off her top and the fact that she wore a black bra underneath (it's easier to spot a black garment in a pack of swarming white uniforms) convinces me that she dreamed about the stunt long before she performed it. By the way, after Chastain showed the world her underwear, sales of sports bras spiked.

Bras are one thing, but how do you get exposure for a product as technically bland as security software for computers? Try daring hackers to penetrate the system and offer to pay $50,000 to anyone who succeeds. That's exactly what Argus System's Group, manufacturer of "Pitbull," did in January 2001. Argus made the challenge during "OpenHack III," a computer-hacking contest sponsored by *eWeek* magazine. The challenge, however, was not so bold as the headline indicated—"Pitbull Double-Dares Hackers." Argus knew that the best hackers couldn't be bated into such a contest because in order to collect the prize they would have had to reveal their hacking secrets. Did the press know that the challenge was essentially bogus? Of course, but the story was too seductive not to cover.

It's highly unlikely that Jerry Springer, Brandi Chastain, and the manufacturers of "Pitbull" said, "Let's prepare for some good publicity by looking for difference, emotion, and simplicity." Instead, they acted on their *intuitive* feel for what would work. That's how most marketing and public relations professionals operate—they have a *feel* or a *sense* of what the news media want. As the result of a lot of experience, a few develop an uncanny ability to feed the Beast its most desired cuisine. For most, it's an occasional hit—but mostly miss—proposition. For those who have no marketing background, it's a big mystery.

Anyone who wants to be consistently successful in grabbing the best that the news media have to offer must apply the Rule of Preparation. Anyone who wants to avoid the worst the Beast can dish out must also apply this critical rule. (I'll talk more about this when we discuss the Hazards, chapters 11, 12, and 13.) Winging it is a bad idea—for the novice and the professional.

The Media Rules are always there whether you use them consciously or by default. For years, both as a reporter and a media strategist, I used the Media Rules. I just didn't know it. As a result, I didn't use them consistently nor utilize their full power. Consequently, I made mistakes that could have easily been avoided. I missed opportunities that were there for the taking. A well-developed sense of what the news media want is no match for a systematic approach based on a reliable model.

It's All about Marketing

All story placement is a marketing proposition. You are selling a product to a newsperson who will in turn sell it to her audience. What is *your* target market interested in? It wants DES—and preferably with as little hassle as possible (chapter 6, Rule of Easy).

In preparing your pitch to the target market, there are three primary questions. What is different about my product? What emotion will my product provoke? What non-essential factors must I eliminate to make my product tantalizingly simple?

McDonald's is one of the world's premier marketers. Leave it to the inventors of reconstituted chicken parts to come up with ingenious ways to stay on top of the highly competitive fast food industry. When McDonald's reinvented the way it prepared food by adding robotized technology, corporate executives wanted everyone to know about it. But why would the news media care that McDonald's had come up with a better way to get orders right and to ship out the burgers and fries a few seconds faster? Isn't that what advertising is for? True. If McDonald's had pitched such a story with no more seductive ingredient than "technology has made us better," the Beast would have yawned and ignored it. But McDonald's got the news media interested by serving up some DES.

McDonald's executives took a calculated risk by inviting 100 of its toughest customers—stock analysts and portfolio managers— to test its new system. In restaurants across the country, stock experts received some quick training and then strapped on the aprons. They inserted buns in toasters, squirted condiments, and monitored customer orders on a computer screen. To make the exercise even more interesting, the investment experts were put on the line during the noon-hour rush. "Financial finaglers frying fries"—it was a different concept that was humorous and simply presented.

Take a close look at just about anything happening on the national scene, be it business, government, sports, entertainment, or politics, and you will see the Rule of Preparation operating underneath the surface. Excellent publicity rarely happens by accident. It is usually the result of methodical preparation.

Liz Kalodner had a problem. She needed some positive "buzz" to promote her online dating company, <SocialNet.com>. Her answer came in the form of an odd use of her own service. At 40 years old and single, Kalodner needed a date. But more than that, she wanted some publicity. So she launched a "Win a Date with our CEO" contest. For several weeks, men from across the country pitched themselves as great date and mate material. The story of

Kalodner's "sacrifice" quickly spread through the Internet and wound up landing her and SocialNet.com in newsprint. By utilizing the three key elements in news seduction, Kalodner didn't just attract a few dates—she drew the affectionate eye of the Beast.

In the late stages of the 2000 presidential campaign, Al Gore and George W. Bush focused most of their effort on winning a handful of key "swing" states that were too close to call. They waged an intensive ground war, zigzagging across the country in order to cash in on as much free publicity as possible. Team Gore knew that just showing up and delivering speeches wouldn't be enough. Their candidate needed a way to get local press coverage in all key states simultaneously. With some creative thinking and preparation, the Gore camp did just that.

Prior to the first big debate with Bush, Gore hunkered down in Florida (the most important swing state) and summoned a special team of "advisors" to help him with debate preparations. Gore's counselors weren't experts in the areas of foreign policy, economics, or education. They were carefully selected working-class people who fit key demographics in the battleground states. Team Gore knew that local newspapers and TV stations would do feature stories on the top Democrat's unconventional confidants. The strategy worked wonderfully. There was blanket coverage in each swing state and in the national press.

The great irony, however, is that Al Gore's excellent debating skills had already been covered extensively in the media. He had just spent eight years as the nation's number two politician and a year on the campaign trail talking to everyday folks from coast to coast. This publicity ploy was as transparent as they get. And yet, it was a great success.

Whether you run a major corporation, a presidential campaign, a small business, or anything else, you must prepare for press coverage with an eye on DES.

A Good Story Isn't Any Good If It Doesn't Stick

If you want to consistently win favorable publicity, the Rule of Preparation is important. If you want to maximize the coverage once you get it, preparation is absolutely critical. The power of publicity isn't just getting exposure. Every day multitudes of people appear in newsprint, on the airwaves, and through the Internet and don't see any noticeable benefit. Their voices simply join the massive roar of information that passes through the culture moment by moment.

It's pretty easy to spot someone who hasn't truly prepared for his or her publicity. After reading, watching, and/or listening to their story, you've got nothing. Zilch. Nada. The story was told, delivered, and received, but nothing stuck. There was no compelling message that made any difference to the news consumer. If you want publicity that counts, find DES in your story *and* your message.

In the made-for-TV drama known as the O.J. Simpson murder trial (the real life version), defense attorney Johnnie Cochran told the world (about the glove taken as evidence at the murder scene), "If it doesn't fit, you must acquit." This one rhythmic line—and the image it evoked—was perhaps the single most powerful reason that jurors found a "reasonable" doubt in the criminal trial. The news media seized this line and allowed Cochran to repeat it over and over via the wonder of videotape (chapter 7, Rule of Repetition).

Cochran's creative and poetic defense, however, didn't make a whole lot of sense. The gloves were designed to tightly hug the skin. Making O.J. wear surgical gloves (presumably to protect the evidence) enlarged his hands. It was also reasonable to expect that sweat and blood may have shrunk the gloves. Did that matter as far as the publicity value was concerned? Absolutely not. Cochran's mantra was just too good. Even though reporters knew that Cochran's line was ridiculous in light of the facts, they couldn't resist using it. The defense attorney's seemingly basic, yet sophisticated, message was a masterpiece of preparation.

President Ronald Reagan became know as "the great communicator" not because of his wit or his ability to ad-lib, but because he smartly prepared comments that stuck. On tax day in 1986 Reagan told the press, "Republicans believe that every day is the 4th of July, while Democrats wish every day was April 15." How could any self-respecting journalist resist such a line? In 1981 Reagan wanted to draw attention to pork barrel spending in the congressional budget: "Cures were developed for which there were no known diseases," he quipped. After years of being criticized for his economic policies, Reagan finally shot back: "A friend of mine was invited to a costume party a short time ago. He slapped some egg on his face and went as a liberal economist." These kinds of clean, snappy (and sticky) quotes don't happen by accident. They are the result of preparation.

> Even though reporters knew that Cochran's line was ridiculous in light of the facts, they couldn't resist using it.

In the world of technology, PR spinners have the nasty habit of weighing down their messages with techno-speak. So it was refreshing to see evidence of creative preparation at the 2000 Comdex convention. Reporters stood by as the leaders of the handheld computer industry debated the merits of their products. It was Palm's "Clie" versus Compaq's "PocketPC." Palm's Michael Mace came prepared to position the Clie as much lighter and less expensive than the PocketPC. Mace said, "One you can put in your pocket, the other you can put in your pocket, and it will pull down your pants." The crowd roared, and the reporters scribbled. Compaq's Ted Clark was ready for that criticism. He quickly delivered a retort that promoted the PocketPC's greatest advantage over the lighter Clie—a vivid color display. To add some humor to his message, Clark mispronounced the name of the handheld while mocking its black and white screen.

"It's too bad he didn't turn on that 'klee.' If you saw the screen on that 'klee,' you would rather use a PocketPC . . . even with your pants down." Again, the crowd cheered, and the reporters took notes.

The Palm vs. Compaq debate at Comdex is a good lesson for anyone who wants the news media's help in positioning a product in the marketplace. Both sides crafted simple, compelling messages, spiked with emotion. That's what reporters (and their audiences) want.

Massage the Message

In any news story, there should be one central issue. The Rule of Preparation commands that you craft a message for this key element. There may be multiple side issues for which you will want a message, but it is the core concern that should receive the bulk of your attention.

The stakes are highest when live cameras and microphones are involved. Just ask former vice president Dan Quayle. In 1988, Quayle was engaged in a live debate with Lloyd Benson, the Democratic vice presidential nominee. Quayle and his managers knew they had to shore up the candidate's most vulnerable attribute—his youthful age. Their strategy was to remind everyone that Jack Kennedy was a young man in his presidency. Therefore, having an equally young vice president would be no big deal. But Quayle's people stopped preparing at that point. It proved to be a mistake that haunts Quayle to this day.

Benson and the Democrats knew Quayle would use the comparison to Kennedy as his defense. What other options did he have? So a retort to the Kennedy defense was prepared and Benson delivered it beautifully. "Senator Quayle, I knew Jack Kennedy. I worked for Jack Kennedy. And you, sir, are no Jack Kennedy." It was a devastating blow. It's nearly impossible for most people to think of a snappy comeback when they've been put down—especially when millions of people are watching.

If only Quayle's people had looked beyond their age defense to what Benson's reply *might* have been, they should have figured that Benson would not have let the Kennedy comparison go uncontested but have a planned counter attack ready. Seeing this as a distinct possibility, Quayle *could have* trumped his opponent. When Benson said, "You're no Jack Kennedy," Quayle could have responded, "You're right, Mr. Benson. I've been faithful to my wife." Kennedy lovers would have been mortified, but Quayle would have been recognized as a man with exceptional wit and moxie—a worthy trade-off.

In spite of the massive amount of news coverage that is generated every day, the number of well-crafted messages is still frightfully few. Why? Most people who find themselves in front of a news reporter don't have a message—at least not the kind that the Beast craves. The reporter asks question after question, and the subject talks and talks and talks. The interviewee incorrectly assumes that it's the reporter's job to find the best message, or that the key point is obvious. You don't want any reporter "finding" your message or having to figure out what you believe is obvious. Prepare your message like you would a gourmet meal and serve it up on a diamond-studded platter.

Mark Twain once wrote a friend a letter and ended it by saying, "I would have written you a shorter letter, but I didn't have the time." Reducing anything to a simple, straightforward message is difficult and often painful work. It won't happen by itself.

Did Muhammad Ali come up with "The Greatest," "Float like a butterfly, sting like a bee," and "The Thrilla in Manila" off the top of his head? *Please*. Ali knew how to massage the news media and, therefore, prepared for that seduction. The media—and the general public—inhaled his compelling message.

NFL lineman Tony Siragusa knows a thing or two about preparing material for the press. Prior to the Baltimore Raven's Superbowl victory over the New York Giants Siragusa became the darling quipster of sports reporters. In one memorable exchange, he took a friendly swipe at teammate Shannon Sharpe—a player known for constantly running his large mouth. "When Shannon first came on the team, he reminded me of Mister Ed, the way his mouth moves and stuff," Siragusa said. "Then I saw his teeth, and I knew it was definitely him." Football fans hear plenty from players and coaches who talk about match-ups, momentum, injuries, and expectations. That stuff they forget. Guys who talk like Siragusa are remembered.

What does Fox sports analyst Howie Long say when radio giant Don Imus asks him about working with the frail-looking Chris Collinsworth? "Don, you know he's one of those guys who gave up a lot of lunch money in his childhood." Did Howie come up with that line off the top of his head? What do you think? Long, who often disagrees with Collinsworth on air, knows that a question about his partner will come up sometime. So, either he thinks up a quip and uses it when the opportunity arises or he relies on his exceptional wit to make himself look brilliant. You decide which it is.

When Democratic Party operative James Carville was asked why he attended the 2000 Republican National Convention,

Carville said, "Every dog show needs one fireplug." In six words Carville painted a vivid scene. Pampered Republican show dogs relieving themselves on the only functional item (Carville) at the pompous affair. But Carville's humorous comment did more than deliver a backhanded slap at the Republicans. It also allowed him to avoid the question he didn't want to answer. Why was a high-level Democratic Party consultant attending the Republican convention? Was he spying? Or did his wife (a high-level Republican Party consultant) prefer that he be there? We'll never know—which is just the way Carville wanted it.

Several months earlier, when George W. Bush's brother Marvin was introduced to the traveling press corps, he wanted to make an impression. Marvin Bush told reporters, "That great sucking sound you hear is the sound of the media's lips coming off of John McCain's butt."

So big deal. Cochran, Benson, Siragusa, Long, Carville, and President Bush's brother all had lots of time to come up with their messages. Wouldn't anybody with a reasonable amount of intelligence be able to do the same thing with days or even weeks to mull it over? Yes, and that's the point: They did the work. Most others don't.

In the Middle of the Blue

Preparing the perfect message for a story you are expecting is a neat and orderly proposition. But what about the call that comes right out of the blue? A reporter is on the phone, and he wants an interview. How do you prepare for that kind of situation? The answer is that in most cases there are no surprise questions. Unless something highly unusual is going on, you should have a good understanding of any topic a reporter might question you about.

Think about it. The reason you are the one being interviewed is that you possess some specialized knowledge of the subject at hand. How many topics in your arena of influence are there? Of those, how many have the potential of becoming a news story? They are pretty easy to spot. The stories are those—good or bad— that possess high levels of DES. How many are there—three, four, six? If you're like most people, it's one or two. But whatever the number, for each and every possibility you should consider your position and how to express creatively that position when the opportunity presents itself.

One client of mine is the founder of a resource center for victims of domestic abuse. She wanted some press to help promote awareness about the center but was apprehensive about doing interviews. "What if I get nervous and say something wrong or sound stupid?" she worried. But once we boiled her topic down to its key elements (simplicity), she realized that there were only a few areas that would be good interview topics. She developed a quote for each and settled on one primary message that she would send in every interview; "The victim of domestic violence doesn't live across town. She lives next door." She's used that line in dozens of print and broadcast interviews. Most of the time that's the quote that gets used.

In April 2000, *People* magazine published a story on a friend and client of mine, middle school teacher Kim Gattone. An accomplished mountain climber, Kim was set to take on her ultimate challenge, Mt. Everest. *People* became interested in Kim because she was going to be communicating with her sixth-grade Calvary Chapel Christian Academy class through her laptop computer, a satellite phone, and the <Quokka.com> website. In fact, students and teachers from across the country would be following the teacher's progress. A great story with a lot of DES, don't you agree? But there was a problem. Kim wanted to make sure that the *People* reporter (and many other reporters to follow) would include the message she most wanted to send. As a devout Christian woman, Kim wanted to tell the world that the climb wasn't just about her endurance and her students' education but about God the Creator. Once she understood the power of preparation, Kim gained great confidence in her ability to make the article a win/win situation. The following passage comes directly from the *People* article:

> A woman of deep faith, Gattone says she'll approach Everest with confidence and humility. "Mountains always seem so *small* to me," she notes. She says she finally understood why while standing atop Cho Oyu, looking at Everest in the distance. "I got a message," she says. "It was, 'Kim, your eyes are on the Creator, so all His creations look small.'" As she challenges Everest, that may be a useful perspective.

Reporters are perpetually in search of something original to print or broadcast. Only occasionally do they find it because very few people speak the way characters do on sitcoms. Archie Bunker, Hawkeye Pierce, Sam Malone, and Bart Simpson are witty because writers spend hours sweating out the set up and delivery of the lines to make their dialogue work. Snappy, insightful, humorous, or profound statements are the result of preparation. Boring, factual, obvious comments are what happen when people haven't taken the time to think of something original to say.

Good Interviews Have Boundaries

Occasionally reporters want to talk to someone who can give an expert's perspective on an issue that could not have been anticipated. In these cases, the opportunity to prepare is somewhat restricted, but it is still in play. When used correctly, the Rule of Preparation will give you time to create a compelling message.

Any time you do an interview, you should also do a pre-interview. This is the moment when you ask the reporter to give you her "angle." Only when you know specifically what the reporter is after should you give her the message that you have, and she wants. Remember, you are putting your name and credibility on a statement that will be publicized. You have the right to be absolutely clear about the context of the story before committing to a public stand.

If a reporter won't agree to a pre-interview, interpret that as a big, red flag with blinking white lights. In this instance you probably have a much bigger problem than worrying about delivering snappy quotes. Journalists who are reluctant to disclose the focus of their story in advance are most often interested in nailing someone to the wall. That's a discussion reserved for the final chapter of this book, the Rule of Ambush.

Pre-interviews allow you to narrow the discussion. Remember, the reporter is on a fact-finding mission. She's going to gather a broad range of information and then whittle it down to a compact story. Your job is to help her accomplish this mission *before* the interview begins. By eliminating irrelevant questions and topics prior to the interview, you have decreased the scope of the discussion. You have told the reporter what few issues are important and what other topics are not. Therefore, the interview is focused. Now you've got a much better opportunity to drive home your message. In other words, *Frame or be Framed.* If you don't frame the boundaries of the interview, the reporter will be free to roam wherever. This type of free-range interview is what gets people into trouble.

Agreeing to answer a reporter's questions "on the fly" is like trying to learn how to ride bulls by just getting on one—no mechanical-bull practice, no training, no boots, and no flack jacket. Either way, you're going to get thrown, and the bull may be kinder to you than the time-strapped reporter.

A Sneak Preview Is Always a Good Idea

Getting critical information before the interview is not as difficult as it seems. If you have a secretary to screen your calls, train that person to quiz any reporter who wants an interview. *"Yes, Ms. Jones would love to speak with you. She's in a meeting now, but she will call you back in less than ten minutes. Ms. Jones would like to know the angle of your story so I can locate any information for her that might be useful."* Now you've got a few minutes to think about the subject, pick your message, and simplify it.

What if you don't have a secretary or suddenly find yourself on the phone with a reporter? This is not a problem. Ask the journalist to give you the angle of his story. What is the focus? What bit of expertise can you provide? What sorts of questions will he be asking? Once you've gathered this information, tell the reporter you have to finish up some business that can't wait and that you'll call back within ten minutes. You'll be telling the truth. Preparing for an interview is very important business that must be done immediately!

Another, more forthright, approach is this: "I'm going to need to think about this for a moment to make sure that I can speak forcefully and accurately. Can I call you back in five minutes for this interview?" Unless the reporter is under extreme deadline pressure, he will happily grant your wish. In fact, the journalist will probably be secretly pleased because the odds of getting a great quote have just increased dramatically.

Think You're Smart Enough *Not* to Prepare? Think Again

Contrary to popular myth, most journalists have no problem doing a pre-interview. When I was a reporter, I always had an increased level of respect for anyone who wanted briefly to discuss the scope of the story in advance. I knew that these people were smart enough not to be paranoid about appearing unsure. I also knew that the ones who were so confident in their ability to speak eloquently with no preparation were not nearly so bright as folks who asked for a little time to think.

When advertising executive Steve McKee got a phone call from a reporter asking about near-term prospects for the industry, McKee knew what to do. He asked the reporter to better define her angle. She told him that a national forecasting company was predicting a sharp increase in advertising in the coming year. She was "localizing" the story by interviewing leaders at the state's top ad agencies. McKee asked the reporter to give him some examples of the questions she would be asking and then told her that he would have to call her back in five minutes. With some time to think, McKee came up with a few answers that reflected his Media Rules training.

On the issue of advertising agencies seeing economic trends before they happen, McKee said, "The state is like a big ship, and our industry is the rudder, so we can feel a change when the ship starts turning." The reporter asked the ad exec about competing for national accounts, to which he replied, "For us, we don't have access to as big a client base, so we have to make bigger leaps. We try smarter." McKee also said, "[S]ince the world is getting smaller, ideas have to get bigger."

Compare McKee's DES answers to what three of his competitors had to say: "We're doing better, yes; but by comparison not as good." What? "Advertising is a real reflection of the economy." Duh! "Nationally I think we could see a dip because many of the dot-coms are struggling." Really? If you were going to hire an ad agency, which executive would inspire your confidence?

Mike Stanford is a bank president, active in his community. As a colorful, straight-talking leader, he has used the Media Rules to become a favorite among reporters. They know he can be counted on to deliver a well-prepared quote. When his state's largest newspaper ran a feature story on him, Stanford said, "My No. 1 customer is my own employee. My basic philosophy is that everything emanates from respect and consideration for other people. Unhappy people don't give good service." When Stanford was asked to give his opinion of the incoming chamber of commerce president, he said, "We always tease him that his demeanor is a lot like James Bond, very suave. He's brutally handsome and doesn't buckle under pressure. It makes me sick, really."

The head of a teacher's union criticized Stanford when he and other business leaders backed a slate of pro-business school board candidates, some of whom had no teaching experience. Stanford responded in the local paper with a counterpoint to the teacher-knows-best assumption. "I don't care if you're a teacher, a baker, or a candlestick maker. Do you really have a clear vision of what it takes to educate children? Can you look outside the box or are you going to be mired down in the system?" It's no coincidence that Stanford's company, First State Bank, has a motto that reflects his philosophy: "Not your typical bankers, not your typical bank."

Intelligence has little to do with the ability to deliver excellent quotes. It has everything to do with preparation. Every day multitudes of smart people are quoted in the press. Most of them sound boring or, at least, uninspired. They do not capitalize on their media opportunity. But that's not the worst thing that can happen to the unprepared—no, not even close.

Foot-in-Mouth Disease

If you have not prepared a message for the reporter, then the chances of his choosing a quote or soundbite that you don't care for increase dramatically. Maybe it will be a quote about a side issue. Perhaps the sound bite will be placed in the wrong context. Worse yet, maybe you'll say something so entertainingly stupid he'll have no choice but to use it.

History is full of examples of people who weren't prepared when the media came calling and stumbled—memorably.

When Sally Field accepted her Academy Award, she said, "You like me, you really like me!" Field's been mocked for her awkward statement ever since.

Actress Alicia Silverstone, star of the movie *Clueless*, told a reporter, "I think *Clueless* was very deep. I think it was deep in the way that it was very light. I think lightness has to come from a very deep place if it's true lightness." For her tangled linguistics, The Plain English Campaign awarded Silverstone its "Foot in Mouth" prize, calling it "the most baffling verbal statement" of 2000. Perhaps she's just clueless.

Testifying during a probate trial over her late billionaire husband's estate, former Playboy model Anna Nicole Smith said, "It's very expensive to be me. It's terrible the things I have to do to be me."

Major league baseball pitcher John Rocker learned the Rule of Preparation the hard way when he told *Sports Illustrated* about his dislike of New Yorkers—especially foreigners, gays, and minorities. Rocker said he would never play for a New York team because he didn't want to ride the subway "next to some queer with AIDS." Among other outlandish statements, Rocker called a black teammate a "fat monkey." The press took Rocker to task, and his career has been abysmal ever since. Even if Rocker stages a comeback, his ill-conceived statements will never be forgotten.

Some of the most notable missteps come from the world of politics. The following are just a smidgen of what have been catalogued by the satirical newspaper *The Onion*.

"I know energy is really important, and that there was a big crisis back in the '70's, but other than that, I'm in the dark."

—Spencer Abraham, the newly installed U.S. Energy Secretary

"Statistics show that teen pregnancy drops off significantly after age 25."

—Mary Ann Tebedo, Colorado state representative

"There are still places where people think the function of the media is to provide information."

—Dan Rottenberg, White House Spokesperson

"I'm not against blacks and a lot of the good blacks will attest to that."

—Evan Mecham, Arizona Governor

"Capital punishment is our society's recognition of the sanctity of human life."

—Orin Hatch, U.S. Senator from Utah

Fuzzy Lock Boxes

There is such a thing as being over-prepared. Using "canned" statements can be more annoying (and even dangerous) than speaking in bland, factual terms.

In the presidential campaign of 2000, George W. Bush accused Vice President Al Gore of using "fuzzy math." Bush's media advisors should have been chastised for fuzzy thinking. While it's important to crystallize your message as succinctly as possible, the media and the public will not tolerate pandering. Canned phrases insult the intelligence of everyone. Team Bush figured this out and stopped using the phrase, but not before late night comedians mercilessly beat him over the head with it.

Not to be outdone, Al Gore told the American public that he would put the social security trust fund in a "lockbox." Ugh. That oft-repeated statement was almost as annoying as the vice president's pronounced sighing during the first presidential debate. Later Gore tried to undue the damage with some self-deprecating humor when he said, "I put all my sighs in a lockbox."

Unfortunately, fuzzy math and social security lockboxes weren't the only canned phrases Americans were forced to endure. Gore repeatedly assaulted us with "the wealthiest one percent," "I'll uphold Roe v. Wade," and "I'll fight for working families." Bush incessantly countered with "mediscare," "leave no child behind," and "a different attitude in Washington."

Perhaps Minnesota Governor Jesse Ventura said it best when he told *Newsweek,* "They're too rehearsed. They're too spun. They're who their parties think they should be to win." Jesse is right. When will politicians learn that the media and the public want clearly articulated, straight talk from their candidates?

The two major parties could have taken a few lessons from Green Party candidate Ralph Nadar, whose polling numbers jumped by as much as seven-percent after the presidential debates of 2000. If you watched the debates, you know why. During their three televised forays, neither Gore nor Bush reduced their arguments into plain English with a message that would resonate. Most of what they said was boring, unnecessarily complex, or canned. Nadar said he should have been allowed to participate in the debates if only to "keep people from falling asleep as they watch the drab debate the dreary."

On ABC's *This Week,* Nadar said, "If Gore cannot beat the bumbling Texas governor with that horrific record, what good is he? Good heavens! I mean, this should be a slam-dunk." Syndicated columnist David S. Broder said of Nadar, "Often in the past a nagging bore, he proved himself a quick and witty TV performer, adept at sharp sound bites." At 65 years old, Nadar suddenly becomes "quick and witty"? I suspect not. Nadar finally learned that powerful quotes rarely just happen. They are the product of concentrated effort.

As of this writing, neither President Bush nor his media advisors have learned to steer clear of canned comments. Three months after the inauguration, columnist David Goldstein wrote an article mocking Bush for his constant use of term "good man." Goldstein rattled off more than a dozen men (and one woman) that Bush had called good, among them, Senator John McCain, Attorney General John Ashcroft, and Federal Reserve Chairman Alan Greenspan. It didn't get any better as the months passed. Following the terrorist attacks of September 11, 2001, Bush repeatedly said, "Make no mistake about it, we will bring those terrorists to justice."

In spite of the continuing canned summaries, the Bush administration has learned a few things about preparing zippy quotes. Following 9-11 Bush unleashed some real zingers. The best among them: "I'm not going to fire a $2 million missile at a $10 tent and hit a camel in the butt. It's going to be decisive." Now, that's a quote worth remembering.

Do You Know Where You're Going?

In order to prepare for something you must know what that thing is. That's why so many people fail to get ready for their encounters with the Beast. They haven't nailed down what the story is about and what their message should be. Why? They have no plan or blueprint for how to get there (no system). Instead, they rely on a feel, an intuition, a sense of what the news media want. While this approach may occasionally work in obvious circumstances, it is not useful for spotting great opportunities that lie beneath the surface. Without a system for getting from point A to point B, most people will never wake up to the possibilities.

But even if an intuitive feel occasionally helps in getting publicity, it will be of little use in maximizing the exposure. It's not enough just to catch a passing flash of newsprint or broadcast time. In order to truly make your publicity count, you have to drive home a well-crafted message.

If you only used the Rule of Preparation as a means to identify and maximize DES, you'd be way ahead of the competition. However, we've only just begun to explore the value of this Rule that is a powerful force in all the other Media Rules to come—especially the Rule that's up next.

◆ ◆ ◆

CHAPTER 6

The Rule of Easy

~ *easy does it* ~

It is the lion in the jungle, the shark in the ocean, the eagle in the sky. It is at the top of the news media food chain. There is no Media Rule stronger than the Rule of Easy.

Anyone who wants to befriend the Beast should memorize this phrase: *Easy does it.* If you want a reporter to notice your story, you better make it as easy as possible to cover. Worried about the reporter getting the story right? Better make sure a fifth-grader can understand it. Want to guarantee the journalist uses the quote you want him to use? Keep your message simple, and make sure that it's *reporter friendly.*

Like the rest of humanity, news people are drawn toward the path of least resistance. Therefore, make your story's path wide and smooth. That's what Bill Gates did, and it made him the richest man on the planet.

Windows into Microsoft's World

In his earlier years, Microsoft CEO Bill Gates clearly understood the importance of the Rule of Easy. Strict adherence to this concept led to massive quantities of news exposure that in turn fueled the creation of the Microsoft empire. Although Gates has lost sight of what it takes to be a master of positive publicity (i.e., the handing of Microsoft's antitrust case with the federal government), we can all go to school on what he achieved in the mid 1990s.

In September 1998, now defunct *Brill's Content* published an exhaustive investigative piece on Gates. It was called "The Making of Bill, How Bill Gate's PR machine helped make him Master of the Universe. And why it's failing him now." In the article, reporter Elizabeth Lesly Stevens detailed Microsoft's obsession with the news media. One conclusion of the story was that the methodical manipulation of reporters was a significant factor in the software manufacturer's astounding success. Gates learned early on that making journalists' lives easier is the key component to winning positive publicity and ultimately greater market share.

Stevens quoted David Kirkpatrick, a member of *Fortune* magazine's board of editors, who said, "Microsoft doesn't control coverage in a conventional way." Instead, the company does it "through massive attention to reporters." According to *Content*, sources close to Microsoft's operation estimated its public relations army to be 500 strong. That estimate was from 1996 when Microsoft employed 20,000 people. By contrast, Time Warner Inc. says it utilizes 300 PR experts for an employment base of 68,000. When you generate the kind of publicity Microsoft does, it takes a lot of manpower to keep reporters happy.

Microsoft's greatest accomplishment (and the one that laid the foundation for its global dominance) was the success of Windows 95. At the time, a relatively small Microsoft engaged in a marketing war with corporate behemoth IBM and its OS/2 operating system. However, as *Content* revealed, it wasn't much of a war. Microsoft utilized the power of the press to crush IBM, even though OS/2 was a superior product.

Stevens quoted former Microsoft employee Rick Segal, who headed up a team called "the evangelists." The people that needed saving: news reporters. Segal said, "The whole key to this whole deal was to make sure no press person ever gets an unsatisfactory experience with our product." Segal told *Content* that Microsoft developed "reviewers' guides" that gave reporters step-by-step instructions on how to use the software. These guides also explained why the Microsoft products were better than its competitor's. Segal said the strategy worked so well that Microsoft's sales pitches became text in published articles. He told *Content* that the tactic "was the result of us thinking, 'We know these people are on deadline, and we know they're lazy, and we can do their work.'"

Segal's view of the news media's weaknesses is only half right. Oppressive deadlines are the problem; laziness is not. The real issue is that journalists are often expected to bring down a buffalo with a .22-caliber rifle. They can't. Therefore, the people who know this, like those at Microsoft, can use the media's busyness and lack of knowledge to their considerable advantage.

The Beast Has Heartburn (and Knows Where to Go for Relief)

Microsoft didn't have to hire a bunch of PR geniuses to pull off the Windows 95 coup. All it took was a fundamental understanding of the Beast's shortcomings (stuff you know well)—he's Handicapped, Hungry, Harried, and Human.

As we discussed in earlier chapters, news people, in general, are set up to fail. In many cases, the reporter only has a peripheral understanding of the stories he covers. Time is always a factor. Deadlines come fast. In-depth understanding of complex issues (such as comparing one computer operating system to another) comes slowly. The newsroom is a pressure cooker. Journalists are underpaid and overworked. They tend to be cranky and cynical. (Who can blame them?) There is no way to catch up. The demand for new content always outstrips the amount of time allotted to gather it. Corners must be cut. Compromises must be made. Entertainment value is a constant consideration. Lunch must be skipped; dinner will be late. Neither is likely to be nutritious. Schedules are inconsistent. All the while the Beast screams for more food. Feed him. Feed the Beast as fast as you can.

Because the Beast refuses to stop running and eating at the same time, he has a bad case of acid reflux. So what does he do? He does what millions of other Americans do. Instead of getting a proper diet, exercise, and rest, he pops a Pepsid or a Prilosec. He swigs Pepto Bismol or sucks on a Tums. Or he goes to the medicine cabinet with a glass of water. Plop, plop, fizz, fizz. . . . Oh, what a relief it is. The artificial cure to the Beast's heartburn is like Rolaids. How does the Beast spell relief? E-a-s-y.

Think about the news you absorbed in the last 24 hours. Didn't it look a whole lot like the news you saw on the same day last year and the year before that? The president talks about taxes or terrorism; a congressman is caught in a scandal; more rioting erupts in the Middle East; an earthquake shakes India; someone is murdered; a bank robber is arraigned; the teacher's union pleads for a pay raise; a university sports team wins (or loses) a big game; it's going to rain or snow or swelter.

As John Allen Paulos astutely notes in his book *A Mathematician Reads the Newspaper*, most news comes from "centralized" sources. Therefore, when a reporter asks the five basic questions that all journalists are trained to ask (who, what, where, when, and why), *where* is the most important query. The vast majority of the time the *where* is one of only a handful of familiar places—Washington D.C., Wall Street, Hollywood, city hall, the state capitol, the police department, the court house, the school district, and the university.

It's tempting to believe that our news emanates from a small number of locations because these are the places "where news happens." To a degree this is true. However, it's my observation (and I believe it will be yours, too, once you think about it) that these places dominate our news diet because they are the easiest. When a news source is centralized, there is a place to go and someone to talk to—quickly and easily.

A Passion for Politics

In researching his book *Deciding What's News*, Herbert J. Gans spent a decade watching journalists at work in four newsrooms—CBS Evening News, NBC Nightly News, *Newsweek* and *Time*. As a result of his study, Gans found that a startling 80 percent of domestic news coverage coming out of CBS and NBC focused on the president, presidential candidates, members of congress, and federal officials. This astounding statistic is no longer accurate. In the 20 years since Gans published his findings, coverage of politics and political institutions has declined sharply—primarily because of the media's new obsession with scandals and crisis coverage. However, Gans' findings are still relevant to our discussion. Governmental institutions (which still soak up a significant portion of what we call news) are attractive targets for journalists because they are centralized.

The problem with government news stories, though, is that the people and the subject matter are often boring and/or complex. Add some drama, however, and watch the Beast come running. Simple titillation always trumps boring bureaucrats because spectacles are a lot more fun—and easier—for journalists to cover. So you can imagine how excited the national press corps became when reporters first heard the phrase "White House intern."

The Center for Media and Public Affairs reported that the nation's network evening news programs produced 72 stories on the midterm elections in 1998 between Labor Day and Election Day. During that same time period, the networks produced 426 Bill Clinton/Monica Lewinski scandal stories. The Bill and Monica story superseded legitimate news about the election of the entire U.S. House of Representatives by a factor of nearly six-to-one.

The network's fascination with the Lewinski scandal didn't just overshadow the midterm elections, it also eclipsed everything substantive coming out of the White House. A NewsTV study showed that in July 1998 the networks devoted 179 segments to the sex scandal. Less than a third of press attention (56 segments) was devoted to all other news not involving presidential adultery and subsequent cover-up attempts. Who wants to talk about education reform, foreign policy initiatives, and campaign finance complexities in the midst of public theater like the Clinton/Lewinski scandal?

A full month after leaving the White House, Bill Clinton (perhaps the greatest media spectacle in presidential history) was pulling down as much coverage as President George W. Bush. It seemed Clinton couldn't resist giving the news media one last flurry of scandals to obsess over: the acceptance of lavish gifts for Bill and Hillary's new homes; the taking and returning of White House property; the attempted rental of pricey New York office space; and the pardon of billionaire fugitive Marc Rich whose ex-wife donated generous sums of money to the Democratic Party.

Of the suspicious quid pro quo pardon, *Washington Post* reporter Howard Kurtz wrote, "It's more absorbing for journalists than the latest maneuvering over Bush's tax-cut plan. For the media, scandal trumps boring Washington substance." In the same week, Jonathan Alter wrote for *Newsweek*, "It's clear that Clinton is more than just another addiction in a nation of substance abusers. He's the gift that keeps on giving—to the media, the lip-smacking Republicans and anyone with any appreciation of the subtleties of character and motivation. It's Razorback opera at La Scala. Everything he does—every success, every failure—is just bigger than anything the rest of American political culture can produce. We'll take Elvis thin, fat—anyway he comes." Syndicated columnist Richard Reeves added, "We cover the Clintons because they are not boring. Most reporters and editors are trying to outrun such boring things as government and politics—and are convinced that most Americans are just like them but more so. In terms of media attention, Bill and Hillary are not competing with the Bushs; they are competing with Eminem and O.J." To cap off the week, "Saturday Night Live" opened its February 24, 2001, show with a Slick Willy skit. Clinton impersonator Darrell Hammond said he was like a Big Mac. "After you eat one, you feel queasy and say you're never going to have one again, but you do because it's tasty." Yes, easy, entertaining political theater is as tasty as it gets.

While this all may be amusing and interesting, you may be asking yourself why you should care. The reason is that there is power in understanding that everywhere you go the news media are the same. Journalists in small towns, medium-sized cities, large metro areas, and those in the national/world arena are all in the same predicament. Reporters, producers, and editors are looking for stories that are easy to cover and, if possible, entertaining. They look first to the centralized, which receive the vast majority of attention. The de-centralized (most businesses, non-profit organizations, and others in the not-obvious category) compete for the leftovers. As if this picture were not discouraging enough, there's another major attraction for the Beast, something called "spot news."

Yippee! It's a Disaster

There's nothing more appealing to news people than an unexpected eruption of activity. Fires, plane crashes, earthquakes, riots, multiple homicides, and, of course, terrorist strikes—these are the stories that reporters crave. And why not? They are a custom fit for all the Seducers—Difference, Emotion, and Simplicity. But the added bonus is that they are easy. The who, what, when, where, and why are all located in one place or in just a few places. It's instant centralization.

Consider the most covered stories in recent memory: The terrorist attacks of September 11, 2001; the Anthrax attacks that followed; the bombing of the USS Cole; Rodney King and the L.A. riots; the World Trade Center bombing of 1993; the FBI standoff in Waco, Texas, with the Branch Davidians; the bombing of the federal building in Oklahoma City; the massacre at Columbine High School; the murders of Nicole Brown-Simpson and her friend, Ronald Goldman, followed by the O.J. Simpson trial and acquittal; the murder of designer Gianni Versace; the murder of Jon Bonet Ramsey and the blundered police investigation; the death of Princess Diana in a car crash; the Elian Gonzales saga; the bungling of election night 2000 by the networks; the accidental sinking of the Japanese fishing boat, the Ehime Maru, by the USS Greenville; etc, etc. If the above list were expanded to include all of the significant spot news stories of the last decade or so (the list would grow considerably), can you imagine how much news coverage that would represent? It boggles the mind. Yes, all of these stories are important, but it's not importance that provokes this obsessive attention. The Beast gorges on spot news because it's easy.

Washington Post reporter William Booth pointed out one of the most illustrative examples of the Rule of Easy. When 150,000 acres of forest had burned on federal and state land outside Los Angeles, Booth was on the story. In his report, he noted that earlier that year fire charred 2 million acres in Alaska and Nevada—more than 12 times the amount in Southern California. And yet, this destruction was almost completely ignored by the national press. Why? Because the Alaska and Nevada fires burned in remote locations and, as Booth observed, "The Southern California fires are burning within the range of television news helicopters."

Take a look at your local community, and you will see the same pattern of spot news dominating newsprint and broadcast coverage. The reason is the Rule of Easy. With spot news, the story practically writes itself. If details are "still sketchy," the story is even easier to produce. The video, sound, or "art" (photos for print people) are readily available. It's a sad commentary on the business, but if you absolutely must be in the news spotlight and don't care how you get there, get yourself stranded on a cliff in a snowstorm. News reporters will track you like a bloodhound.

If you want to snatch the publicity prize, you should understand at the outset that you are outgunned. Scandals, crime, politics, spot news, social conflicts, and governmental activity are always going to take the lion's share of available news coverage. Why? They're easier. Competition is stiff for the leftovers. But hey, may the easiest story win.

The Beast Does Not Have ESP

The biggest component of Easy is access. If it's restricted, so too are your chances of grabbing the publicity prize. The question is, what's standing in between your story and the journalists who may want to cover it? Could that barrier be you?

I once covered a story about increasing violence on a high school campus. In the course of the story, a group of students took me to a bush, where a club had been hidden. The students claimed that many other weapons had been stashed on or near the school grounds. When I asked the high school principal about this disturbing bit of information, she became incensed. "Why do you reporters only come around when there's a bad story to tell?" she wailed. "Why aren't you interested in the positive stuff?" she screamed. The principal went on to tell me about students honored the previous week for outstanding academic achievement. When she was through chastising me, I asked her whom she had contacted about the student success story. She hesitated and then sheepishly admitted, "nobody." If the news media don't know about a story, they don't have access to it.

Sometimes that's all it takes—just letting a journalist know that a good story is ready for a telling. It sounds obvious, but you would be surprised at how many great stories get overlooked.

After attending a Media Rules conference, the public relations director of a small, non-profit organization that helps the handicapped realized he had overlooked a golden publicity opportunity sitting right under his nose. When he returned to work, the PR man called a newspaper reporter and told him about 21-year-old Michael Ortega. At 18-months-old Ortega had contracted meningitis, which numbed his brain and partially paralyzed the right side of his body. In spite of his handicap, Ortega went on to receive a high school diploma and, with the help of the non-profit, landed a job as a U.S. District Court custodian. Because of his exceptional job performance, Ortega was nominated for—and won—the "Yes I Can" award given by the Foundation for Exceptional Children. Ortega was one of 35 winners selected among 2,500 candidates in the United States, Canada, and the Soviet Union. This was an easy story to tell, and it had plenty of feel-good DES. But none of that mattered until a reporter actually heard about the young man and the wonderful non-profit organization that helped him achieve a dream. Ortega's story subsequently appeared on the front page (Sunday edition) of the *Albuquerque Journal*.

I had a similar experience with a marketing specialist at a large HMO. I know what you're thinking, good press for an *HMO*? Good luck! But we didn't need any luck. Just letting some reporters know about a great story was more than enough.

Following his Media Rules training, the HMO marketer outlined the story of Valerie Pinto. The 21-year-old woman cannot walk or speak because of cerebral palsy. Valerie lives on the Navajo Reservation. She enjoys herding sheep and visiting her great-aunt who lives a half-mile away. But Valerie had a difficult time enjoying her favorite activities because her thin-wheeled wheelchair would bog down in the sandy terrain. The HMO fixed that problem by supplying her with a high-tech, fat-wheeled replacement. It was a great story that only a few people knew about—that is, until a few reporters were called. After the HMO delivered a well-prepared pitch, the story appeared on the front page of their major daily newspaper's Sunday edition. Several smaller newspapers picked up the story and the region's top-rated television station ran a two-minute feature.

Getting great press can often be a difficult process, but sometimes you can find it by simply looking at what's right under your nose.

What They See Is What You Get

For a reporter, good access means access at any time. Therefore, be prepared to jump through hoops on weekends, nights, or holidays, if necessary. If a reporter can't come to you, offer to go to him. If the story requires additional interviews, provide him with contact names and phone numbers. If there is a visual component to the potential news item, make it easy to photograph or videotape. Your mission is to examine every aspect of your story and remove all unnecessary inconveniences.

Almost any obstruction to a reporter's easy access can be removed if you think creatively. Take a lesson from major corporations and government agencies that are often the subject of news stories. It's not easy to get pictures of Intel workers making microprocessors inside a "clean room." Nor is it convenient to get video of Army troops in training or of cars being made at a General Motors plant. So Intel, the U.S. Army, General Motors, and multitudes of other public and private organizations have come up with a wonderful compromise—

. . . the Beast is always drawn to news of the one-stop-shopping variety.

stock footage. They shoot the hard-to-get videotape themselves and then supply it to the news stations that cover them. When a story pops up, news organizations don't have to invest the time and effort into getting new video (and occasionally photos). They don't even have to look up old stories to capture file tape. All the pictures they need are already in house, sitting on the shelf. *Easy does it.*

A more sophisticated approach to getting news coverage via easy pictures is something called a "video news release" (VNR). Every year large corporations spend a small fortune producing their own "news" on videotape. They use professional photographers, (many of them refugees from television news) to create a gift-wrapped story for time-strapped TV stations. These stories have newsworthy hooks that prominently feature the corporation's product or service. Sometimes television producers will run them as-is. Most of the time the VNRs are cannibalized for their video and relevant information. But even when a reporter or producer dissects a VNR, the corporation that produced the original piece usually gets a mention or has its product or service shown in the video. Mission accomplished.

You don't have to be a major corporation or government agency to take advantage of the Beast's need for photographic images. Under the right circumstances, news organizations will use your video or photography. "Circumstances" usually means that the news organization is interested in your story but doesn't have the time or resources to get the pictures the story requires. You might have a chance at providing those images if they are shot well, using high-quality equipment. The relatively low cost of good digital cameras has made this option more practical for news people and for you.

On the fourth of July 2001, a community group staged a parade in my neighborhood. Hundreds of kids decorated their bicycles, their scooters, their dogs, and even themselves. Some firefighters brought over an engine to lead the procession. We told the local television stations about the parade. One was interested, but because of other news and a lean holiday staff, their photographer wasn't able to make it. Enter the Rule of Easy. With a steady hand, I shot the parade with my own digital video camera getting all the wide, medium, and tight shots I knew the producer would want as well as a few short interviews with children. I then delivered the videotape to the TV station along with the relevant facts. The station dubbed the tape and featured the parade on two evening newscasts. Everybody loves a parade. It's easy.

A "Happy Meal," Please

Because gathering information is often an inconvenient, time-consuming process, the Beast is always drawn to news of the one-stop-shopping variety. The Beast doesn't have time for a sit-down meal. It's got to happen on the go—and if at all possible, by way of the drive-through. That's why books, studies, and surveys, with all their pre-packaged data, are publicity magnets.

When the World Wildlife Fund releases a report that predicts rapid extinction as the planet warms, reporters get out their notepads. When the U.S. Education Department completes a study that says high school seniors are goofing off in class, producers start setting up interviews with school administrators. When the Institute of Medicine releases a scathing report on too many Americans receiving inadequate, outdated, or unsafe therapy, newsroom keyboards start clacking. At first glance, you may believe these kinds of stories are like the fire that sucks up the oxygen (publicity) in the room. To a degree, this is true. However, if you look a little closer, you'll see opportunity where once there was only faster competition.

Architect Sarah Susanka enjoys designing small homes. In America, where the average house has increased by 825 square feet in the past 30 years, she's in the minority. Susanka's dislike for the cavernous domicile was so intense that she wrote a book *The Not So Big House*. Sure, she was bucking a trend, but in any market dominated by one idea, there is always a backlash. Because her book cut across the grain (difference), it received widespread publicity and became an instant best seller. Susanka followed up the book with *Creating the Not So Big House*, a practical guide for homebuilders and re-modelers. Fueled by press coverage, the architect's books became so successful that Susanka decided to stop building houses. She went on the lecture circuit, and as of this writing her web site <notsobighouse.com> is receiving 4,000 hits a day.

Authors such as Susanka are easy targets for press coverage: they are completely accessible and present tightly packaged facts, figures, ideas, and emotions. And if it's a good book, the information is timely (chapter 10, Rule of Timing). That's good news for the authors, but what about everyone else? The Rule of Easy says: allow the authors to do the work while you cash in on what they produce.

Let's say you are a contractor who builds smaller homes. Read the book. Along the way, collect every tantalizing tidbit related to what you do as a homebuilder. Package your material and sell yourself to a reporter as someone who is on the leading edge of a new trend. The book provides the credibility. You are the easy example of what the best seller is preaching. In any city, reporters are always anxious to "localize" a national story.

News organizations, especially the networks and national magazines, are drawn to surveys, studies, and reports like flies to cow flop. Look for them and then try to establish some leverage.

When the *International Journal of Obesity* released a study that suggested the existence of a "fat virus," the press came running. Can you blame them? Who could resist the claim that a person might "catch" a spare tire in the same way that he or she might catch a cold? And if it's true, might there be a pill that could combat the fat bug? It's a great story, one that could be exploited in dozens of ways. A fitness club could pitch the story as just another bizarre example of how people want to find an easy way around the necessity of exercise. An obesity support group or therapist could discuss the emotional impact that such an announcement has on the overweight population. Heaven knows, the audience for such a story would be huge. Others in the health, food, and dieting industries could also mine the study for some free press.

In March 2001, *U.S. News & World Report* ran a short story on the hazards of riding bicycles—especially when you've had a drink or two. The article was triggered by a study of 124 seriously injured bicyclists in Maryland. One third of those fatally injured had elevated blood-alcohol levels. There have to be ten different ways a bike shop owner, a chapter of Mothers Against Drunk Driving, or even a government agency could turn this article into easy publicity pickings.

The flow of new studies, reports, and surveys can be found in just about any industry. Lifestyles are constantly changing. New innovations are impacting the way people live. Old theories die, and new ones emerge. All of this pre-packaged data is a prime source of information for expanding awareness about your organization through public exposure. Of course, if ambitious and creative, you could always just produce the data yourself. In chapter 9, the Rule of Invention, I'll show you how.

Making the Message Hum

Colorful, humorous, shocking, or otherwise unique quotes are what drive any story. Without quotes, the story is like an engine with no sparkplugs. It just sits there, lifeless. If the reporter has to ratchet in some crusty, factual, boring comments the engine will run, but not well. What the reporter wants most are some fresh-out-of-the-box plugs that he can quickly spin into place with his bare hand. It's fast, convenient, and, when the job's done, the engine hums.

You'll be glad to know that the Rule of Easy has nothing new to teach you where quotes are concerned. If you are diligently applying the previous four Media Rules, your quotes *will* be easy. Just ask yourself a few questions. At the core, what is the story about? What is the message I want to send about that key issue? How can I frame my answer so it is different in context, simple in meaning, and emotive in flavor? When you have walked through these steps (preparation to seek out DES), what should come out at the other end is a bright, shiny plug that can be spun into the engine block with no trouble at all. And as I have mentioned previously, the framing of a good quote will dramatically increase the chance that your primary message will be used, while significantly decreasing the risk that what you say will be taken out of context.

Read the following dissimilar quotes and see if you notice a consistent quality.

"Never in the field of human conflict was so much owed by so many to so few."

—Winston Churchill

"When you go into the lion's den, you don't tippy-toe. You carry a spear, you go in screaming like a banshee and kick the door in and say, 'Where's the son of a gun?'"

—Brian Billick, NFL Football Coach

"I always thought of losing my virginity as a career move."

—Madonna, Pop Singer

"If the Democrats wanted Gore to be president so bad, they should have voted for impeachment."

—Unknown

"If you're looking to save the whales, call Oprah. If you're sleeping with a whale, call us."

—Richard Dominick,
the "Jerry Springer Show"

"Golf is like life in a lot of ways—all the biggest wounds are self-inflicted."

—Bill Clinton

Notice how each of the above quotes is self-contained. The reporter doesn't have to strain himself to make the comment work. There's no stretch to ensure accuracy. All the writer has to do is set the story into motion and plug the quote in where appropriate. That's a luxury every reporter appreciates. Also, good reporters are always on the lookout for quotes that create a theme for the story. A thematic tale is not only more entertaining; it's easier to write.

A college basketball player I worked with used his Media Rules training when he was interviewed for a story about an injured teammate named Brian Smith. "Have you ever heard the old farm story when the horse has a broken leg?" he asked the reporter. "You just put him to sleep, put him out of his misery. It came to a point this year, I thought I was just going to have to put him [Smith] to sleep. I told coach, 'we just got to call it a day and finish him.'" The headline for the story became, "Smith's A True Workhorse." The reporter began the story by calling Smith a "consummate workhorse" and then wove the injured-equine theme throughout.

Reporters absolutely love people who can concisely use words to make complicated issues easier to understand. Physical therapist Terri Lohnes is a case in point. She has a simple explanation for why America's health industry is so inefficient and why health insurance is so expensive. She compares the maintenance of the body to that of an automobile. For instance, if a car company gave you a free engine every time you blew up the old one, would you bother to change your oil? She says that's the problem with health insurance. Many people are not motivated to maintain their bodies because when something breaks down, their insurance pays to fix it.

Lohnes ran this theory by a business reporter who loved it so much he built a story around it. The journalist even praised her easy explanation in his article, saying, "Since Lohnes is a physical therapist she speaks plainly. Were she an economist, she would say something like, 'the information content of the health system pricing model is deficient.'" The reporter is only partially correct. Being a physical therapist is not the reason Lohnes speaks in easy quotes. She gave him a gift-wrapped analogy because she was actively using the Media Rules to win her company some publicity. Both the reporter and the physical therapist got what they wanted.

If you want positive news coverage for your company or organization, follow the path of least resistance—not yours, theirs. Schedule your event at a convenient time. Prepare your material in a tight, easy-to-understand package. Make bold, compelling, or colorful comments in the interview. Keep your message focused.

Knowing Makes It Easy

If you are a public information officer, public relations director, marketing manager, or are otherwise in charge of handling the press, your sole preoccupation should be figuring out ways to make reporters' lives easier. It's your best shot at getting publicity and making it count when you do get it. It also can be the ultimate tool in minimizing bad press when trouble arises.

In spite of this seemingly obvious fact, "flacks" who just don't get it continually frustrate reporters and editors. They stage events at the wrong time of day or on the wrong day of the week. We'll talk a lot more about this in chapter 10, the Rule of Timing. They don't provide clear, concise information, which will be taken up in chapter 8, the Rule of Resource. And some even engage in power struggles with the press—chapters 11 and 13, the rules of Ego and Ambush.

If you step back from the book for a moment, you can see that Easy's fingerprints are all over the first four Media Rules. Reporters are attracted to different stories because they stand out. They're easier to spot. Emotive issues are preferred by the Beast for much the same reason—they rise above the mundane. People are not easily moved by the facts of this world but throw in some emotion and watch them gyrate. Complex stories turn off not just journalists, but the people they serve. It's the simple that we want—cut, dried, and easy to digest. And because we understand the premier importance of difference, emotion, and simplicity, we should carefully prepare our stories and our messages in order to take advantage of this reality.

As you will continue to see in the chapters that follow, the Rule of Easy is at the core of every media rule. It's the "plop, plop, fizz, fizz" of the Beast's diet.

◆ ◆ ◆

CHAPTER 7

The Rule of Repetition

~ say it again, sam ~

What do McDonald's, Starbucks, The Rolling Stones, Honda, H & R Block, Stephen Spielberg, Coca-Cola, *Time* magazine and Hertz have in common? They're all highly successful, of course, but what is it that makes them successful? The answer is that they have all achieved momentum by accomplishing three tasks: 1) They broke out from the pack; 2) established a leadership position, and 3) kept cranking out that thing that makes them so good. As hard as it is to accomplish the first and second tasks, the real winners know the greatest challenge is the third task—consistency over time.

Be Committed or Be a Loser

When it comes to the work of winning positive publicity, people tend to fall into three categories. First, there are the uncommitted. These are people who would love to get the benefits of news exposure, but for any number of reasons (too busy, scared, or otherwise distracted) they don't even try. Second, there are the pseudo committed. These folks are more successful than the first group because they actually give it a shot. Once in a while they contact a news organization about something they're doing. Maybe they get some press, maybe they don't, but either way they stop thinking about the news media until the next project comes along. A lot of large companies fall into this category. The pseudo committed are more pretenders than performers. These two groups make up the vast majority of folks who talk about feeding the Beast. They never get much success because they fail to harness the power of Repetition.

> Most publicity seekers give up too easily or celebrate too soon.

Then there are the thoroughly committed. These people make getting publicity of all kinds a top priority. They constantly look for opportunities and thoroughly exploit the ones that are found. The end result is as amazing as it is predictable. The top ten percent of publicity seekers win ninety percent of the positive press.

Most publicity seekers give up too easily or celebrate too soon. Win or lose, they don't keep on keeping on. In order to earn valuable exposure, you have to carefully package your story and message and keep putting it in front of any member of the media who will listen. If you can't get the Beast's attention, take a hard look at what you're selling, fix it, and try again. If it still doesn't work, drop it and move on to the next possibility. If a reporter bites, great, but don't stop there. Repackage your material for a different audience (if that's even necessary) and go for it again. If one news organization thought the story was worth reporting, chances are another one will, too.

We can all learn a lot about the Rule of Repetition from the half-breed known as the freelance writer. This individual is part journalist, part PR specialist. The freelancer doesn't just write the story; she also must sell the story to news organizations. If she isn't committed to the Rule of Repetition, she won't last long in the profession.

Before any successful freelancer will begin collecting material for an article, she will first consider who might purchase it—and will probably have it pre-sold to a number of publications. For example, a story on work stress would be equally relevant to a local newspaper, CNN, *Popular Mechanics*, *Wired*, an industry newsletter, and who knows how many other information outlets. With a little tweaking, the same core story can be sold to a wide number of targets. So, if the freelancer puts twenty hours into a story that she sells once for $300, she makes a paltry $15 per hour. After taxes and overhead, she would be better off working as a secretary. However, if she sells the same story to eight customers for the same price, she makes $120 per hour. Repetition is a beautiful thing.

You should look at all publicity opportunities the same way a freelance writer does. Ask yourself, how many different news organizations can I sell this to? How can I reposition the facts to make the material more relevant to a different organization? How can I get the same news organization to "buy" the story multiple times? The goal is to get your name out there at every possible opportunity. Many people fail in this endeavor because they mistakenly think once a story has been told, that's it. On the contrary, once you've succeeded in making a story work, keep making it work.

In the early 1990s, a national news magazine published an article on an innovative program to combat diabetes on the Zuni reservation. The chief photographer of the TV station where I was working showed me the article and suggested we do a series on the diabetes fighters. So we did. It was a powerful story. In fact, the series received an Emmy nomination. It went out on the feed to other ABC stations, and someone at the network liked it as well. Correspondent Tom Foreman gave me a call to get some details, and several months later Foreman did his own story for the network. And it's still a great story. In January 2001, I was thumbing through *U.S. News and World Report* and saw another article on the Zuni program—one of many since we visited the reservation years earlier. The woman who runs the Zuni Diabetes Center hasn't stopped selling the program, in spite of the fact that the story has been told many times in local, regional, and national media of all kinds.

The best Seducers of the Beast aren't those who constantly come up with new ideas. It's those who take the same idea and beat it like a drum—but with a different beat. All the while they're on the lookout for the next great opportunity.

If at First You *Do* Succeed, Try, Try Again (Two Case Studies)

Repetition can take many different forms. Sometimes it requires throwing a broad net over multiple news outlets. Several journalists tell the story to multiple audiences across multiple mediums. In some instances a print article becomes a broadcast story—or vice versa. Local publicity goes national, and national publicity gets localized. Industry news hits the mainstream, and the reverse also occurs. Sometimes a story catches fire, and it takes on a life of its own (more on this to come). And, as is often the case, there will be a combination of the above. But no matter what form it takes, positive repetition for a created story is nearly always the result of someone who is dedicated to making it happen.

I got the opportunity to demonstrate the power of Repetition in

May 2001. One day I opened the morning newspaper and was astonished to see that the New Mexico Public Regulation Commission (PRC) had voted to give the state's most densely populated region—Albuquerque/Santa Fe—a new telephone area code while allowing the predominately rural portion of the state to keep the existing code (505). The decision—which was to be implemented in only two months—made absolutely no sense. The bulk of the state's business and industry as well as its government offices is located in the Albuquerque/Santa Fe corridor. One expert estimated the cost to change the area code in New Mexico's urban center to be 50 million dollars more than it would cost for the rural region to change. So why did three of the five members of the PRC vote for an urban switch? Because their districts, and the people who vote for them, are located mostly in the rural area.

I didn't want to allow the PRC to get away with such nonsense. So I contacted a lawyer (David Campbell of Vogel, Campbell, Bleuher, & Castle) and a public relations specialist (Gene Grant of DW Turner & Assoc.). The three of us formed the "505 Coalition." Our first mission was to announce our arrival on the scene. I sent out a press release on a Sunday announcing a "Keep 505 Rally" in Albuquerque's downtown civic plaza the following Tuesday. The ABC affiliate interviewed me and ran the story that day on their 10:00 P.M. newscast. Did I stop there? Of course not! The next day I called the state's number one talk radio station and was invited to speak on the issue for an hour during the afternoon drive. I also contacted several newspapers, all of which interviewed me. A reporter from the state's top daily, *The Albuquerque Journal*, said the story would run Tuesday morning. All five local television stations ran the story on Monday night newscasts. Was it time to slow down yet? No way! The next morning I did radio interviews with the top AM and FM stations. The CBS and ABC affiliates interviewed me for their noon newscasts. Our attorney, David Campbell, was interviewed by several reporters from various mediums as well. That afternoon we staged the Keep 505 Rally at, when else, 5:05 P.M. All of the TV stations aired live reports from the rally, and I did several newspaper and radio interviews before and after the event. We were the big story on all the late newscasts and landed on the front page (above the fold with large photos) of the *Albuquerque Journal* and *Albuquerque Tribune*. Was it time to stop? Not even close.

We set up a web site, wrote several op-ed pieces, and continued to work every opportunity. The 505 Coalition forced the PRC to conduct an additional public hearing, followed by another vote that generated another flurry of stories. (The second PRC vote was identical to the first, so we appealed to the state supreme court.) A dozen newspapers got involved, not only covering the story, but producing their own editorials and cartoons. Our attorney and I logged more hours on morning and afternoon drive talk radio. The issue was picked up by the Reuters news service, Washington, D.C., based *BNA* (which produces more than 200 news and information services, including *The Daily Report for Executives*) *USA Today*, and others. In the end, the 505 Coalition stirred up the biggest state story of 2001, by generating hundreds of news reports across all media. It didn't happen by itself. We made it happen and kept making it happen.

The protest, and all the media attention that kept it going, was a big success. During the battle, local and federal officials discovered that they could delay adopting a new area code in New Mexico for many years by simply implementing some telephone number conservation measures. The Rule of Repetition saved us from flushing tens of millions of dollars down the drain.

Of course, controversial topics (such as area code battles) have a much greater chance of generating repeat coverage. However, non-controversial stories can be highly successful as well—if you're willing to keep on keeping on. Lenya Heitzig's Mercy BANDs prove this truth.

In the days following the terrorist attacks of September 11, 2001, Heitzig, an author and pastor's wife, watched the horrific pictures on her television and prayed for a way to help the families of the victims. Heitzig believed that, like herself, Americans everywhere were feeling overwhelmed by the enormity of the tragedy. She thought that people could not emotionally grasp thousands of lives lost, but that they could connect to one victim and that person's family. That's when the Mercy BAND (Bearing Another's Name Daily) idea came to her—silver wristbands engraved with the names of 9-11 victims.

In only two weeks, Heitzig pulled together everyone she needed (designer, manufacturer, web site developer, printer, media specialist, and others). The program was launched during weekend church services. I sent out press releases on Saturday and called media contacts. The local TV stations all ran stories on their early evening and late evening newscasts. One station ran multiple follow-up stories over the next ten days. Unfortunately, the newspapers didn't bite on the story right away, but we kept working our sources. Lenya used her contacts (chapter 8, Rule of Resource) to arrange a meeting with the publisher of the *Albuquerque Journal*. Two days later her color photo and story appeared on the front page. We sent a package to *The Oprah Winfrey Show*, and I e-mailed a reporter friend at CNN. Lenya did multiple radio interviews, including one with Decision Today, a large radio ministry of the Billy Graham Evangelistic Association. Freelance writer Jeremy Reynalds wrote a story about Mercy BAND, which was picked up by more than a half-dozen Internet news sites. As the result of our media exposure and other efforts, the *Dallas Morning News* published an article on the front page of the paper's metro section. A

Producer from ABC's "Nightline" saw the *Dallas Morning News* article and used Mercy BAND in a show dedicated to 9-11 charities. The story snowballed from there as it was picked up by CNN, <NYTimes.com>, the *New York Daily News,* the *Washington Times*, the *Minneapolis Star Tribune*, New Jersey's *Star Ledger*, the *Charlotte Observer*, and many other newspapers, magazines, Internet news sites, radio and TV stations across the country.

The important thing to take away from the 505 Coalition and Mercy BAND projects is that they were successful because of the momentum that was first generated and then accelerated by a deliberate effort to keep the story moving.

Follow the Leader

Most journalists like to consider themselves independent thinkers, and many of them are. However, as you know, the Beast is human. And, like everybody else on the planet, journalists are greatly influenced by their industry's leaders. Once a journalistic giant puts its seal of approval on a story, it becomes legitimate, and a whole lot of other media outlets will instantly decide they want a piece of it. Nationally, this group is known as the "media elite" (chapter 12, Rule of Balance)—the networks, *Newsweek, Time*, the *New York Times*, the *Washington Post*, the *Wall Street Journal*, and a handful of others. When one of these news organizations takes hold of a story, look out, the impact can be enormous.

The proprietors of Three Dog Bakery felt the cascading effect of getting a media leader's attention when a *Wall Street Journal* reporter happened by their store. The reporter loved the unique idea (Difference) of selling all-natural baked goods for canines. So he wrote an article about the store and its products, including Pup-Cakes, SnickerPoodles, and Great Danish. On the day the story was published, the people at the bakery must have felt like three-legged dogs—they just couldn't keep up. The store was overwhelmed by phone calls for two solid weeks from people wanting to know how they could get biscuits and product information. Two days later the bakery was ten weeks backlogged. It was an overwhelming response to a single story, but Three Dog hadn't seen anything yet. Following the *Wall Street Journal* story came a flood of interview requests from other media outlets, including *USA Today, People, Entrepreneur,* the *New York Times Magazine,* National Public Radio, "The Oprah Winfrey Show," "The Tonight Show," and many others. All that media attention helped launch Three Dog Bakery into an international franchise with dozens of stores across the United States as well as Canada and Japan. How did *I* find out about it? I read an article on *Inc. Magazine's* website, <Inc.com>.

When a media leader latches onto your story, big things are bound to happen. Steve Hanks was just another starving artist until *The Wall Street Journal* alerted the world to his stunning talent for creating fine art on an Etch-a-Sketch. In as little as thirty minutes, Hanks could "draw" anything—an object, a person, an entire scene —and do it with extraordinary accuracy. Producers from "Good Morning America" saw the story and invited Hanks into the studio to Etch-a-Sketch the "GMA" crew. *People* magazine featured the artist, as did dozens of other publications. Hanks eventually ditched the Etch-a-Sketch because he didn't want to become known as a gimmick artist. But he used all the media interest to draw attention to his previously under-discovered talent of watercolor painting. He is now recognized as one of the nation's premier watercolor artists.

It's too bad there is no way to control the Beast once he gets a taste of a story he likes. How wonderful it would be if all of the Beast's minions would patiently wait in line for their turn. But that's not the way it works in the real world. When a media leader blesses a story, a horde of others comes all at once. The result can be a curse.

Lyle Bowlin had set up an Internet bookstore, <PositivelyYou. com>, and was making a fair profit. The *New York Times* believed that Bowlin's modest success was an indicator that almost anyone could make a living on the Web. So the *Times* featured the Iowa resident's business in an op-ed column. *Time* magazine ran a profile piece on Bowlin's venture. Then came coverage from "Good Morning America," Fox News, and a swarm of other media outlets. As you might have expected, business for <PositivelyYou.com> increased by more than 2,000 percent almost overnight. Unfortunately for Bowlin, his little company was unable to handle such a sudden, dramatic rise in business. Less than a year later, the virtual bookstore was forced to close its doors—the "victim" of too much publicity.

If you think this section doesn't apply to you because you have no chance of getting the attention of a big-time news provider, think again. Three Dog Bakery, <PositivelyYou.com>, and Steve Hanks were all complete unknowns before their big publicity hit came. The same can be said for thousands of other little people and organizations that suddenly find themselves the subject of media elite stories every year. But even if the *New York Times* never comes calling, it's still important to understand the power that media leaders have to influence other news organizations because the same dynamic is at work in your city, state, and region.

Monkey See, Monkey Do (or Not)

No matter where you go, journalists are the same. They love to lead the pack, but they also tend to be paranoid second-guessers, who, incidentally, are always on the lookout for a good story. Therefore, like their national counterparts, local news organizations compulsively monitor the competition. In doing so they can: a) reassure themselves that their news judgment is sound; b) feel superior because they got a story that the others didn't, and c) find out what they've missed. To a degree, they are all influenced by what the others are doing. If a story gains legitimacy in a newspaper, TV and radio stations will often pick it up, and, vice versa.

There is, however, a peculiar little glitch in the Rule of Repetition that every publicity seeker should be aware of. On the one hand, news organizations look to one another to determine what's news and what isn't, and they also use each other as a resource for story ideas. On the other hand, they are fiercely competitive and jealous, which sometimes leads them to minimize or even ignore a legitimate story simply because another news organization has gotten there first.

In the case of Mercy BAND, we received blanket coverage from the television media on the first day. But one station took the lead, giving Mercy BAND much more time in its initial reports, and then followed up with more stories later. The result was that the other TV stations lost interest. The same type of thing happened with the newspapers. The morning newspaper picked the story up first, so the afternoon paper ignored it. After the *Dallas Morning News* ran a feature on Mercy BAND, I called WFAA in "Big D" to let them know that their sister station in Albuquerque had produced several stories on the silver wristbands and would probably be willing to send them some video (chapter 6, Rule of Easy). But the assignment editor balked, saying that the *Dallas Morning News* had already "been there and done that."

As a media expert, shouldn't I have known that WFAA wouldn't pick up a story that had run in the *Dallas Morning News*? Absolutely not. On a different day, under a different set of circumstances, the TV station might have eaten it up. Some news organizations try not to "steal" stories from the competition. Others couldn't care less. Local television stations in small- to medium-sized markets typically have no compunction about lifting stories right out of the newspaper on a daily basis. But no matter the "policy," the media tend to do whatever is convenient at the time. One day they ignore an issue because "it's been done." The next day they snatch up a juicy item that they just learned about from the competition. Because it can be difficult to tell in advance how various media are going to handle a story, it's best not to guess. Sell it to as many reporters as you think might buy it, and be prepared to sell some more as the story twists and turns. And don't be too surprised when the unexpected happens.

When we were in the middle of the 505 area code issue, I wrote an op-ed piece for the *Albuquerque Tribune.* I had also written an op-ed for the *Albuquerque Journal* due to be published the following morning. Once the afternoon newspaper was out, I got a call from the editor of the *Journal.* He informed me that he was pulling my piece because of what I had written for his competitor. I was taken aback because the two op-eds were completely different. But did we give up? Of course not. I asked the editor if he would publish the piece if it had our attorney's name on it instead of mine. He agreed and ran it a few days later.

The thing to remember is that the Rule of Repetition works in every direction—up, down, sideways, diagonally, locally, nationally, across media, and within media. If a story doesn't move in the direction you think it should, don't worry about it. Just concentrate on making it happen in as many places as possible.

What's Up Is Also Down

The Rule of Repetition is a great purveyor of information. But there is a danger here. Repetition does not make any distinctions between what is accurate and what is not. With so much intentional and unintentional disinformation out there, fact and fiction can become a muddled mess.

The pressure to pump out news product has become so intense

that reporters often don't have the time to check each other's work. The "facts" presented by one reporter are assumed to be accurate. Consequently other reporters will use them in their stories. If the facts turn out to be erroneous, before long the inaccuracies get repeated so many times by so many reporters that they are generally accepted as truth.

In the frantic hours following the massacre of students at Columbine High School, reporters rushed in from across the country. As the death toll mounted, we began hearing reports that the teenage gunmen had specifically targeted classmates who were minorities and athletes. This "fact" emerged when it was learned that Isaiah Shoels, a black athlete, was one of the twelve students and one teacher murdered. It was a compelling piece of information, so, of course, it was repeated countless times in the days and weeks following the massacre. Before long, articles that explored the "targeting" of minorities and athletes began appearing. However, it wasn't true. Shoels was the only athlete and only minority student killed. It was later learned that the gunmen *did* single out a certain group for execution—born again Christians. As the two killers roamed the school picking victims, they asked several if they "believed in God." Those who said "yes" were murdered. This truth, however, is lesser known than the minority/athlete disinformation.

Former president Richard Nixon recently *benefited* from the Repetition of inaccurate information. In the days following the near dead-heat election of 2000, the national press was hungry for a historical comparison. Bush front man James Baker was happy to give it to them. Baker talked about the extremely close election of 1960 and how Nixon nobly conceded to John Kennedy even though Kennedy's margin of victory in more than a half-dozen states was razor thin. There were also rumors of voter fraud in Illinois, Texas, and elsewhere. The news media didn't challenge Baker's claim because Nixon's noble sacrifice was "common knowledge" in political circles. So the press picked up the story of Nixon's high-road stance and collectively asked if Gore should do the same. Nixon's magnanimous gesture became a persuasive argument for a Gore concession. But it wasn't true.

Historian David Greenberg published articles that proved Republican officials (including Nixon aides) had doggedly challenged results in eleven states late into November. Nixon publicly stayed above the fray but undoubtedly endorsed the election challenge. Greenberg's facts, however, are no match for the Rule of Repetition. Come the next close election, you can count on partisans to use Nixon's patriotic sacrifice as reason for the loser to concede gracefully.

Remember when Clinton administration staffers vandalized the White House before they turned it over to George W. Bush? It was another widely reported scandal for the king of presidential indignity—only this one wasn't completely true. The story started with a report that White House aides had removed the "W" key from some of the keyboards. Then we were told about severed computer cables, snipped phone lines, graffiti on the walls, overturned desks, and filing cabinets glued shut. Air Force One had reportedly been looted. The story peaked when *U.S. News & World Report* published rumors that the White House was spending a whopping $10,000 a day to fix phone systems vandalized by Clinton staffers.

Journalist David Goldstein debunked the scandal as completely false and a fresh wave of "accurate" information was sent to Americans. But a funny thing happened after Goldstein had apparently set the story straight. Representative Anthony Weiner, a Democrat from Brooklyn, held a press conference insisting that the Bush administration apologize. Instead of an apology, White House spokesman Ari Fleischer gave Weiner a detailed list of the vandalism. The damage included graffiti in six offices, 10 sliced phone lines, and 100 inoperable computer keyboards. Turns out, Clinton's staffers did indeed vandalize the White House, although not to nearly the degree that was first reported.

Where did the inaccurate extremes of information come from in this story? Nobody seems to know. Tom Rosenstiel, Director of the Project for Excellence in Journalism, admits, "The dirty little secret of the information revolution is often there's not a lot of verification." But there is a lot of Repetition.

Somebody Said It, So It Must Be True

Repetition is as much a factor on the local level as it is on the national scene—perhaps more so. As I mentioned earlier, at TV and radio stations across the land, assignment editors (and others) scour the local papers for story ideas. The ones they like have a decent chance of becoming a broadcast story. If there is a factual error in the print version, there is a strong likelihood that it won't be detected and corrected before news time.

Rooting mistakes out of TV news stories in particular can be as difficult as killing Bermuda grass in your garden. Unless you achieve complete eradication, the pesky nuisance will reappear. Communication within TV newsrooms is amazingly poor. There is typically little conversation between the early-morning crew, the day timers, and the evening crowd, but they all rely on each other's work.

Let's say a dayside reporter makes a mistake on a 5:00 P.M. newscast. You catch the error and call the station. Chances are you'll talk to some uninterested party (an intern, perhaps) who will listen to your complaint, hang up the phone and say, "What a whiner." If you manage to speak with the reporter or someone else who actually cares, the assignment desk may get notified. But your troubles aren't over. If a different reporter picks up the story for the 10:00 P.M. news, he will pull facts from the earlier script, which, of course, probably has not been corrected. So the mistake is repeated.

A more common scenario occurs in the early morning hours. A mistake happens on one of the previous day's newscasts, and a few key people are alerted to the error. The mistake probably won't happen again on the evening shift, but without a corrected script the misinformation can still resurface. The morning producer writes a new story using an old script, and the mistake rises again. Who knows, the noon producer might even use the morning script to write his own yarn.

If a mistake is repeated a few times, it becomes harder to kill because many people have seen, read, or heard this "fact" and will continue to believe it true. If the issue resurfaces in the future, reporters, anchors, and producers may write new stories based on a tainted memory. It all starts over again.

Minimizing Mistakes

When dealing with the press, imagine that you are navigating your way through a swamp where quicksand is a constant hazard. The best course of action is to carefully plan each step. But if you find yourself sinking, focus all your energies on getting to dry land quickly. With every passing minute your chances for a positive outcome slip away.

The way to protect yourself against damaging inaccuracies is to combine the Rule of Simplicity with the Rule of Repetition. Resist your desire to tell the reporter everything there is to know about your subject. Restrict your comments to only the relevant facts and give the reporter a one-sheet summary of the subject. Come up with a primary message—the quote you would pick if you could write the story. Send your message in the pre-interview, multiple times during the interview, and even after the interview is over. Leave no room for error.

If in spite of your best efforts the reporter gets the story wrong and you believe the inaccuracy will be damaging, don't delay.

Spring into action. Call the reporter(s) who got the story wrong. Tell them about the error (be nice about it) and ask that they correct the past scripts/articles and notify the assignments desk/editor and anyone else who may pick up the story. If a newspaper reporter is the culprit, call any media outlet—TV, radio, local Associated Press office—that you think might pick up the story and alert them to the misinformation.

Your job isn't done yet. Monitor as many news sources as possible. Enlist the help of coworkers or friends if necessary. If the mistake pops up again, go right to the top of that news organization. Tell the person in charge what's going on and ask him or her to help stop Repetition of the error. If that doesn't fix it, see the news boss in person. Be firm but friendly. Only as a last resort should you get nasty or call a lawyer. It rarely pays to upset the Beast (chapter 11, Rule of Ego).

The lesson, therefore, is to use the Rule of Repetition to your advantage. If you've got a message to send, send it often. If the wrong message starts to flicker, don't reach for a glass of water—grab a fire hose.

Interviews Are Not Conversations

From a very young age we are told not to repeat ourselves. There's no telling how many times I have told my son, "Say it once, and I've got the message." This isn't always the case, but how else can you explain to an eight-year-old that you don't want to be pestered about what's for dessert?

When we get together to talk, Repetition is annoying. Thankfully, most of us have strong conditioning to avoid it. The interview, however, is not a conversation. It is an opportunity for you to send a message to an audience through a news filter. The audience is not going to hear everything you say (except in a live interview, which we will discuss later). In most cases, the audience is only going to receive one or two short comments. Everything else will be edited out. In order to make sure the reporter chooses the right one or two quotes, you need to say them repeatedly. Say it, and then, *say it again, Sam.*

One of my great frustrations as a reporter was the reluctance of my interview subjects to repeat themselves. While my photographer was setting up his camera, I would start priming the pump. "What do you think is the key issue in this story?" I would ask. Often the person would say something absolutely wonderful—the perfect soundbite. But once we started the interview, the subject would resist saying the same thing in the same way. I could tell that consciously or subconsciously the person was thinking, "I've already said that; I shouldn't say it that way again." Nonsense. In the interview, turn the rules of conversation upside down. Act like an eight-year-old who's worried about getting his dessert.

Think of the reporter as a gravel pit sifter. In the interview, you pour in your messages—sand, pebbles, and rocks. The sand and pebbles fall through the holes (reporter simplifying the story) while only the rocks remain. The best rocks are big (Different), bright (Emotive), and smooth (Simple). In stark contrast to the smaller, dingy rocks still in the screen, they stand out and completely overwhelm the sand and pebbles that the reporter quickly sifts out. The journalist examines the DES rocks and then picks one or two for her story. If the interview subject has done his job right, several of the DES rocks will repeat the primary message in slightly different ways. At least that's how the interview is supposed to work.

Unfortunately, since most people don't prepare for interviews, they don't throw in DES rocks. After sifting out the sand and pebbles, the journalist is left with a bunch of small rocks, none of which is all that attractive. The reporter is none too pleased because she doesn't have any terrific rocks for her story. Worse yet, you've made her job more difficult because she has to rummage through a large pile of relatively unremarkable stone.

For your benefit—and the reporter's—don't make the interview such drudgery. Apply the Rule of Preparation. Pinpoint your most important messages. Stick to only one or two primary points, if possible. Figure out different ways to send the same message. In the interview, concentrate on your message and hammer, hammer, hammer. When the reporter is finished, she'll have a limited amount of sand and pebbles, a smattering of small, unattractive rocks, and several large, eye-catching gems (your message[s]). This is how an interview should work. With a couple shakes of the sifter, the reporter quickly gets what she wants—and so do you.

Quotation Quicksand

The Rule of Repetition is equally important when speaking with print or broadcast reporters but for slightly different reasons. The print reporter typically has more time to write his story and more space to explain it. Interviews last longer and go deeper, so there is a greater chance that a print journalist will stray into areas that are distracting and unimportant. By repeating your messages, you bring him back to the key points that matter most, lessening the chance that the journalist will take the story in a direction you don't want it to go. And there is another advantage to repeating yourself. If you drive home the same point several times, you significantly reduce the room for confusion in the busy mind of the reporter. The person who uses the Rule of Repetition tends not to get misquoted. He also gives himself an advantage over the person who is on the opposite side of an issue.

Let's say the reporter interviews someone else who has a viewpoint contrary to yours. But that person doesn't utilize the Rule of Repetition. When the reporter sits down to write his story, whose message is going to be the clearest in the reporter's head? Yours will, and consequently, the odds are very good that the article will favor your point of view.

In broadcast interviews, the technology creates an additional set of problems. If you stumble in the middle of a quote, it doesn't show up in print, but in television or radio an extended pause or stumble kills the message. A good reporter will edit around the dead spot, if he can, but that takes up precious time and energy. A bad or extremely busy reporter might just leave it in. But the awkward soundbite won't be a problem if you give the reporter three better quotes to choose from.

Audio and videotape present other troubles that Repetition will overcome. The tape is an abused tool in the broadcast industry. As tapes are repeatedly used, they develop glitches and dead spots. But because many managers of TV and radio stations are pressured to stretch their budgets, used tapes tend to hang around longer than they should. If your only good quote happens to hit a bad spot in the tape, the reporter can't use it. High-quality half-inch videotape has greatly reduced this nuisance, but it's still a hazard.

Another nasty problem that hasn't gotten any better is unexpected noise. No telling how many dozens of great quotes I lost in my TV-news career because some numbskull just had to honk his horn while driving by my interview. I can remember getting a terrific soundbite from a high school student (not an easy task) only to have the last few words blown out by the school bell. I once interviewed a cowgirl who had split open her chin after being thrown from a saddle-bronc. With blood all over her face and shirt, the pretty young woman fought back tears and tried to talk tough. It was a wonderful, classic contrast—until her horse blew his nose into the microphone. By the time I re-asked the question, the moment was gone.

These awful noise interruptions are everywhere, and they tend to happen at the worst possible times. Someone nearby laughs real loud. The phone starts ringing. An obnoxious fan sounds off, or an air conditioner kicks on. A guy drives by on his Harley. A plane flies overhead. The photographer sneezes (or the reporter does). It's a constant hazard for anyone who makes a living holding a microphone. It's your hazard, too, if you don't utilize the Rule of Repetition.

There's one more good reason to chew your cud twice (make that 3 or 4 times) during TV and radio interviews. It increases your chances of being quoted in multiple stories. Because there is more news time to fill and fewer resources to get the job done, an increasing number of stories are appearing on multiple newscasts. The ones that get chosen for additional play are those that have the best material—good, fresh quotes are high on the list. At the very least several compelling, distinctive sound bites can result in more airtime and face-time for you. Without a new and interesting sound bite, a TV producer is likely to turn the second telling of a story into a V/O (voiceover: anchor reads script with video), as opposed to a VOB (voiceover with bite: add quote to the story). Give a radio announcer several good snippets, and he's going to want to use them all.

The First Word, and the Last Word—Live

Even though a live interview can feel a lot like a conversation, don't be duped—it's not. The Rule of Repetition still applies.

In a short interview, say ninety seconds or less, you may not get the opportunity to hit your message more than once. But you should still be prepared, nonetheless. Because of limited time, the reporter will want to immediately get to the core of the issue. The first question will lead right to your message because you've set that up in the pre-interview. If there is a follow-up question, use that as an opportunity to support what you have said.

There is always the possibility that the journalist will ask you a question of lesser importance that will eat up your precious time. In that case, do what a lot of savvy politicians do—don't answer the question, at least not immediately. The exchange goes something like this:

Reporter: "Senator, how do you think this new treaty will impact U.S./China relations?"

Senator: "Bob, first let me say that this treaty would never have become a reality without the hard work of the president."

Once the senator has delivered the message he came to send, he will then answer the original question or let the reporter re-ask it in a follow-up.

In a longer format, such as a live radio program or TV talk show, follow the same rule that broadcast journalists use when they write their stories: Tell them what you're going to tell them. Tell them. Tell them what you've told them.

It's been my observation that even people experienced in giving live interviews will start with a bang but end with a fizzle. Any decent host will set up the interview with a preview of what you have to say. Hitting your message at the top is easy. That's what you're there for. But the real experts shine in the middle and at the end where most others fail. As the host starts extending the discussion into side issues, it's easy just to sit in the back seat and let him drive. Don't do it. Provide answers to the smaller questions, but then steer the interview back to the heart of your argument.

Good hosts will give you a chance to summarize your thoughts at the end. That's your chance to finish strong. For example, Bill O'Reilly, host of "The O'Reilly Factor," typically wraps up interview segments by telling his guests, "I'll give you the last word." Some seize the opportunity to return to the beginning and hammer away at their message. Many do not.

Don't count on your host being as skilled as O'Reilly. As a former radio talk show host and TV news anchor, I can tell you that managing the clock during live interview segments is not easy.

Make sure you tell the host and the show's producer that you would like to finish with a quick summation of the main point. In longer radio shows, remind them of this priority in the break just before the interview is over.

As I was Saying . . .

The Beast intimidates the ignorant, leaving them confused and cautious. They give up quickly, and that thins out the competition. However, those who understand the Media Rules know that publicity success is not an event but an ongoing process. You win a few and you lose a few, but you never stop trying. It's much easier to remain diligent and not get discouraged when you know that Repetition is necessary for everyone who wants to be successful. It's as true for McDonald's, Honda, and the Rolling Stones as it is for you. Sustained momentum is the goal, and it is achieved through Repetition.

We are now halfway there. You have learned the Seducers—the three core elements that attract the Beast—Difference, Emotion, and Simplicity. We've just completed the Enablers—the Rules that put the Seducers to work. Great exposure and excellent quotes rarely just happen; they are the product of Preparation. We prepare not just for ourselves but also for reporters, editors, and producers who are desperate for something Easy. And finally, success is defined by momentum, which is generated through persistent Repetition.

Now it's time to get moving. You are ready for the blue-collar section of the Media Rules—The Aggressors. In the next three chapters, we will answer the question "How do I get there—a lot—from here?"

◆ ◆ ◆

CHAPTER 8

The Rule of Resource

~ feed 'em before you need 'em ~

We've all heard it, and no doubt most of us have said it—but don't believe it. "It's not what you know, but who you know." This piece of folk *wisdom* would be a lock to make the top ten list of All-time Most Used and Abused Half-truths.

Of course, *who* you know is important. In fact, the bulk of this chapter is focused on that very thing—the critical importance of relationships in the publicity process. However, it is a fundamental mistake to discount *what* you know. Expert knowledge is a staple of the Beast's diet.

It's All About Self Help

People pay attention to news for two reasons: to entertain their curiosity and to improve their lives in some way. Anyone interested in reaping the benefits of publicity should consider himself or herself to be in the life-improvement business—their life included.

The power of being a resource for the Beast is found in an exchange of trustworthiness. As an expert, you give a journalist's story credibility. And because the reporter chose to talk to you instead of countless others, you are endowed with a higher level of legitimacy. In the mind of the news consumer, you must be *the* expert.

For the businessperson, the legitimizing effect of press attention puts his or her product/service at the top of the list. The politician who gets the most ink and air usually gets the most votes. This credibility exchange also works for anyone else who needs to extend her/his sphere of influence through the press. Those who can be a resource in a curiously entertaining way are even more successful.

In the Rule of Easy, we got a look at the Beast's ravenous taste for studies, reports, and books. The ease with which stories can be generated from such information makes using these resources very attractive. People are extremely curious creatures. We enjoy seeing reports that validate what we believe to be true as well as information that debunks stereotypes.

Did you know that the amount of time kids spend doing chores has taken a steep dive in the past twenty years? Have you noticed that the hands of a lot of today's children have never touched a weed or a broom or a hoe? I suspect that this news flash has hardly taken you by surprise. Nonetheless, when the Institute for Social Research at the University of Michigan released a study confirming this cultural shift, journalists were eager to tell us all about it. *U.S. News & World Report* picked up the story, interviewed senior research scientist Sandra Hofferth, and filled out the article by interviewing two more experts. Dorothy Rich, president of the Home and School Institute, explained why the trend is occurring (lots of kid activities and parents too exhausted to crack the whip). Anthony Wolf (child psychologist and author of *Get out of My Life, But First Could You Drive Me and Cheryl to the Mall?*) provided some solutions—start by age 4, make them work on weekends, supervise. *World Report* and other news organizations depend on people like Hofferth, Rich, and Wolf as resources. It's a mutually beneficial arrangement that meets everyone's needs, including those that provide, purvey, and consume the information. The end user, in this case the reader of the news magazine, receives helpful advice that can be used to make life better. In other words, don't be dupes, Mom and Dad. Make those over-indulged kids clean the garage and vacuum the carpet while you get a long overdue break. And don't feel guilty about it either!

Did you see the news magazine show that featured the Parkinson's disease patient who improved remarkably after brain surgery? You know, the one in which the woman didn't actually have the surgery but thought she did. Or maybe you saw the *Newsweek* article written by Dr. Howard Brody that retold the story. It suggested that we can all live longer, healthier lives by simply believing we can. In publishing his article, Dr. Brody became a resource to *Newsweek*, to the magazine's readers, and to himself. By freely giving of his expertise, the Michigan State University professor generated more momentum for his book *The Placebo Response: How You Can Release Your Body's Inner Pharmacy for Better Health.*

Wanted: Experts (Ethics Optional)

The national news industry, including infotainment shows, needs a steady flow of expert data and opinions. It's the drug that keeps them going. Watch any network or cable newscast, and you will see experts being interviewed. News magazine shows such as "Dateline," "20/20," and "60 Minutes" rely heavily on information generated by specialists. Oprah Winfrey and Larry King are addicted, too. And for good reason—people sit in front of the warm glow because they want to be entertained or helped. If the program they're watching doesn't deliver, they'll start clicking until they find one that does.

These shows are so desperate for experts that they will sometimes invite guests who lack credibility. Self-described psychic

Sylvia Browne, for example, has been on "The Montel Williams Show" more than twenty times and has been a returning guest on "Larry King Live." Browne claims that she works with police agencies to solve crimes and that she sometimes uses her psychic powers to help families find missing loved ones. The FBI and the National Center for Missing & Exploited Children, however, tell a different story. They say there is no evidence that Browne or any other "psychic detective" has solved even one missing person case. The James Randi Educational Foundation goes even further to expose these frauds. It offers $1 million to anyone who can prove psychic or paranormal abilities. So far, there have been no takers.

We don't need to turn over rocks to find examples of the news media's reliance on expert ineptitude. Just listen to any of the stock market prognosticators who feed the financial press. If you are an investor, a stock market soothsayer has probably burned you. Did you listen to the hordes of Wall Street analysts who had fallen in love with Enron? Everywhere a reasonable and prudent investor looked there were financial experts who were urging "buy, buy, buy!" To the very end, even when it became clear that Enron was cooking its books in devious ways, media analysts did not tell their audiences to sell.

The Enron debacle, of course, is only the tip of the proverbial iceberg. Beneath the surface are countless examples of the public getting bad advice from ethically challenged financial experts. Perhaps you listened to Henry Blodget, the "star" analyst who kept telling people to buy Pets.com during its free fall from $14 per share to $2.50 per share, where he issued another "buy" rating. The descent continued until the company was dissolved. Not surprisingly, Blodget's employer, Merrill Lynch, had a financial interest in the success of Pets.com because it took the business public.

Unfortunately, Blodget and Merrill Lynch appear to fit the rule rather than the exception. In a recent study of high tech stocks, researchers from Cornell and Dartmouth universities found that investment banks rarely downgrade a company's stocks to a "sell" rating if they have a relationship with the company. The result is that a lot of so-called "analysts" are pushing stocks that they themselves wouldn't buy.

If you have an interest in the conflict-of-interest inherent in the financial press, you may want to pick up *The Fortune Tellers* by press critic Howard Kurtz or order a videotape of a PBS documentary called "Dot con" at <http://www.pbs.org>.

My goal here is not to disparage the syndicated TV shows, cable news, or the financial press. (I would, however, be interested in knowing if Sylvia Browne can find any unbiased analysts on Wall Street.) I simply want to drive home the point that news providers rely heavily on people who produce or analyze information that people want. The Beast's craving for helpful experts is so intense that it sometimes overpowers its desire for reliability.

Mega Magazine Marketplace

The *New York Times,* ABC News, "Dateline," *Time* magazine, and the other top-tier news and information providers are much more selective than their TV counterparts when it comes to choosing expert resources. Consequently, for most of us the thought of winning national exposure is pure fantasy. Thankfully, the opportunities that lie beneath the big boys are vast and deep.

Valerie Lichman runs a small marketing and public relations firm in New York. And yet she scored a nice two-column story (with large photo) in *Inc.* magazine's January 2001 issue. How did she do it? By providing some helpful advice. Lichman's story described how she made the same mistake that so many other sole proprietors make in their first year of business. In her desperate attempt to win clients, she left herself open to unscrupulous bottom feeders who didn't pay her for work and didn't reimburse her for expenses. *Inc.* liked her solution, a set of common sense rules to protect her company, such as not beginning work until the first check has been received and a complete halt to work if any subsequent payment is 30 days late. In addition, she stopped wasting her time producing 20-page proposals for which her hit rate was only 50 percent. Her new two-page pitches are far more successful. Now that's some useful small business information.

In 1999, Mark Zagorski started WorldNow, an Internet solutions company. Two years later, Zagorski landed himself in one of the nation's hottest business magazines, *Fast Company.* He did it by offering a unique and fun solution to a widespread problem— the tendency of corporate culture to erode as new employees are added and others leave. Zagorski's fix: the creation of a company icon that would symbolize the heart of the business. Once a month a top-performing employee is presented with "The Team Drill," an old tool that is continually modified by its caretakers. The winner has 30 days to put his or her personal stamp on the drill. As *Fast Company* reported, "One staffer added a Bart Simpson trigger. Another made the drill wireless by adding an antenna." A new rule for how to care for the drill must also be instituted. (You'll notice that Zagorski's news item is DES.) Zagorski explains, "the dented old drill captures our unofficial mantra of 'drilling down to solve problems.'" That includes his need for publicity.

I could go on and on citing examples from other publications such as *Entrepreneur, PC Computing, Better Homes & Gardens, Muscle & Fitness, Success, Home Business Magazine,* and hundreds of others. The 2002 edition of *Writer's Market* lists more than 1,400 consumer magazines and nearly 500 trade journals. Magazine Publishers of America <www.magazine.org> claims a stunning total of 18,000 consumer magazines. All of these publications are looking for fresh material—always. Can you help?

The Beast Loves to Share

National exposure need not be national in its origins. In other words, your best shot at widespread publicity may be as close as your local newspaper, television, or radio station.

Virtually all newspapers have cooperative agreements with other publications. For the vast majority that means a membership with the Associated Press. AP serves more than 1,500 newspapers and 5,000 broadcast outlets in the United States and more than 15,000 news organizations worldwide. The AP also has its own army of reporters—more than any other news organization in the world. It has bureaus in all 50 states and 72 countries. Through its wire service, the AP allows members to share article content. A good local story will be put on the "state wire," where it can be picked up by other news organizations in that state. A story with broader appeal can "move" regionally and then nationally.

There are other news services as well (NY Times, LA Times/ Washington Post, Gannett, Scripps-Howard, Reuters, and Knight Ridder). They all essentially do the same thing in slightly different ways—share information.

Knight-Ridder is the second largest newspaper publisher in the United States with 32 dailies and 26 non-dailies. It operates the Real Cities Network, which includes 36 regional news websites. Then there is the Knight-Ridder/Tribune Information Services (KRT). This group shares stories between more than 40 newspapers, which can be picked up by any one of 350 subscribers in the United States alone.

This kind of cooperative story swapping between print organizations has been going on for a long time. But now there is a new wave of synergy that would have been unthinkable in the "good old days." Many, if not most, local television stations now have cooperative agreements with newspapers and radio stations. It's a marriage that works well. The newspapers get a chance to spread their influence over the airwaves, and the broadcast outlets get more and better reporting at no cost. The TV and radio stations act like a "tip service" for people who then turn to the newspaper for the full story. If it's your story that's being shared, you've just hit a publicity jackpot.

That's not the end of it. Most local television stations are owned by, or are associated with, media conglomerates that share stories. And then there is more news trading that takes place over the Internet. In short, the point is that national exposure can take many forms and is more accessible than it seems. Every day editors and producers are looking for stories that have broad-based appeal. Good, helpful, interesting information that works in Birmingham will also work in Boston, Bakersfield, Bloomington, and beyond. Be a resource for your local reporter, and you've got a shot at influencing people and reaching customers in multiple time zones.

Reach Out and Touch a Reporter

The reason I so dislike the "it's not what you know, but who you know" axiom is that people tend to use it as an excuse rather than a motivation. If your success is tied to people you don't know—and presumably have no access to—then you're off the hook. "Hey, I'm a pretty sharp guy, but I can't get ahead because I'm not connected to the right people." That excuse may fly in some industries, but in the news business it's horse manure.

Anyone with a telephone and a voice has easy access to local reporters, editors, producers, and many others who are directly connected to the publicity process. And contrary to what many folks have been led to believe, news people want to hear from you—provided you have something worthwhile to offer them. Don't believe me? Pick up a phone, send a letter or fire off an e-mail. You'll be surprised.

Remember the lesson from chapter 1—the Beast suffers from a

strange disconnect. The mission of the journalist is to inform the public about events and issues that are important to her/his audience. But because of intense pressures within the industry, news people tend to isolate themselves from those who are the very reason for their existence—the rest of us. Consequently, a bizarre irony is formed—journalists need daily help from people they do not know.

I did say help—not to be confused with hindrance. Anytime you contact a reporter, have your act together (chapter 5, Rule of Preparation). Your news item needs abundant quantities of DES, and you should be able to explain it in 60 seconds or less. Have a one-page description at the ready that answers the reporter's five W's. Put that package together, and you've got an excellent opportunity for some ink, airtime, or pixels.

Before you do anything, consider the context of what it is you have to offer. If it's a decent story, but nothing spectacular or pressing, don't call. Write it down in a tight paragraph or two, and send it in the mail. Use e-mail if that's what your contact prefers.

Your goal is to become a name and voice that a journalist recognizes as helpful.

Even though news organizations are constantly looking for legitimate material, they are also continually burdened by kooks and others who don't understand deadline pressure. They work a lot like the single woman in her mid-30's who suddenly hears her biological clock ticking. She's eager to consider any guy who's worthy husband material, but she's got no time for pretenders. Once you have won a newsperson's trust, he or she will gladly give your material fair consideration—and that's a great deal any day of the week.

Reporters Know Their Sources

I worked in five newsrooms as a reporter and anchor and in every one of them a few media-savvy people who wanted to be my resource targeted me. I was glad to have them. These folks would call me from time to time to tell me about news stories they thought would spark my interest. If I liked the story, I would pitch it to the assignment editor as something I wanted to do. If I thought it was a decent news story but didn't want to do it, I would write it up and suggest another reporter take the assignment. Either way I scored points with my bosses. The number one complaint management has against newsroom labor is that they don't generate enough story ideas. Give a reporter a few timely ideas, and you can become her new best friend.

One strategy I highly recommend is *feed 'em before you need 'em.* Don't just call, e-mail, or write news contacts when you want their help. Make a point to contact them anytime you see something genuinely tasty. For example, one day I was driving home, and I noticed a road crew ripping up an intersection that had been built only months earlier. I called a reporter friend who got a pretty easy scoop. Turns out the contractor hadn't mixed the cement properly, which resulted in premature cracking. On another day, I happened to look out my window and see that an apartment complex under construction had caught on fire. I grabbed my cell phone and called a news anchor. I fed him information while the station hastily dispatched a live truck and a helicopter.

If I see something in a national news magazine that has local implications, I send it over to a newsperson or two. If I hear something juicy at a party or a business meeting, I do the same. Sometimes I get e-mails with good news potential or come across something compelling on the web. When that happens, I don't keep it to myself. Then the day comes when I—or one of my clients— really want a newsperson's help. When I call, the journalist knows who I am and is ready to listen. Because I've been a resource, he or she has a strong motivation to return the favor.

Keep in mind, I'm not recommending that you contact a journalist every time something the least bit interesting pops up. You don't want to become a pest or be perceived as a publicity hound. Make sure you only sell stories that are truly good news hits. If you attempt to sell weak stuff, your credibility will be shot faster than the Beast can say "buh-bye." Try to work the same people but not too frequently. Establish several news contacts in different mediums.

The Girl Next Door (and in the Next County)

Someone once admonished me: "Don't overlook an orchid while searching for a rose." That's excellent advice, whether you're looking for a date or some powerful publicity. The tendency of many of us is to focus on what we see straight ahead without ever looking left, right, down, up or behind. Therefore, we see only our local newspaper and TV stations right in front of us. But beyond them are large magazines. And way off in the distance are the networks, the *Wall Street Journal, New York Times,* and the rest of the "big time." If you have the motivation and the material to hit those targets, by all means, go for it. If not, take a look around. Opportunities are everywhere.

Perhaps the most overlooked venue for positive press is the smaller newspaper. In most communities today, there is one dominant publication whose readership dwarfs all others. However, the little guys still reach enough people to have a rewarding impact on your organization, should you choose to become a resource.

Business publications in particular are great targets for exposure. The audience for these publications is typically small; however, it's a powerful group. If you have a product or service to sell, this category of newspaper could become your most potent marketing tool.

Another neglected source of excellent exposure is talk radio. Talk show hosts are constantly under the gun to come up with new and interesting topics for their programs. Local politics, spot news, playful games, and controversy can only fill so much airtime. The rest is wide open to local people who have something entertaining and helpful to say. And it's not just one-time guests they want. Most stations will create space for experts who make regular appearances. Take a listen and you will hear stockbrokers, veterinarians, auto mechanics, psychologists, healthcare professionals, contractors, lawyers, and people from many other professions dispensing wisdom and commentary. Even media consultants can receive their fair share of airtime.

A few years ago, the 50,000-watt powerhouse of the Southwest, KKOB-AM, lost its evening talk show host. The station decided to sponsor a contest where local people could audition for the job. Although I had no interest in being paid slave wages to host a radio show five nights a week, I cashed in on the chance to grab some free exposure. I spent my two hours discussing the shallowness of local television news, much to the delight of the listening audience. A longtime anchor even called in to yell at me, which made the show that much more entertaining. A short time later, when Princess Diana was killed and the news media obsessed, the station's hugely popular morning drive host invited me on for an hour of expert analysis. The station later gave me my own Friday night show, and I also became a fill-in host for the afternoon drive. The Rule of Resource (and Repetition) was hard at work establishing me as the resident media expert.

The most recent census should wake us all up to a giant market that has quietly emerged around the monolingual public. In a growing number of markets, Spanish-language TV and radio stations are competitive with mainstream broadcasters. In 2000, Spanish-language TV revenue alone had reportedly grown by almost 20 percent. Univision Communications, the dominant Spanish-language television conglomerate in the United States, with 28 stations and 940 cable affiliates, is gaining viewers while the networks are losing theirs. From 1992 to 2000, Univision picked up nearly a million viewers while ABC, NBC, and CBS all lost at least that many over the same time period.

Contrary to what many believe, this is not a one-dimensional audience of uneducated immigrants and laborers. Spanish television and radio are attracting increasing numbers of working and professional class people who enjoy getting news and entertainment in their native language. For many, it's a way of staying connected to their heritage. For others, it's a practical method for maintaining their Spanish speaking abilities. No matter the reason, this exploding market force should not be ignored. By the way, not being fluent in Spanish does not exclude you from this market. Most of the journalists in these organizations are bilingual, and they can translate your message to their audience.

Of course, there are other niche markets that have a need for expert input. Some local cable stations, for example, have decent-sized audiences. Your challenge in considering these options is to do your own cost/benefit analysis. Only you can decide where your time is best spent. In some cases it might be more beneficial to get five hits with a small news source than one hit in a larger one. The opposite could also be true. While you don't want to overlook lesser opportunities, you also don't want to squander time that could land you a much bigger and better publicity prize.

A Little Elbow Grease

Before the more observant among you start screaming, "Wait a minute!" please wait a minute. I haven't forgotten about the Internet, small town newspapers, trade journals, newsletters, and the like. I saved those for this section, the one that requires a little more effort on your part. We'll begin with the high-tech stuff.

At this writing, the Internet is a powerful force that has yet to live up to its hype. It's like a machine gun loaded with a handful of live rounds but many more blanks. Occasionally a bullet is going to hit the target, but much more often there's just a bang but no measurable results. Nonetheless, every day it's becoming a more legitimate forum to hunt the Beast.

There are services on the web that give journalists direct access to industry experts, two of the better-known sites: <experts.com> and <profnet.com>. For a fee, specialists are registered under their specific area of expertise. Journalists need only cruise the site and pick a resource out of cyberspace. The key to using such services is to take them for what they are—professional dating companies. They make the introduction but no more. It's your job to be so smart, convenient, and helpful that the journalist will want to come back to you again and again. On the first date, you simply provide information. On the next outing, you're quoted. By the third date, maybe you write a guest column.

It's a nifty concept that, like the Internet itself, could have a big impact on how news people do their jobs . . . or not. If you've got a few bucks, some time, and ample motivation, it's worth a shot.

There is a multitude of other ways that the Internet is being used to exchange information. Most of these, such as web page partnerships and link exchanges, fall more in the category of general marketing. If you have a strong interest in using technology for exposure in a number of different ways, check out Susan Kohl's book, *Getting @ttention.*

Some of the most attractive out-of-the-way goldmines are in smaller communities. These newspapers are run by small, dedicated staffs that would make a beaver look lazy. They can always use the help and the assistance they like best—someone who can write copy. If you've got something to say on a topic the editor believes is useful, most papers will welcome your prose as a special guest column. If your material is lively and relevant, you'll be welcomed back frequently. You might even be offered your own column. Don't be intimidated. Anyone can do it.

In college, I took a photography class that required the publishing of a picture in order to get an A. So I visited the editor of a small town weekly and asked if he would be interested in a feature story on a nearby national monument. He said sure. I went to the site, conducted some interviews, shot a roll of film, and wrote up the story. A couple weeks later, I had my first published work accompanied by three photos. For me, that was a primer lesson in the power of being a resource. Since then, I have been a ghostwriter for business and community leaders as well as a guest columnist to many other publications. If it fits into your project needs, you can do the same. For some, being featured in a small town newspaper has no value. Almost no one is going to drive 100 miles to get their car fixed or to buy minor products or services. However, if distance isn't an issue, you've just expanded your market.

One day my life insurance agent told me he could lower my premium by half. I told him to come right over. After signing the paperwork, I asked him how many people knew about the recent changes that allowed people like me to save money. "Not many," he said. So I told him to write a short article and then offer it to newspapers across the state. He did and several papers published it. The agent later told me he made $14,000 in one week as a result of the exposure. When people in little towns read his guest column on lowering rates, many of them ignored their local brokers and dialed long distance to get new policies. But that wasn't all. One publication asked him to be a regular columnist, and the host of a radio show on finances asked him to be a semi-regular guest.

If you have an expertise and can write, or have the money to hire a writer, the opportunities to spread your message are endless. Identify any group under the sun—legal aides, nurses, coin collectors, accountants, bird watchers, physicists, you name it—and there is at least one trade journal or newsletter serving that group. While the readership of such publications is typically small, some reach audiences of thousands. The important thing is that these are "target-rich" environments with many people who are likely to have an interest in what you have to offer.

Writing isn't the only way to be a resource to specific groups. Being available for an interview works just as well, if not better. Many professional associations have tape-of-the-month clubs. Twelve times a year these groups will record a question-and-answer program with experts on a given topic. Recently, my wife and I were interviewed by Marita Littauer of the National Speakers Association (NSA) for the group's "Voices of Experience" audiotape program. More than 4,000 copies of that interview were sent to NSA members. Upon release of the tape, my website was bombarded. I received multiple inquiries, which resulted in subsequent consulting work. Too bad this book wasn't available at that time. My publisher would have been thrilled.

In this category of "author your own press," I've saved the best for last. It's the op-ed (opposite editorial) page. Although studies have shown that a majority of people read the lifestyle sections of their newspaper, the power players of any community skip the fluff and go right to the op-ed page. The *New York Times* says, "The op-ed position should be viewed as the single most valuable position to reach top government, social and business opinion makers." The op-ed page is so valuable that the *Times* can't resist making big bucks on it. Unlike most newspapers the *New York Times* sells quarter-page op-ads. The price tag for one day of this real estate: $30,000.

The requirements for submitting an op-ed piece are few. The topic must be connected to a current event. You must be an authority on the subject or have an otherwise relevant point of view. And the piece should be well written and meet the word-count requirement of the publication. That's it. We'll talk more about the practical application of the op-ed column in chapter 10, the Rule of Timing.

The Shaky Front Line of the PR Army

Many thousands of them are out there—people who carry the title of public information officer (PIO), public relations director, and community relations specialist. Then there is a whole other army of folks who work for PR agencies. All of these people essentially do the same thing in two different ways. They spend part of their time connecting their organizations to the outside world through direct marketing such as advertising, special events, and community activism. The rest of their time is dedicated to trying to win free publicity. Finding the right balance between these two time-consuming endeavors is a difficult task that many organizations fail at miserably.

It's been my observation that most leaders do not appreciate the power of publicity. They have no idea how much time it takes thoroughly and creatively to work the Beast. As a result, their PR people (including young staff members at P.R. agencies) get little or no media training. The idea of making a reporter's life easier is only a fuzzy concept. To make matters worse, their bosses saddle them with so many other jobs, such as writing newsletters, managing special events, and attending endless meetings that they have little time to think about how to be a resource. It's the tyranny of the urgent. Marketing matters take precedence, and the Beast is not considered until he is needed.

Jennifer Comiteau, senior features editor for *Adweek,* suffers the consequence of this priority problem every day. In the October 2000 issue of her magazine, she wrote a column harshly critical of unskilled PR practitioners. Says Comiteau, "Some people get it. Most don't." She complained about the constant stream of lame e-releases and phone calls from PR people who don't understand the value of a journalist's time. "Rule No. 1: Don't squander mine (time), or anyone else's," Comiteau railed. She went on to point out the irony of the problem she and others like her endure. "The journalist ends up educating the PR person; to be effective, you need to flip that equation." In other words, use the Rule of Preparation and the Rule of Easy to fulfill the Rule of Resource.

Don't get me wrong—I'm not indicting the entire profession. Public Relations people provide a valuable service to journalists. Every reporter and editor knows it—even if they do refer to PR people as "flacks." Like Jennifer Comiteau, I've worked with some excellent PR practitioners that I valued immensely. Unfortunately, I've suffered many more who didn't have a clue.

Interestingly, some of the best "resources" are people who don't even work in PR or marketing. These are folks who aren't out to "spin" the Beast. They simply see that they are in a position to help a time-strapped journalist and help themselves along the way.

While working in Central California, I did numerous stories with the California Conservation Corps. (CCC). The director of the program routinely called me with story ideas. As a result, the CCC got a lot of positive coverage from my station. He also did something few others have the discipline to do. He tried to keep an "evergreen" (a story that can be done most anytime) within reach if I ever called in desperate need of something to point a camera at. I did call, and those stories did get told.

A resource is someone who makes himself and his organization available anytime a reporter needs him. I was the sports director at a station in South Carolina that made me do a "tips" segment once a week. I wound up having to do it on my own time—it was always a hassle. A local resort manager made the chore easier. He made his golf and tennis pros available whenever I needed them. Sometimes that meant two or three hours early in the morning so we could shoot multiple stories. It was a huge help to me and golden exposure for the resort. If any of the other nearby clubs had called, I would have let them be my resource, too. But the others only made contact when they wanted something such as coverage for an event. They had no idea how many great opportunities they were missing.

Being a true resource can also be a great benefit when you're caught in a jam (We'll get into this deeper in chapter 13, the Rule of Ambush). Reporters are only human. If they know and like you, they're not going to want to hurt you. They'll naturally be more inclined to understand your point of view or go out of their way to let you tell your side of the story.

I once covered an ongoing dispute between a newly appointed county fire chief and a longtime volunteer chief. The new boss was trying to make changes, but the volunteer chief was resisting and had the support of a core group of firefighters. The volunteers staged raucous meetings in which they tried to discredit their boss. Of course, the news media came; it was emotionally charged and easy to cover. But the new chief was a lot smarter about how he handled me. He called many times to explain complicated issues in simple terms. He gave me ways to advance the story on weekends (hard days to find "hard" news). While the volunteer chief was a difficult-to-schedule, hotheaded complainer, the paid chief was genuinely likable and always accessible. Even though I tried to present balanced stories, there's no question the paid chief's viewpoint was better represented in my reports.

Press Release Madness

The knee-jerk response of many publicity seekers is to put out a press release, cross their fingers, and hope for the best. For a national target, that may be your best shot. However, on the local level, it's a big mistake. While a press release can be a useful tool in the hands of a reporter already assigned to a story, it is a relatively weak publicity attractor. The most effective way to initiate publicity will always be a relationship with a newsperson. That said, press releases are still a necessary part of the process—even with a relationship. Write them according to the Beast's preferred formula, and your pitch will rise to the top of the stack.

Newsrooms are continually flooded with press releases. They come in the mail, over the fax, and now via e-mail. A small news organization will get dozens every day. Larger shops receive hundreds. Ask any editor whose job it is to wade through the stream of paper and electronic pitches, and she will tell you that very few press releases actually trigger a story. It's a safe estimation that well over 90 percent get less than 30 seconds consideration before their demise.

> The vast majority of press releases are ditched in just a few seconds . . .

The vast majority of press releases are ditched in just a few seconds for one reason. They violate the Seducers. A press release must immediately convey its message in the headline, sub-headline and first few sentences. Everything below the third sentence becomes useful only when the editor's attention has been seized. Without a clear, emotion-provoking, or curiously different headline, your release will quickly be trashed—literally.

Here are a few examples of how press release headlines/sub-headlines are typically written, immediately followed by an example of how each might be improved.

U.S. Forest Service Changes Policy

*Some fires will be allowed to burn themselves
out to clear dangerous undergrowth*

Smokey Bear Now Says, "Let it Burn!"

*New research proves that putting out fires too quickly
is a dangerous policy*

The idea is to get the editor's attention. A policy change at the U.S. Forest Service is about as compelling as watching a tree grow. The editor needs something hot and flashy to catch her eye, so give it to her. What about the media focusing on the line "Let it Burn"? Isn't that, well . . . inflammatory? So what. If the local newspaper or TV station does the story, the forest service gets a chance to explain what the new policy means. Isn't that the goal?

Insurance Industry Responds to Increase in Dog Bites

*Agencies may now consider discontinuing homeowner
policies of those who own dangerous dogs*

Message to Dog Owners: Beware of Dog

*Insurance Industry now advises carriers to drop
policyholders with vicious canines*

Headlines should always be simple and different from the norm. The first example sounds like industry-speak. The second headline forces the editor to stop and visualize a "Beware of Dog" sign that faces *inside* the fence. It's a twist on the familiar. News people salivate like Pavlov's dog when they see a fresh angle on an old story. As you now know, that's what news is.

Chamber Sponsors City Council Debates

Voters will ask questions of candidates

Voting is Unpatriotic! . . . If it's Uneducated

*Chamber invites voters to educate themselves
at city council debates*

Few public relations directors would write the headline above for fear of offending someone. But how could the public be offended if it never sees the headline? The purpose of the press release is to get the editor's attention and to provide core information for the reporter. That's it. In the event that a reporter bites on the "unpatriotic" angle, it still doesn't matter. It then becomes the reporter's angle. If the chamber of commerce is pinned with it, so what? Who is going to fault the chamber for trying to educate the voters? The alternative is to write a boring headline and fail to get anyone's attention.

Another dominant problem among press release writers is their tendency to slip into industry-speak that is unintelligible to the non-flack. Try to decipher this one that I recently came across in a business publication: "A next-generation set of tools designed to dramatically enhance the value end-users receive from trading hubs." What? Is this PR person talking about a) a digital telephone network, b) Internet software, or c) a new system for international currency exchange? The reporter who read this techno-gibberish off a press release openly admitted his confusion. After a lot of straining of his gray matter, he finally figured the thing out. In the column that followed he said, "The idea was astonishingly simple considering how complex the PR made it sound." By the way, the correct answer is: b) Internet software.

But it's not hopeless. At long last, we are beginning to see a reaction in the business world against techno-speak. The Gable Group, a Los Angeles–based PR firm, operates a website called <jargonfreeweb.com>. Posted on the site are examples of jargon-inflated press releases, written in amazingly convoluted language. One PR person writes about "a comprehensive set of commerce-related design tools and transaction modules, including auctions, aggregated and distributed catalogs, exchanges, RFP's/RFQ's, and structured negotiations." Believe it or not, the author of this mess was actually trying to *communicate* an idea to the press.

It's not just jargon that journalists hate. Overused buzzwords drive them crazy as well. To battle-weary editors it must seem as if the czar of the PR world decreed that every press release should contain at least two of the following words: "solution," "leading," "best," "first," "seamless," or "robust." To quote Rob Calem of the *Wall Street Journal Interactive,* "Please don't write to me about solutions anymore . . . they have become a problem." To combat this PR heresy, many major publications are now reportedly using e-mail filters to immediately trash messages that contain any "leading-edge" words that promise "end-to-end" success.

If you're not going to write a simple, different, and emotion-provoking press release, then don't waste your time because otherwise you're wasting the editor's time—a high crime, indeed.

A Helping Hand Often Needs a Glove

Knowing how to be a resource—the kind that isn't also a pest—is the most important skill of any publicity seeker. It's the ticket to a level of press access that few PR professionals ever find. However, being the kind of resource that regularly scores with the Beast requires more than just offering the occasional helping hand. It also demands an aptitude for dressing up that hand so it gets noticed.

Very few of us are in a position to be a resource on a consistent basis with the good opportunities that may or may not pop up around us. So, if you're going to be serious about your publicity quest, you'll have to become something of an inventor. You don't have to be as smart as Thomas Edison to do this, but it helps if you learn to think like him.

◆ ◆ ◆

CHAPTER 9

The Rule of Invention

~ must see publicity ~

In newsrooms everywhere, reporters can be heard repeating the tongue-in-cheek phrase "Don't let the facts get in the way of a good story." If you want to pursue publicity aggressively, that cliché should become your new mantra.

As you now know, the Beast isn't too concerned about just the facts. It's all the different, emotive, simple, and easy to capture stuff that excites him. And that's the rub. The material that many of us have isn't all that compelling, or it's annoyingly complex. But that's no reason to give up. If what you have to sell can't be stretched to fit the media's requirements, invent something that will.

Inventor's Inventor

Thomas Edison, the greatest inventor of all time, should be an inspiration to all who crave the publicity spotlight. After he created the incandescent light bulb, the world was amazed but still extremely cautious. Few people could imagine the possibility of having a light source inside their homes that did not come from a flame. Edison demonstrated the practicality of his mysterious invention by installing the first commercial electric utility in New York's Wall Street district. The system worked great, except for weak insulation around the cables buried in the street, which soon resulted in a massive public relations problem. One day after a soaking rain, a faulty line electrified the street, killing several men and horses.

So how did the great inventor combat the public's fear of electric power? He invented some publicity. In one case, Edison sent a parade of 400 men through Manhattan with glowing light bulbs on their heads. The spectacle was powered by a horse-drawn, steam generator and electric lines concealed inside each man's sleeve. In another stunt, Edison hired an entertainer to tap-dance across an electrified floor at an exhibition in Philadelphia. As the man danced, his shoes would send an electric current to a light on his helmet. While the helmet pulsed to the rhythm of the dancer's feet, he handed out pamphlets touting the safe and practical use of electricity. The press swooned, fear subsided, and progress was served.

Manipulating the Media

The next time you watch a newscast, read a newspaper, flip through a magazine, or click through a news website, look for Invention. You'll be astonished at how much "news" is actually the product of media manipulation. Excluding spot news, most of what we receive from the Beast is at least partially manufactured.

In this chapter, we will examine the ways in which various groups manipulate the news media to serve their own agenda. If you think your particular group wouldn't stoop (or elevate itself) to this level of free marketing, think again. Anyone serious about getting press does it. If you don't, you won't succeed.

Before getting into all the different ways to attract the Beast through artificial means, we should first mark the news media's love of Invention itself. Earlier chapters in this book have proven this point. Remember the green ketchup, the trap cap, the gambler's exercise bike, and the fat-tired wheel chair? News people will always be curious about the newest, latest, greatest thing out there.

When <Inside.com> published a story that famed inventor Dean Kamen was working on something big, the press went bonkers. It was nearly a year before the invention would be unveiled, but still the media could not resist constantly speculating about what "It" could be. The project, which Kamen said could "profoundly affect our environment and the way people live worldwide," provoked breathless anticipation across all media. Periodic and intentionally vague mentions of the device (also code-named Ginger) kept the media in a controlled state of hype. Then, on December 3, 2001, Kamen unveiled the Segway Human Transporter on ABC's "Good Morning America." The two-wheeled, gyroscope-stabilized vehicle was a huge hit. The press went bonkers all over again, and this time they even had pictures! The Beast loves new gadgets, even if the world could get along just fine without them.

When Brill Hygienic Products released the electronic toilet seat cover, the press went nuts. Reporters marveled at how the computerized toilet seat electronically rotates a fresh plastic sheet cover into place with the touch of a button. No more wrestling with those clumsy paper covers. The plastic sheets are four times more expensive, but what the heck; they're newer and cooler than pre-packaged paper kind. We could talk about how unnecessary a toilet seat barrier invention is (paper or plastic), but that's a subject for a different book.

Did you know that you can greatly extend the life of your home's water heater by periodically flushing it? I didn't, until I read an article about a device called Kwik Kleen, which automates the flushing process. Just hook up the low-voltage unit to your water heater and forget about it. Once a month the device will flush away the corrosive sediment that cuts into the lifespan of your H_2O warmer. Of course, you can always save a few bucks and flush your system manually. But who wants to do that now that you know there is a gadget that will do it a dozen times a year while you sleep? Leave it to the news media to give us a solution to a problem that most of us didn't know existed.

Ever heard of using Cheez Whiz to clean the salsa off your Calvin Klein jeans? If you haven't, you're in the minority. Joey Green, author of *Clean Your Clothes with Cheez Whiz*, has carved a highly profitable niche out of finding wacky ways to use ordinary products. In his many books, Green explains how you can do such things as polish furniture with pantyhose, catch fish with M&M's, or clean your toilet with Gatorade (or Country Time Lemonade). News and entertainment providers, of course, love this guy. Green has appeared on the "Today" show, "Good Morning America," "The Tonight Show," and the "Rosie O'Donnell Show." He's also been featured in *USA Today*, the *New York Times*, the *Los Angeles Times*, *People*, *Entertainment Weekly* and many other publications.

> ... the most sophisticated ... form of invention is that which appears unforced.

Couldn't we just drink the Gatorade, clean our toilet with Sani-Flush, wear the pantyhose, and save the dusty furniture for Pledge? Yes, but if you're asking this question, you're missing the point. The Beast loves a good Invention, and not just the gadget kind. As we will see, he's also attracted to stunts, events, protests, marketing ploys, and even spectacles that are created by the media itself.

Be the Ball

Anyone applying the Rule of Invention is actively working an angle to get publicity. Even so, the most sophisticated (and often the most successful) form of Invention is that which appears unforced. This seeming contradiction of "effortless power" is true of any human endeavor. The classic comedy *Caddy Shack* captured this concept when Chevy Chase advised his young protégé to "Be the ball."

When Fred Couples hits a tee shot, his body motion looks almost nonchalant—and then you see his ball run 285 yards down the center of the fairway. Michael Jordan slides by hapless slow-motion defenders, uncontested to the hoop. Easy. When reading a novel by John Irving, you feel as if you were eavesdropping—the mechanics of eyes pulling words off paper goes unnoticed. You never see Meryl Streep act—she *is* the character. It works the same way in the publicity game. If you want to score consistently, learn how to be the ball.

The best inventions are those that seamlessly connect three things: 1) the invention; 2) the product, service, organization, or person that the invention represents, and 3) other marketing efforts.

Southwest Airlines found this seamless connection in 1990. Airline executives were looking for a way to make a big media splash for their 20th anniversary, which would officially take place in early 1991. Knowing that a mere announcement or even a party would have attracted little, if any, attention, Southwest came up with a great idea. As a tribute to 20 years of flying out of its Dallas, Texas, hub, the airline painted a big blue star on a brand new plane and called it "Lone Star One." The anniversary unveiling attracted widespread attention in all media within the state and nation.

The Invention was such a publicity success that Southwest followed up with "Arizona One" in 1994, "California One" in 1995,

"Nevada One" in 1999, and "New Mexico One" in 2000. Each of these new state planes was also greeted with overflowing news coverage. Southwest flies four other signature planes, three Shamu aircraft, which advertise the company's relationship with SeaWorld, and "Silver One," which was christened on the 25th anniversary. In this case, Southwest's general marketing effort and a specific publicity invention have become almost one.

While it's difficult to see a "seam" between paint and airplane, it's even more difficult to see a connection where one doesn't exist. The product, person, or service is a news seducer in and of itself. The Ice Hotel in Quebec, Canada, is one such example. About 250 tons of ice and 4,500 tons of snow are used to construct this winter "hotel" where the average temperature inside is 26 degrees. Believe it or not, the inn is full nearly every night (when it exists between December and March) with people willing to spend between $80 and $190 to shiver underneath deerskin blankets. The Ice Hotel is an invention of the Quebec Tourism Department, which stole the idea from the Ice Hotel in Jukkasjaervi, Sweden. The objective is to promote winter tourism in the Canadian province. I'd say it works, considering how the press attention has translated into a busy reservations department—even if the guests are a little numb between the ears.

Internet consultant Philip Kaplan unexpectedly discovered his seamless publicity niche when he created a website that mocked the dot-com disaster of the new millennium. Kaplan gave the site a vulgar name (let's euphemistically call it <screwedcompany.com>) that was intended to make fun of *Fast Company,* the information source preferred by new economy believers and touters. As more and more Internet startups turned into closedowns, Kaplan posted the carnage on his website. People began coming to the site for several reasons —to laugh, to predict the next dot-com implosion, to snoop on the competition, and even to scout for newly unemployed talent. *U.S.*

News & World Report called it "a cyberspace must-read: part dot-com obituary page, part intelligence-gathering tool and part comic relief for stressed-out employees at flailing Internet startups everywhere." While it did turn into an excellent publicity Invention, the site is not merely a publicity tool. It stands by itself as a viable enterprise. Long after the dot-com disaster the website lives on as a bizzare blend of commerce, complaining, crudeness, and camaraderie. How about that? Momentum generated by the Beast has kept *screwedcompany.com* from appearing on its own website.

The best publicity Invention is one that is so tightly integrated to its reason for existence and other general marketing that the three different elements appear to be one. When such an opportunity fails to present itself, shake off all inhibition and invent something that will splash.

Ground Breaking the Mold

The most common publicity event is the press conference, followed by staged ceremonies such as when ground is broken or when ribbons are cut. If you're wondering which one is better . . . don't. They both stink. Reporters loathe them. The reason why is obvious. What Difference, Emotion, or Simplicity is there in talking heads seated at a table or in eight suits sinking shovels into the ground? Boring. Press conferences and perfunctory ceremonies are like repellent to any self-respecting journalist. They will only come to such an event if they believe they *have* to. Politicians, cops, school superintendents, and other community leaders can often get away with unimaginative "photo ops," but to everyone else it's a killer.

Do I mean to say that you should never hold a press conference or celebrate the beginning or end of a construction project? Absolutely not. What I am suggesting is that you avoid them, if at all possible. But if you must, search for every scrap of DES you can find and invent something that will attract a camera. Events must be visual.

While consulting with Gateway on a new call center facility, I knew we had a problem. The construction site was located about 30 minutes away from the nearest TV station—a nasty violation of the Rule of Easy. Getting the local stations out to the grand opening, however, wouldn't be difficult because at least then there would be something to look at. Our challenge was to figure out a way to get the attention of producers who would be asking, "Where's the beef?" Why should they care if the actual building and its benefit to the community were still months away from the groundbreaking ceremony? The answer was to show them the beef—literally.

As you may know, Gateway's corporate symbol is the Holstein cow box, a tribute to the CEO's dairy farming lineage. You can see what's coming, can't you? I called a nearby dairy and asked if I could rent a cow. We eventually wound up with a 4-H Club teenager and his sizable black and white heifer. Of course, I let all media outlets—especially the TV stations—know ahead of time that a cow would be part of the ceremony. It worked. The event that would have been largely ignored was widely covered.

Even though ribbon cuttings and grand openings are an easier sell to the news media than a patch of dirt and shovels, they can still be a challenge. Newspapers understand the importance of new businesses and new jobs to a community, but local TV stations typically don't get it or just don't care. TV producers need to be sold in a visual way. And even if the newspaper editors don't require as much persuasion, they still appreciate a good picture. The motto of Invention is: *must see publ*

When Sprint PCS was ready to open a new customer support facility for its wireless telephone service, we needed something distinctive for the ceremony. I suggested that instead of cutting a ribbon, we cut one of those curly telephone cords that connect handset to receiver. Sprint PCS executives loved the idea. So did the news media.

While consulting with Victoria's Secret Catalogue on the opening of a newly purchased facility, I was instructed by the PR staff that there would be no ribbon cutting at the ceremony. Delighted, I asked about what creative alternative they had in mind. The PR manager said the company president would be cutting through a flank of hand-painted wallpaper. Wallpaper? "It's gorgeous," I was told. And it was, but what sense did it make to cut through wallpaper for a company that sells lacy underwear? For once, an actual *ribbon cutting* ceremony was completely appropriate. When the wallpaper arrived the night before the event, the PR rep agreed it was a bad idea. After a panicked dash to a fabric store we strung up a beautiful four-foot-wide band of bright pink lace that spanned the 30-foot entrance to the building. The sexy ribbon was prominently featured in newspaper pictures and even mentioned in the copy. TV photographers and reporters also picked up on the symbolism and leaned heavily on it in their stories.

Every visual enhancement to a ceremony helps. Sometimes a compelling picture will make the difference between getting coverage or not. However, the extra energy will always make the story better than it would have been.

When I was assisting Intuit Inc. in a grand opening event, we had a company executive stand in front of a giant TV monitor to demonstrate the function of its cutting-edge software. (Intuit is the producer of financial software programs Quicken, QuickBooks, and TurboTax.) The camera-friendly bonus no doubt contributed to the excellent media turn out.

At another event, the opening of a new senior living community, we used athletes in their 60s, 70s, and 80s to bring the swimming pool and exercise room to life. Empty pools and vacant rooms do not make for good stories.

Creating a visual enticement for your event need not be confined to manipulating elements within a ceremony. Sometimes the thing you want publicity for doesn't have a ceremony. In that case I would advise inventing the whole thing. I once consulted with a small city chamber of commerce that was about to reach a major milestone—its 500th member. It was big stuff for the business community, and the director wanted big publicity. But merely announcing the good news was not going to get the job done. The solution to the chamber's dilemma would have to be invented.

Because the mainstream media doesn't care a lot about business, we knew that the story's hook had to come from somewhere else, and it had to be something with a lot of emotive appeal. We didn't have to look far. The growing city was in such desperate need of schools that it had created a school made up entirely of portable buildings. It was a pathetic looking facility, absolutely without any landscaping. We drew attention to the chamber by drawing attention to this stark campus.

The chamber asked the 498th, 499th, and 500th members to purchase five large trees each. A local nursery threw in a few more and donated the labor to plant them. The event was portrayed as a way to "give back to the community." The mayor hosted the tree-planting ceremony in front of the school's entire population of students, teachers, and, of course, news cameras and reporters. When life gives you lemons, make lemon meringue pie—and put colorful sprinkles on top.

Does the Beast know when it is being manipulated by the Rule of Invention? Certainly. Does he care? Not really—so long as the story is worthwhile. If the story is a dud, journalists grumble about all those clueless "PR flacks." In the previous example, news editors knew that the school district's money problem was one of the most important issues to the community. Covering a positive story related to such a hot topic was an easy hit. If the Invention hadn't made the grade, it simply would have been blown off like the other dozens of manipulation attempts for that particular day. If the news media don't allow themselves to be manipulated, editors and managers would have a difficult time getting their jobs done.

Voilà! News from Nothing

Winning publicity through a news conference or ceremony can be gratifying, if only because you've managed to draw reporters to something they would really rather avoid. But the thrill is much like cajoling a child into eating eggplant. Yes, it's a triumph, but it lacks originality. The true ecstasy of Invention comes when you create a publicity magnet from nothing more than your own imagination. This is the heart of the Rule of Invention—its truest form. Few find it.

Not even Thomas Edison could say he entered the heart of publicity Invention, for Edison's inventions *were* the source of his press interest. No, the best examples of news Invention come from two of the 20th century's greatest showmen—Harry Houdini and Evel Knievel. Houdini created the spectacle of the seemingly impossible escape where none presumably existed. He stepped onto the world stage with nothing but his own wits and imagination. Evel Knievel essentially did the same thing, only with a motorcycle instead of chains, shackles, and ropes. If you didn't see Knievel's jumps at Caesar's Palace or at Snake River, you've no doubt heard about them or seen the spectacles on TV.

The Beast loves people who invent things. It finds stunts especially irresistible.

When it was announced in summer 2001 that the space station Mir would be guided to a crash landing in the South Pacific, Taco Bell began inventing. The fast food chain hastily put out an order for one huge, inflatable target for the decrepit spacecraft to crash on. If Mir had miraculously defied impossible odds and hit the target, Taco Bell promised free tacos. Who would get these free tacos? I don't know. The question isn't even relevant. The total absurdity of the stunt is what matters (Difference), and that's what got the Mexican-food chain national exposure. One executive was interviewed on the "Today" show by host Katie Couric, who asked the obvious question and then answered it herself: "How effective is this type of thing? Well, it got you on the 'Today' show, right?"

Weird contests and competitions are always a good media draw. The public loves this kind as stuff—as evidenced by the success of shows such as "Survivor," "Who Wants to Be a Millionaire," "Jeopardy," and a spate of others. What the people want, the news media wants to deliver, no matter how ridiculous. The good news is you don't have to escape from a submerged box, jump a river, or spend a fortune on an inflatable target to get a reporter's attention. Just be creative.

Lisa Kanarek knows a few things about whipping up publicity out of thin air. The consultant to home-based business owners held a contest to find the strangest places where people have set up shop. She received more than 50 bizarre entries including a man who runs his business from a sailboat in the Caribbean to the owner of a construction company who spends part of his time working out of his bathroom. Kanarek's little contest just dripped of DES, so much so that it became the centerpiece of a *Wall Street Journal* article.

Staging a quirky contest can be one of the cheapest marketing attempts you can engage in. It's like the pie-throwing booth or the dunk tank at the county fair. A few folks contribute some of their time, resources, and expertise, and a crowd gathers to watch the fun.

Creating a contest isn't as difficult as you might think. Simply identify something connected to your specialty that people can identify with and then twist it in a funny, ironic, or silly manner. For example, everybody loves to hate the company copier, right? These wonderfully frustrating machines seem to break down every day. So, if you are an office equipment dealer, why not hold a contest to find the "World's Worst Copier"? Give the winner a new machine and write it off as an advertising expense. It will work. I know—a client of mine did it.

I recently saw a newspaper story about a homebuilder's show that was accepting nominations for the "Ugliest Bath." The winner received a $7,000 remodeling job, with the expense absorbed by the organization at wholesale cost. Anyone nominating his or her bath for the dubious honor was admitted for free. Undoubtedly, the contest brought in some extra people who were unhappy with their pitiful bathrooms, but that wasn't the point. The idea was to spread the word that a homebuilder's show was coming up that would be of interest to anyone planning a home-improvement project.

When you are contemplating a contest or any other publicity stunt, don't confuse the Invention with the goal. The attraction is only the tool that gets you the prize.

Kansas City–based Camp Fire Boys and Girls was looking to expand awareness of its children's programs. A typical effort from such an organization would have been to invent a contest. But kids' lives are filled with contests these days. Therefore, the novelty that works in the business world would probably have flopped in the child arena (Difference). The Camp Fire group understood that the publicity Invention only required an indirect connection to the organization. So they created something called the "Absolutely Incredible Kid Day." The idea, a takeoff on Mother's Day and Father's Day, is to have adults write letters to children in need of encouragement. Any kid will do, and anyone can participate. The event gets press coverage every year. First, the reporters talk about the positive impact the letters have on the lives of the children. Then, the stories inevitably move toward a discussion of Camp Fire programs —mission accomplished in more ways than one.

Someone could fill a book with examples of stunt publicity, and it wouldn't take long. It's everywhere. Just look for it. When Microsoft co-founder Paul Allen donated a piece of his large fortune to the Experience Music Project, an interactive music museum, he christened the building with a stringed instrument. Newspapers all over the world published a photo of Allen in the process of smashing a glass guitar. United Airlines gives sick kids a "Fantasy Flight" to see Santa Claus at Christmas time. The plane taxies around the runway and then drops the children off at an airport gate not far from where the plane "departed." The Desert Nature Park raises money for its program by hosting a "Bug Banquet." People pay a fee to watch community leaders eat "gourmet" worms, beetles, crickets, and other insects. The event raises a nice chunk of cash, but heightened awareness about the park is worth far more.

Stumping without a Stump

In general, politicians are lame publicity inventors. The primary reason is that they usually have pretty easy access to the press, which blunts their incentive. Another reason is in this PC age most politicos have been emasculated by hyper-concern over offending someone. That's too bad, because in the political arena opportunities abound.

The crazy thing about political blandness is that it need not be that way. If a community leader isn't directly attacking someone, the fear of being burned is somewhat irrational, especially when weighed against the potential name-recognition benefits. But the more experienced a politician is, the more unfair press treatment he has witnessed or experienced. The fact that an official's own dumb mistakes and a lack of press understanding contributed to his wounds is not given much consideration. Therefore, some of the more inventive politicians tend to be those who are the least experienced and most needy.

Rookie state legislator Joe Mohorovic attended a Media Rules conference and afterward told me he was going to put the training to use. During the next legislative session, he got his chance. A dispute between the governor and legislative leaders had held up a bill that was needed to pay for the session's paperwork. Without the passage of this bill, there would have been no money to pay for the printing of all the bills. While state leaders bickered, Joe invented. He came to the next day's session with a giant copy of a check in the amount of $234.00, the cost of printing the bill he wanted passed. That little stunt landed him on the front page of the state's newspaper of record. The big check stunt has been used innumerable times. But in the stale air of the political chamber, a small puff of creativity can have a blustery effect.

I once advised a young candidate who was running against the 30-year veteran who was also a longtime speaker of the New Mexico House of Representatives. My client's best attribute was his youth. He wasn't married to, or responsible for, a failing state bureaucracy. As a way to contrast his youthful energy against his opponent's old tiredness, I suggested he declare his candidacy at a community center basketball game (the candidate was an excellent player). This different kind of ceremony would have suggested many messages to the voters including youth, vitality, community spirit, boldness, and creativity. Unfortunately, input from the political establishment killed the idea. However, wise use of the Media Rules in a variety of other ways played a role in his defeat of a man who took office before Watergate became a household word.

While most seasoned politicians are about as creative as a bricklayer, occasionally we are treated to some notable exceptions. In Chapter 5, the Rule of Preparation, we took a look at Al Gore's use of "advisors" prior to his debates with George W. Bush. Gore didn't need any advice from workaday folks. Hadn't he been listening to the ordinary people he encountered on the campaign trail? What about his eight years as vice president? Wasn't he listening then? No, Gore wasn't looking for a last-minute debate strategy. He was desperate for easy press in the swing states that his advisors came from. Gore's powwow with everyday folks in Florida (ultimately the most important of all swing states) was a calculated publicity Invention. And it was a good one that sent the message he wanted: Al Gore is a good guy. To quote Gore "advisor" Joseph Austin, "A lot of people think Al Gore is stiff and boring, which is not the case at all. He's very personable. I think our opinions will be valued greatly."

The Democrats weren't the only ones creatively to invent the day's news during election 2000. Republican National Committee (RNC) chairman Jim Nicholson pulled off one of the campaign's more imaginative stunts that mocked Gore's claim to "rural roots." More than a dozen camera crews recorded Nicholson as he drove a mule-drawn cart in front of the upscale Washington, D.C., home that Gore grew up in.

In another ploy, the RNC sent out an April 2000 press release headlined, "Reporters Held Hostage." The copy complained that Gore had not held a press conference in 51 days. An accompanying illustration featured two prominent campaign reporters locked in a stockade. The *Washington Post* and the *Los Angeles Times* soon ran stories about Gore's avoidance of the press.

The following month, the RNC released a CD entitled "The Best of Al Gore." The mock musical compilation featured 17 of the vice president's most notable verbal gaffes. The party sent it to 1,000 radio hosts, and many of them obliged the RNC by playing cuts. At least ten major news operations had reportedly mentioned the CD within a week after its release.

After the election, the Democrats regrouped. As President George W. Bush attempted to sell his tax cut to the country, Representative Dick Gephardt and Senator Tom Daschle staged a Capitol Hill photo op. The two stood in front of a $43,000 Lexus and behind a table that displayed an old muffler. Gephardt and Daschle told the press that Bush's tax cut would give millionaires enough extra cash to buy the car, while average working Americans would only be given enough to buy a muffler. Now that's an Invention that shines, purrs, and gets traction like a fine automobile.

Your Inner Inventor

The beauty of the Rule of Invention is that anyone can use it. You don't have to be a politician or a business owner or any other kind of mover and shaker. If you can manufacture something worth paying attention to, journalists will give you a shot at some free exposure. And they're always suckers for a good cause.

Remember the movie *Forrest Gump*? A broken-hearted Forrest decides to go running and winds up traversing the continent three times. Once the press gets wind of this obsessed runner, he becomes an instant celebrity. Of course, Forrest Gump is only a fictional character, but the storyline works because it rings so true.

No telling how many people have walked or run from here to there to win publicity for their cause. So many have done it that the stunt has become something of a cliché. Nonetheless, if you can add a twist, reporters will pay attention. Toby "Twist" Johnson is an excellent example.

At 39 years old, Johnson had to undergo an angioplasty operation to clear a 90 percent blockage in his right coronary artery. A year later he walked across the state of Illinois to raise money for the American Heart Association. He collected a lot of press attention and $10,000. What's so great about walking a mere 333 miles in 33 days? Johnson accomplished the feat on a pair of stilts that make him nine feet tall.

Stilts are a wonderful bit of difference, but you don't have to be a former circus performer (like Johnson) to get reporters to pay attention to what you're doing. Sixty-three-year-old Michigan native Billie Gardner is proof of that. She just walked—for 2,448 miles—along historic Route 66. Her cause was birth defects. Her twist—she's a grandmother of five.

Steve Gutierrez doesn't walk; he sleeps. The 50-something social worker spends cold December nights holding a sign out to passing cars asking for blankets for the homeless. When the traffic thins, he bunks down on the sidewalk. It's not too comfy, but with the press exposure he receives, Gutierrez has brought in hundreds of blankets and food donations.

All of the above examples are a little askew (difference), which is what makes them work. Although I don't advise it, really wacky stuff works as well. Maybe you've heard of Jim Moran, the guy who went to Alaska in 1938 to sell a refrigerator to an Eskimo. He found a buyer and some fame. Perhaps you've seen videotape of Los Angeles' Pancake Man. This guy flips flapjacks in a skillet—while running in marathons. You've read these kinds of stories in your local paper and seen them on the news. Why? People are easily captivated by silly stunts. Just ask anyone who is a regular viewer of late night television. Two of David Letterman's most popular recurring segments are "Stupid Pet Tricks" and "Stupid Human Tricks." Have you seen the guy who squirts mustard across the stage by squeezing the plastic container between his butt cheeks?

There's no need to digress further. The point is that anyone can use the Rule of Invention to win high-value press coverage. It's done in business, politics, education, philanthropy, entertainment—and yes, even in the news business itself.

Pot to Kettle: We're Black

It happens every February, May, July, and November. These are the ratings months for local television stations. Some sort of stunt is pulled to bring in the highest number of viewers possible.

Have you seen a reporter or anchor undergo Lasik eye surgery live on the air? I've witnessed it twice in the same market. It's a little silly watching a doctor operate on someone's eyes on the 10:00 or 11:00 P.M. news, but who can argue with success?

This type of inventive "news" is, of course, nothing new. TV stations have been "stunting" (as they call it in the business) for decades. Sometimes it's a contest. "Watch Eyewitness News tonight, and win a bucket of cash!" "Win a car!" "Win a vacation!" "Win a Sony PlayStation 2!" Other times it's some sort of spectacle. "Tonight at eleven you'll see something blown up!" "Watch a former car thief actually steal a car. . . . Live at eleven!" "Our very own investigative reporter tips a few and gets tipsy to prove a point about drunken driving!" Then, there are the call-in shows. "Tonight at six, financial experts will be manning the phones to answer your investment questions." In the next rating period, the experts might be doctors, lawyers, or parenting experts (Resource).

The networks enjoy a good stunt as well. After "Today" show host Katie Couric's husband died of colon cancer, NBC videotaped her colonoscopy and shared the story with the world. It was highly successful in raising awareness about colon cancer. In fact, Couric later interviewed three people who saw the colonoscopy segment, got tested, and were found to have the deadly disease.

Newsmagazine shows are built on the Invention premise. On one show they dust kitchens for traces of e-coli bacteria. They sting unscrupulous auto mechanics who charge exorbitant prices for parts they don't even install. Hidden cameras are taken inside jewelry store showrooms where diamond dealers under-appraise stones that they over-valued when they sold them days earlier. Is all of this stuff "news?" Yes. I don't have a problem with it, and nor should you. But we should call these stories what they are—Inventions.

Of course, newspapers, magazines, Internet news providers, and especially radio stations are also happy participants in the

Invention game. There's no need to belabor the point with examples from each of these areas. I simply want to emphasize the fact that journalists are always up for manufacturing a little news. Knowing this should give you confidence as you plot your own grab for publicity.

Want a newspaper or TV station to cover an event? Ask a reporter or anchor to be the emcee, hand out awards, or be a judge. News providers are always looking for ways to demonstrate that their people are "part of the community." As we discussed in chapter 1, study after study has demonstrated that the public and the press know there is a "culture gap" between journalists and everyone else. Bridging that chasm, or at least making an attempt, is a priority in many newsrooms.

TV anchors and reporters as well as radio personalities typically have a monthly quota of public appearances they must make. Even if a specific number isn't given, the practice is strongly encouraged. That's one of the reasons I got roped into participating in three bachelor auctions in three different states. My wife and I have handed out countless plaques and certificates. We've also received a few, which is another ploy organizations can use to get free exposure.

One night my wife's TV station aired a story about her co-anchor, who had been invited to fly with the Thunderbirds. Following the story, Dianne wondered out loud in front of the viewing audience why she too hadn't been given an opportunity to break the sound barrier. That prompted a call from the New Mexico National Guard, which cheerfully offered her a spin in one of its F-16s. She took them up on the offer, and the "Taco Squadron," as the unit is affectionately known, got some great PR. The Tacos received some more publicity when Dianne's story won a feature award from the Associated Press.

Make It Sing Before You Ring

Talk to any producer or editor about people who invent publicity opportunities and they will sigh heavily and mumble something about a need to gas all the "PR hacks" along with the lawyers. Don't be dissuaded by such grumbling because it's disingenuous. Journalists don't loathe invented news. They love it—but only when the item is highly creative and packed with lots of DES. What news people hate is wasting their time sifting through pathetically lame publicity pitches. They pour in non-stop through the mail, computer lines, phone lines, and the front door. People will even approach journalists at the grocery store, the park, or the doctor's office to expound on some "great" story idea. It's exhausting.

Therefore, remember the number one rule for the Rule of Invention: don't go off half-cocked (chapter 5, Rule of Preparation). Work over your idea with the same kind of diligence exhibited by Edison, Houdini, and Knievel. If your Invention is worthy, it will probably work. If you're not convinced that it will succeed, work it some more.

In this chapter, we have concentrated on the "what" aspect of the reporter's W's (who, what, when, where, and why). But honestly, the "what" isn't worth diddly if it isn't paired with its twin sister, "when," the focus of our next Media Rule.

◆ ◆ ◆

CHAPTER 10

The Rule of Timing

~ busy blows it ~

Do you like Oreo cookies? I do. The Beast does too. In fact, they may be his favorite dessert. After wolfing down train derailments, school shootings, stock market analysis, presidential politics, and countless other entrees and side dishes, the Beast loves to savor a delicious Oreo cookie. It's so good because it's the right treat at just the right time. As we all know, "timing is everything," right? Wrong. Timing is not everything. It is the creamy, white center of the Oreo cookie.

If you don't fully understand that opening paragraph, that's okay. It was not meant to immediately enlighten, but to challenge a conventional way of thinking. The Oreo is a metaphor that debunks the mystery surrounding excellent timing. Contrary to the myth, fortuitous timing is not some sort of serendipitous event that finds the haves and dodges the have-nots. It is one part of a three-part formula—just like the beloved black and white cookie.

The top wafer in our timing Oreo is Preparation. The bottom

wafer is Invention. Sandwiched in the middle is opportunity, which presents itself in the form of Timing. Learn this recipe, and you'll have the Beast eating out of your hand.

The Trained Eye of Timing

Mark Twain once lamented, "I was seldom able to see an opportunity until it ceased to be one." Don't be fooled by false modesty. As one of America's greatest writers, Twain knew exactly how timing works, and in this pithy quote he attempts to instruct the rest of us.

What Twain wants us to realize is that excellent opportunities rarely plop in our laps and scream, "Here I am!" As a rule, they quickly stroll by in plain view. Most people are so busy they never even notice an opportunity's sudden arrival and departure. Others catch a glimpse of what could be but are caught flatfooted, mouths agape. Sorry, it's too late. Only those who are *looking* for publicity prospects are nimble enough to snatch this thing called Timing and use it to their benefit before the chance evaporates.

Think of publicity this way. Preparation is the chocolate wafer that is constantly looking for the tasty white filling to present itself. When it does, Preparation catches the filling and momentarily holds it in place so the Invention wafer can be slapped to the other side. Voilà, now you've got a treat that the Beast will devour.

News events gain or lose significance because of time.

In this chapter, we will examine four different methods for using the Rule of Timing. The first is the way of the "sniper," the discipline of pouncing on the most fleeting of opportunities. The second is "bandwagon," an approach that requires more work but allows more time for planning. The third scheme is "target," a way of placing a media Invention within a specific time frame. The final method is "avoidance," a way of keeping from being stepped on by the competition. While sniper and bandwagon are tied to other events already in the news, target and avoidance are not.

Each of these four methods is based on a recurrent theme in this book—that journalists are obsessed with the passage of time in every conceivable way; they never have enough, so they are always looking for ways to find more. News events gain or lose significance because of time. The inevitable consequence of this time obsession is that the Beast's attention span is pitifully small. Understand the time warp, and you will be prepared to catch the publicity prizes that constantly appear, develop, and either pass away or are capitalized upon.

A Sniper Always Has a Finger on the Trigger

The number one hindrance to winning publicity is the "big busy." Our entire culture is stricken with this malady in the worst way. For reasons beyond my comprehension, busyness has become a badge of honor. It is an implied definition of our self-worth. If you're not busy, you must be lazy or, even worse, unimportant.

Separating yourself from the big busy is the first step in using the Rule of Timing (and all other media rules for that matter). It's impossible to seize opportunities that momentarily appear when your head is always down working on other things. The most successful publicity hounds are those who keep their eyes and ears wide open to the possibilities. They create time in their schedules and space in their brains to think about their own free marketing. The best of these people qualify as snipers, folks who have trained themselves to be patient and alert so they can quickly pick off whatever may come by. Snipers know what all successful publicity seekers know: *Busy blows it.*

Remember Joe Mohorovic, the state legislator from the last chapter who offered to pay to get his own bill printed? Mohorovic knew that the stalemate between the governor and the legislative leadership would last for no more than a day or two. There was no time to spare. He immediately printed up his large check and took it into the House chamber the next day. Score!

When I was still in the TV business, a local gymnast, Trent Dimas, won an Olympic gold medal on the high-bar. Upon his return home, a party was thrown in his honor. During the ceremony, a jeweler presented Dimas with a stunning diamond ring commemorating his victory. Of course, I interviewed the jewelry store owner, and my photographer got several close-up shots of the ring. We were all amazed at how quickly the jeweler was able to craft his beautiful gift. This was the shot of a sniper. He saw his opportunity and fired without hesitation. His alertness was duly rewarded with some high-powered exposure.

In the Rule of Timing, the more creative the invention, the more time you will have to pull it off. The legislator and the jeweler had to act quickly, but not instantly. This is not the case when publicity potential should be plainly obvious to anyone paying attention. In these circumstances, every minute counts.

One day I opened up the morning newspaper and saw the large headline, "Belen Family's Only Auto Stolen at Hospital." Below the headline was a photo of a sad man and woman, standing with four children in front of a trailer home. The story explained that while the family had been at the hospital getting chemotherapy treatment for the oldest boy, who has leukemia, their car was stolen. What followed was a tale of hard luck and despair for these recent immigrants from Mexico. They did not have insurance, and now there was no way to get the boy to the hospital or get his father to work.

When I saw the story, I cheerfully told my wife, "I can tell you what the lead story on tonight's news will be and tomorrow's front-page headline as well." I showed her the story, and she agreed that a car dealer would donate a vehicle to the family, thereby raking in loads of free publicity. Of course, we were right.

The coverage was amazing. The story ran for two days on TV and radio. The following day's front-page headline read, "Donated Van Gets Family Back in Gear." The family received more than a half-dozen offers for a free set of wheels. Others called to give money and provide rides to the hospital. Having that car stolen was probably the best thing that ever happened to these folks. But the real winner in this deal was the owner of the car dealership whose good deed was praised extensively in the press. You can't buy that kind of incredible PR, and even if it were possible, who could afford it?

A sniper does not hesitate when the target pops up. This is as true on the national level as it is locally. In the post-election skirmish of 2000, the national media focused on the "butterfly" ballot in Palm Beach County, Florida. Many people who had voted in Palm Beach said the ballot design was confusing, and as a result, they had mistakenly voted for Pat Buchanan for president instead of Al Gore. Others had voted for two candidates, which automatically voided their ballots. The timing was right for a little experiment, and at least two elementary school educators took a winning shot.

Ron McGee, a school psychologist in Georgia, designed a butterfly ballot with Disney characters. Seventy-four second graders were told to vote for Mickey Mouse (the Gore position), and not one cast an incorrect ballot. Dane Wilson, a third-grade teacher in Bowling Green, Kentucky, did essentially the same thing. She created an exact duplicate of the ballot on a computer and asked her students to vote for Al Gore by pointing the digital arrow to the correct hole-punch. All 19 kids cast a correct vote. The local and national press, of course, ate these manufactured stories. And why wouldn't they—with so much DES and perfect timing?

Granted, the car dealer and the educators are probably not true snipers. These people are not constantly monitoring press coverage to look for their next publicity hit. However, they are opportunistic sharp shooters, and the lesson still holds. They saw an opportunity and moved quickly. How many other car dealers saw the story in the newspaper and then promptly dropped it to answer the phone? What about all the others who could have cashed in on the butterfly ballot hysteria if only they hadn't had their heads down in the big busy? A printing or copying company could have held a mock election. How about holding an election at a bar at 1:30 A.M. in the morning when most of the patrons are inebriated? A retirement community could have matched its wits against the voters in Palm Beach. The possibilities were endless—for a time. Then they vanished.

All Aboard!

The bandwagon approach to winning publicity is the same as being a sniper, except with less pressure. To score you don't have to shoot immediately. There is more time to think about how to connect yourself or your organization to high-profile items already making news. I'm not talking about a lot of time here—usually only a few days to a week or two, depending on the weight of the story. The underlying pressure, however, is the same. The Beast has a short attention span. Feed him while his interest is peaked or don't bother wasting your time.

Former president Bill Clinton was a master at using the news media's attention deficit disorder to his advantage. That's quite an accomplishment when you consider that the president of the United States has more power than anyone—by far—to command the attention of the press. Even so, Clinton hitched his wagon to every national event possible to advance his agenda. When the nation was fixated by the O.J. Simpson trial, Clinton talked about race relations. If there was a flood, an earthquake, or a fire, Clinton was there to "feel your pain." After school shootings, Clinton was quick to promote more gun laws. Former Clinton advisor George Stephanopoulos made note of Clinton's timing skills in an August 21, 2000, column for *Newsweek* magazine. Stephanopoulos wrote, "[T]he president realized that cutting through the clutter required becoming one with it. Clinton saw that he could take advantage of the Media's short attention span by making policy points off breaking news." Good point, George.

One of the more impressive uses of timing I've seen involved the handiwork of a private investigator. When Wayne Brewer read a story about a drunken driver who had eluded prosecution for more than a year after nearly killing a man, he was incensed. This private eye also saw a way to generate more name recognition for his business. Within six days of reading the story, Brewer had tracked down the criminal and told police where to find him. The fugitive landed in jail, and Brewer landed a big headline and some instant credibility.

Back in chapter 5, the Rule of Preparation, I told you about a client of mine who runs a center that helps women get out of abusive relationships. She uses the Rule of Timing a half-dozen times a year. When police arrest a high-profile athlete for domestic abuse, she talks to reporters about the epidemic of violence within relationships. When a new law is proposed, she's there to tell the stories of abuse victims. After a woman's boyfriend kills a child, my client is there to express her outrage. When new domestic violence statistics are released, she's advancing awareness of her cause through print and broadcast media (chapter 7, Rule of Repetition).

If you want a free publicity ride, keep your eye on the horizon. When you see the wheels of the bandwagon kicking up dust, start running. You'll be at full stride and ready to jump on at just the right time.

One excellent publicity opportunity that's often overlooked is the op-ed page. Guest columns can be an easy hit if you are an expert in your field (chapter 8, Rule of Resource). And, remember, the op-ed page is the most powerful section of a newspaper when it comes to reaching community decision makers. Of course, I try to follow my own advice.

When neighbors of two TV stations began complaining about all the noise generated by the station's helicopters, I saw a chance to get some free press. (Even media consultants need to feed the Beast.) I also saw a ticking clock. That day I wrote an op-ed piece explaining that TV news helicopters are completely unnecessary in all but the largest of cities and that they are primarily marketing tools. If I had waited more than a few days to send in my comments, they probably wouldn't have made it into print.

In chapter 7, I told you about the fight to keep the 505 area code in the Albuquerque/Santa Fe corridor. We were looking for every opportunity to send our message to the public, and that included writing our own op-ed pieces for several newspapers. But, of course, the best possible time for writing those columns came when the battle was at its peak. I was absolutely swamped with my own work as well as that of the 505 Coalition. Our attorney was buried, too. We could have just put our heads down into the big busy, but we knew that our short window of opportunity would close very quickly. So we put in some even longer hours to get those articles written, and the 505 Coalition was rewarded for our timely effort. The Beast waits for no one.

In the summer of 2000, American children—and the news media—went nuts over the latest release of the Harry Potter book series. But don't include Yale professor and renowned literary critic Harold Bloom among its admirers. The author of the top-selling *How to Read and Why* wrote a scathing editorial to the *Wall*

Street Journal, calling the book "foolish," "horribly written," "a mass of clichés," and "inferior to many comic books." Ouch! Hey, Harold, tell us what you really think. By the way, we noticed your nice use of the Rule of Timing.

Hit the Bull's Eye

In its simplest terms, the Rule of Timing tells us to grab the Beast's attention when his interest level is at the highest point. Sometimes that means jumping on issues about which journalists are currently reporting. In other instances, it's picking the best possible time to launch your own material.

One of the great launchers of another kind, Sammy Sosa, gives us an excellent illustration. On September 13, 1998, Chicago Cubs slugger Sammy Sosa hit his 62nd home run of the season. He had broken the record of 61 homers set by Roger Maris in 1961. The following day the *Chicago Tribune* printed an extra 43,300 newspapers. Impressive, but not when compared to what had happened in St. Louis five days earlier. The *St. Louis Post-Dispatch* published an extra 400,000 copies after the Cardinal's Mark McGwire hit his 62nd home run. Sosa's triumph measured about one-tenth that of Mark McGwire's—all because he was five days late breaking a 37-year-old record. *Strike* (or in Sosa's case, *hit a homer*) when the time is right, otherwise the news media won't care, or won't care nearly as much.

The concept behind the "target" method is this: pick a time frame for your story that syncs with the priorities of the Beast. Perhaps no other group of people does this better than political leaders.

New York governor George Pataki wrote a book titled *Where I Come From*. When did he release the book? One day after announcing his bid for reelection. By lining up the two events on successive days, Pataki created an effective burst of media attention. If he had separated the two events, even by a matter of weeks, his total press coverage would have been significantly less. Instead the New York governor manufactured the illusion of momentum. But Pataki's strategy was small potatoes compared to what an alliance of politicians can do.

In 1998, the House of Representatives was poised to vote on the impeachment of President Bill Clinton. The report from independent counsel Kenneth Starr had been released weeks earlier. No substantive new information had come out since then. In fact, the bulk of the case against Clinton had been out for months. Yet, during the final days before the House vote, Republican representatives from all over the country began holding press conferences. Suddenly, previously "undecided" House members were now going to vote for impeachment. What had taken them so long? And why did these Republicans come out in a rising wave of conviction that crested right before the vote? The Rule of Timing provides the answer. The representatives were building a perception of momentum. If the Republicans had announced what they were going to do weeks or months earlier, they would have shot all their ammo prematurely.

A word of caution: the Rule of Timing is not *just* about the Beast's clock. It's about the entire Oreo cookie. Preparation and invention are two-thirds of the equation. Keep that in mind as we look at some practical applications for picking timely targets.

Blind Dates Are for Losers (Keep Your Eyes Open)

Snatching the Oreo's creamy filling need not always be a tricky endeavor. Sometimes it's as easy as spotting the perfect date on a calendar.

Remember the grandmother in the previous chapter who walked from California to Illinois to raise awareness about birth defects? She didn't select her route and timing at random. She chose to amble down old Route 66 on its 75th birthday. She strengthened the hook to her story by marrying her walk to the anniversary of the historic roadway. Any recurring event can provide a timely connection. The most obvious occasions are holidays. Christmas, Thanksgiving, Halloween, St. Patrick's Day, New Year's, and all the rest are like magnets to publicity entrepreneurs, which is precisely why I don't recommend them. Who needs the competition? The idea is to take your shot when the Beast is most likely to pay attention. Being one among many makes it tougher than it need be.

Use the most important media rule—the Rule of Difference— to choose the right time and place to attract the Beast. Be creative. Stand out like a bright white canvas painted with consecutive red circles. Your creativity is likely to be more important than a strictly logical connection between timely events.

Here's a case in point. Let's say you want to get coverage for a big chess tournament, and TV exposure is your highest priority. When would you think is the best possible time to hold the event? Of course, it's a trick question. There is no good time to air a story on such a visually unappealing subject. How desperate would a TV station have to be? Well . . . maybe there is one day that this story would have a decent chance of making the evening news.

You might be surprised, but I think the best day to see TV chess is on Superbowl Sunday. Think about it. What else could be newsworthy on a day when television attracts its largest audience of the year? Answer: a story about those who couldn't care less. The contrast is fantastic. At one end of the scale, 90 million Americans are watching gridiron goliaths pound each other into the turf. On the other end, a group of intellectuals watch pocket-protector participants match wits. Any feature reporter would love to exploit the contrast between the two. Can you imagine the story? The quarterback is crushed by a 300-pound tackle. Then the video cuts to a four-eyed, pimple-faced kid taking a bishop with a knight.

The possibilities are limited only by your imagination.

You own a bike shop. When do you think would be the best time to get some free exposure? Combine the rules of Resource,

Invention, and Timing, and you've got your answer. The end of the school year is a time when journalists are especially receptive to stories about children. A story about keeping kids safe during summer vacation has those all-important timely and emotive elements. Can you see where I'm going with this?

As a bike shop owner, you could offer a free cycling safety course. Try to get the local school district, YMCA, or city recreation department to partner with you, even if it's only to add their name for extra credibility. Turn it into a big contest and give away free prizes. Hold it about a week prior to the end of school as a preview of summer cycling hazards. Tell the press that you have two objectives. The first is to teach the kids to ride safely. The second is to remind drivers that two-wheel traffic is about to increase exponentially. With a package like this, how could you miss the target?

Did you remember to change your smoke detector batteries at the end of daylight savings last fall? If you didn't, don't blame the fire department. Chances are pretty good that your local television stations and newspapers produced stories encouraging you to "change your batteries when you change your clocks." Every October fire departments across the country give out free batteries and stage other publicity events to help protect us from our own forgetfulness. But is there any connection between smoke detectors and changing clocks? Actually there is. The hazard of home fires increases slightly in the winter months. It's a weak connection (or story hook), and that's precisely the point. The attractiveness of the story has as much to do with *when* it occurs as *what* it is.

Shoot the Bull Before *or* After the Stampede

The next time you're looking for some cheap Saturday night entertainment take a trip to the video store and rent the 1987 film *Broadcast News*. It offers lots of comedic insights into how reporters think.

In one scene, a journalist played by Albert Brooks is attempting to interview a Vietnam veteran who does not want to talk. In retaliation to the persistent questioning, the vet spits a string of profanities into the reporter's microphone and then asks, "Can you use that?" Brooks responds, "It depends on how slow a news day it is."

This scene teaches all publicity seekers an important lesson: picking the right time to engage the Beast often means not picking the wrong time. In other words, go where the competition isn't.

How many thousand charities help disadvantaged people during the holidays? I don't know, but I do know this—most of them get no publicity for the good work that they do. In any city, dozens of organizations host Thanksgiving and Christmas feasts or food drives for the homeless, the elderly, the seriously ill, and others. It's a wonderful thing to do, but it's the wrong time to do it. Not only is there an enormous amount of competition for print space and airtime, news organizations quickly tire of the "holiday charity" story. My recommendation—be first, or pick another target date.

Every year Samaritan's Purse sends about four million shoeboxes filled with goodies to needy children all over the world. It's called "Operation Christmas Child." Because the organization makes its big push in mid-November, at the front end of the holiday season, Operation Christmas Child always gets excellent publicity. All the press attention has helped the program continue to grow.

One national organization that plays the Christmas avoidance strategy well is "Christmas in April." This group, which has chapters in all 50 states, specializes in repairing rundown homes for elderly and disabled people who can't do the work themselves. Volunteers from local companies replace water heaters and stoves, fix leaky roofs and faucets, clean up yards, and generally make dilapidated homes livable again. Companies that participate rake in bushels of great publicity because nobody else is playing Santa Claus in the spring.

I've used charitable causes to illustrate this strategy, but avoidance can be applied to absolutely any media situation. If your organization is planning an event or an announcement for which you want publicity, take a good look at what else is happening on that day. This is true for any news item, but especially for anything not considered to be "hard" news. Only a small amount of space and airtime is reserved for feature items. Therefore, check the community calendar to make sure your event doesn't fall on the same day as a big fair, festival, or any number of other celebrations.

Frequent Flyers Leave Early

It's never possible to know for sure how busy a news day will be. Unpredictable "spot news" happens all the time—murders, earthquakes, stock market dives, accidents, nasty weather, etc. When breaking news happens, stories deemed the least significant get dropped. That's the reality of the business. Nobody is immune from being pre-empted by a major news event. However, some time slots are safer than others.

Dealing with the news media is a lot like commercial flying. If your plane takes off first thing in the morning, you've got a pretty good chance of arriving at your destination on time. But as the day wears on, bad things happen. Planes break down, storms hit, flights get rerouted, crowds form, frustration builds, and by the end of the day, it seems everyone is frazzled, late, and completely distracted. Welcome to your average newsroom.

Events that can be held any time of the day should be scheduled for the morning, before the day gets messy. As a media consultant, I've staged dozens of large events. As a reporter, I covered hundreds. With very few exceptions, the most successful were those held before noon. Does this sound like common sense? It is, but it's not put into practice nearly enough.

Every day massive numbers of press releases are sent out inviting reporters to come to this thing or that at 4:00 or 5:00 P.M., or at some evening hour. Are these people nuts? The worst time to seek the news media's attention, especially for TV, is in the mid or late afternoon. Late in the day, most journalists are pulling together stories launched in the morning. Editors and producers are making decisions about where to put "breaking news." It's often a scramble. If a low-level story that happened in the morning is already "in the can" (completed), it still has a chance of airing. Late afternoon or evening items, however, have to compete with everything.

Some reporters start their day in the early afternoon, but now you're talking about trying to hit a smaller target. Most news operations dedicate far fewer resources to the "swing" shift. Additionally, swing-shift reporters are likely to be assigned stories that began developing earlier in the day. There's also the hazard of those awful meetings that start about 7:00 P.M. (school board, city council, etc.). If there's no compelling reason to face this competition, don't.

Early usually works best, whether it's the time of day or the day of the week. The news machine runs non-stop, but it is not immune to the Monday morning blahs. Most of the important decision-makers in a news operation work Monday through Friday. So there is a vulnerable moment when the baton is passed from the weekend to the weekday crew. That's a great opportunity. On Monday morning, editors immediately feel the pressure to fill the pipeline. But news is a slow starter, like everything and everyone else. Faced with the choice of having a reporter sitting idle or sent out to cover a not-so-sexy news event, the editor will reluctantly dispatch the reporter.

Use the clock and the calendar to your advantage. Often times your publicity success will have more to do with how busy journalists are when your story happens than the allure of the story itself. So, do yourself a favor—fly through the newsroom in the morning and avoid all the competition that pops up later in the day.

There's no way to cover all possible scenarios. I'm not going to do it, nor should you. You need only to keep in mind that the Beast worships the almighty clock. It has to. Time controls virtually every aspect of the news industry. Therefore, pay close attention to *when* things happen. As long as you remember the Oreo cookie, you will enjoy the sweet taste of free exposure.

Take a Time Out

As each chapter has progressed, you may have noticed that the Media Rules are a lot like teenagers. They love to travel in packs, they tend to dress alike, and they require constant monitoring.

In this chapter, I used the example of the DWI fugitive caught by the private detective to illustrate the Rule of Timing. The same example would have fit nicely in the Rules of Invention, Easy, Preparation, Difference, Emotion, and Simplicity. This same kind of overlapping of the Rules applies to all other examples in this book and, indeed, to all publicity. That's why it's so important to apply a systematic structure to engaging the news media. Without it, everything blurs, and there's no way clearly to understand why some stories work and why others don't.

Ask any public relations specialist, journalist, or advertiser what made Muhammad Ali so successful, beyond his obvious physical talent. What you'll get is an earful about charm, charisma, bravado, and intelligence. That kind of description is of little use to anyone who wants to go to school on Ali's example.

In contrast, the Media Rules give you a clear description of the tools Ali used to become one of history's all-time media darlings. His personality overflowed with Difference, Emotion, and Simplicity —the three requirements for news interest. Ali didn't pursue the heavyweight championship by treating the press as a necessary evil. He used reporters as partners (Rule of Resource), carefully preparing every match, every interview, and every quote (Rule of Preparation). He wisely chose the messages he wanted to send and sent them repeatedly (Rule of Repetition). An accessible sports figure, Ali constantly put out fresh material. He wasn't just "The Greatest." He was also the "easiest." Ali used the Rule of Invention to re-create himself in a compelling image, and his Timing was impeccable.

Foremost we learn from Ali (and other media darlings) that using the Beast as a means to promote your success requires sustained effort. It demands that you make the news media an ongoing priority. Aggressive publicity seekers don't just schedule a block of time to consider ways to win free exposure and then move on to the next thing. They constantly keep their eyes and ears open and know exactly what to do when opportunities present themselves. In short, they refuse to allow the "big busy" to keep them from grabbing all the free exposure they can get.

Please, don't let the prospect of "another time commitment" drag you down. The Media Rules do not "take" time. In fact, they *save* you time because with each potential press hit, you streamline your method overall. With a little practice, you'll do so with increasing skill and success. Before long, the Media Rules will become integrated into how you see the world.

In the first nine chapters, we have focused on understanding the Beast in order to pursue him. Along the way, I have stressed that poor execution of the Seducers (Difference, Emotion, and Simplicity), the Enablers (Preparation, Easy, and Repetition), and the Aggressors (Resource, Invention, and Timing) will get you into big trouble. Annoy the Beast, and you're likely to get bitten. However, getting nipped because you broke a Rule or two is a lot different from being mauled in a direct attack. Therefore, in the next three chapters, I'll describe how the best defense is a good offence. The conditions under which the Beast is most prone to attack—or to be used by others for attack—are described in the *Hazards*.

◆ ◆ ◆

CHAPTER 11

The Rule of Ego

~ experience does not equal skill ~

It was late in the day. I was in a big hurry. My script for the 6:00 P.M. news had to be finished in less than ten minutes. Of course, I hadn't realized that it had begun raining outside. I hardly even noticed the clap of thunder above the newsroom clatter. But how could I not be distracted by the sight of our lead anchors rushing to the door? In spite of my looming deadline, I left my desk and hurried to the door to see what was the matter. To my astonishment, I saw the anchors standing in the rain, smiling, and waving as lightning crackled across the horizon. Two photographers—apparently unimpressed by the spectacle—were standing just outside the door casually smoking cigarettes. "What in the world are they doing?" I excitedly asked the disinterested photogs. "What does it look like?" one of them answered. "The bubble-heads think they're getting their pictures taken."

Sorry. I couldn't resist. Anchors are such easy targets for disparaging humor. Don't feel bad for them. It's one small price they pay for their fame.

There's no denying it. The news industry is driven by people with substantial egos. If there was such a thing as an ego-meter, I suspect that journalists would rank near the top—right behind entertainers, politicians, doctors, and lawyers. It's a business that draws the self-assured like flies to a mirror. Oh, what a feeling it is to see your thoughts and your name in print. Oh, what ecstasy to speak to thousands or even millions through the miracle of modern technology. Oh, what pleasure it is to say, "I'm a journalist." And that's not even the half of it. Such great satisfaction comes from telling a good story or helping to right a wrong. To have access to the politically powerful and the culturally desirable is a very cool thing. Working in and around the news spotlight is exciting. If you don't have a hefty ego, you don't have any business being in the business.

With that said, get ready for a sudden jolt. While the news industry is full of self-important personalities, that's not the focus of this chapter. The Rule of Ego is a lot more about yours than theirs.

In the next few pages, I will discuss the "ego-factor" that exists within the business. However, the primary purpose of this information is to give you a better understanding of the journalist. Then the real work begins, which is dealing with your own issues. They can express themselves in a number of dangerous ways.

The Beast Has a Fat Head

Ask any newsperson to tell you tales involving egomaniacal colleagues, and you're apt to get a response like, "How much time you got?" Anyone who has spent more than a few years in the news business has a load of stories to tell. I'm certainly no exception.

There was the time when I nearly got into a fight with a weekend anchor over a measly 30 seconds. I had spent the entire day traveling to and from a football game in another state. This was no ordinary contest. It was a Division 1-AA playoff game for the Citadel, a team that rarely made post-season appearances. This was one of the biggest games the Bulldogs had ever played. My weekend sportscaster needed the extra half-minute to give the story the coverage it deserved. So I (the weekday sportscaster) asked the anchor if we could have 30 seconds of *his* news time. Without hesitation, he said no. I couldn't believe it. How could he deny our sports audience 30 extra seconds on such a big day? Aren't the weekends mostly about sports anyway? A photographer and I had devoted 16 hours of our lives to this story, and the station had picked up the tab for overtime and gas. Worse yet, his newscast was pretty boring. Words were exchanged. Tempers flared. More words were exchanged. Cigarette smoke was blown in my face. "Let's take this outside," I said and marched out the door. He followed. Thankfully for both of us, our hastily summoned boss drove into the parking lot before any blood was spilled. Did I get the 30 seconds? Yes.

Sounds crazy, doesn't it? Two guys are ready to fight over a lousy 30 seconds? Well, that half-minute was pretty important to *my* story. It was also a chunk of *his* face-time. Ego can make people do some pretty silly things.

In the early 1990s, I spent nearly two years investigating and reporting on an international scandal involving the Catholic Church. For decades the church had been sending priests—who had sexually abused children—to a treatment center in Jemez Springs, New Mexico. After some "rehabilitation," the priests were returned to parish duty in New Mexico churches, where they often began molesting children again (primarily prepubescent boys). The story got a lot bigger, and darker, when "60 Minutes" discovered a possible connection between the church's ambivalence to child molesting priests and the leader of the Santa Fe Archdiocese. Sources told "60 Minutes" producers that the Archbishop of the diocese had been having sexual relations with a woman. The speculation was that guilt over violating his celibacy vow had kept the Archbishop from acting on dozens of complaints against the priestly pedophiles. A source leaked the information to me a few weeks before the "60 Minutes" story was due to air. I immediately arranged an interview with the chancellor of the archdiocese who had agreed to confess the church's sins to our camera. This was big! I was waiting outside the chancellor's office reviewing my questions for him when the news director called, summoning me back to the station. My boss decided that the climax of the story I had been working on for two years should be given to the station's longtime investigative reporter. Why? I was told he had some "exclusive" information that he couldn't give to me. (Sound a little fishy?) "Exclusive" turned out to be an exaggeration at best. The truth was that the investigative reporter's ego wanted a boost, and my story was a quick and easy way to get the adrenaline rush. So I did all the work, and he swooped in to steal the glory. Nice.

Oh, the stories that could and should be told about journalistic Ego. I once did a midday newscast that featured a daily interview segment. It was the most enjoyable part of the show because it allowed my co-anchor and me some room to flex our personalities. One day she hosted the segment, the next day I did—that is, until she decided that this choice piece of broadcast time should belong exclusively to her. In a devious power play, she managed to get her way. It did wonders for the show's "chemistry."

Then there was the general manager who said he was going to fire my weekend sportscaster and fill the position with someone who would report news during the week. Apparently, production among news gatherers was lacking. To head this off, I told the GM that some of the news reporters had been allowed to slack off and that a little whip cracking would solve the problem. The news director didn't appreciate my analysis (oops), so he decided I had to go. When the next "window" in my contract opened, I was introduced to my replacement and was shown the door. (A "talent window" is a nasty little clause in an anchor's contract that allows the station to fire the anchor for no justifiable reason. If this happened to me in a corporate or government job, I could have sued and won.) That was a fun time in my life.

I tell you these stories—my stories—for three reasons. First, it's fun to relive the *good old days* (My ego must need the boost). Second, it demonstrates how widespread the problem is. I didn't need to search high and low for the best stories I could find. All my friends in the business have just as many ego-tales of their own—if not more and better. Third, and most importantly, it demonstrates something you should understand about the Beast. In the ongoing war of news Egos, the battle lines are usually drawn *inside* the newsroom or *inside* the business. Journalists would much rather attack one another than bother with you.

Even though the possibility of a newsperson's ego damaging you or your organization is relatively small, it's still important that you look inside the strange world these people inhabit. Having an understanding of the Beast's skewed reality will help you keep a tight rein on your ego, which is where many media problems originate. It will also enable you to massage the Beast's Ego, while being careful not to step on his tail.

Borrowed Status

Being a member of the news media is a lot like being rich—except without the money. The moment you become a member of the working press, people treat you differently. Your card has been punched. You are now a member of a pseudo-elite class of people—

like the poor cousin who has a passkey to the mansion. Although you aren't a *real* member of the club, everybody fears your rich, temperamental uncle. Therefore, you are bequeathed with instant—albeit tarnished—status. Of course, the larger your news organization, the richer and crazier your uncle.

I remember my entrance into this bizarre world. One day I was a poor college student who would have had trouble getting a janitor's attention. The next day I was interviewing a senior member of the United States Senate. He even called me by my name. Imagine that! With lightning speed, the power of my employer was transferred to me. It took weeks to get used to this alien phenomenon called respect.

It's one of the great perks of being a news gatherer. You get to meet all sorts of powerful and fascinating people—politicians, entertainers, athletes, and other folks on the culture's list of who's who. Because this chapter is the Rule of Ego, I'm going to drop a few names of people my wife and I have interviewed or otherwise rubbed elbows with: Oprah Winfrey, Ted Turner, Red Skelton, Tom Seleck, Patrick Dennehey, Gayle Sayers, Payne Stewart, Lee Trevino, Andre Agassi, Bob Feller, Eddie Money, Bette Midler, Sam Donaldson, Jimmy Carter, Bob Dole, Norman Schwarzkopf, Colin Powell, Bill Clinton, and who knows how many others I can't remember. Impressed? Don't be. Anyone who hangs around the news business for any length of time has a list of people he or she has met with a guest pass to the mansion.

As a member of the club, you also get front-row seats to some of the most incredible drama on the planet. I was one of the first people to see the wreckage of PSA Flight 1771, in which all 47 people on board perished. I was on the scene moments after a police officer was murdered in the line of duty. I've been flown in to witness the devastation of train wrecks, tornadoes, fires, and floods (Never got an earthquake, though—Darn the luck). Car accidents, murders, and courtroom decisions—I've been there and done that more times than I can count. Feel yourself slipping into the warped world of the Beast?

As disturbingly intoxicating as the high-drama is, it's not the best part of being a member of the club. When you're a journalist, you get to go to all sorts of neat places to see and do fun things. There are concerts, athletic events, festivals, rodeos, missile launches, war games, riots, and much, much more. And at most of these events, there's free food and VIP parking

Live in this world for a while, and it becomes difficult not to let the strange environment warp your perspective. The longer you have occasional access to the mansion, the more natural it is to think that you're entitled to preferential treatment. And why not? The commoners, who have seen your face or your byline, begin to treat *you* like a celebrity. They ask for your autograph and want you to speak at their functions. They offer you free desserts, free tickets, and lots of other free stuff. With all this attention, it's easy to begin thinking that you could enter the mansion even without a rich, crazy uncle.

However, there is a dark side to the Beast that skews Newsland even further. While journalists are often treated like members of the upper crust in the outside world, back in the newsroom they are constantly reminded that they are merely interlopers.

Meanwhile, Back at the Newsroom . . .

Think back to chapter 1, where I described the difficult conditions that news people must endure. Here's a quick review: slave wages, inconsistent hours, unrelenting and unforgiving deadlines, grumpy coworkers, messy workspace, unappreciative bosses, a bottom-line corporate mentality, bad diets, loads of stress, and lots of moving around. Remember all that?

No telling how many psychotherapists have put their kids through college on the bounty of news people who feel so "conflicted." Outside the newsroom, they are respected, feared, and even pampered. Inside the newsroom, they are disrespected, mocked, and driven to produce more and do it faster. It's like being an abusive man's trophy wife. In public, you sport a huge diamond ring from an adoring mate. At home, you clean the tile grout with a toothbrush while the man of the house stands over you with a belt. By the way, do you know if schizophrenia is only a genetic disorder, or can it be caused by environmental factors?

Okay, maybe I've stretched the analogy a little too far, but you see my point. Even in the best of newsroom environments, there is still a startling disconnect between the inside and outside worlds. Of course, the contrast between these two worlds is typically greater for "on-air talent" and lesser for print people and others who work behind the scenes.

So how do news people manage to cope with the difficulty of working in a constant state of ego whiplash? They handle it just like the *real* members of the club—with denial, therapy, and/or self-medication. Unlike the true elite, journalists usually lack the resources to fully indulge their condition. So quiet desperation, alcohol, cigarettes, or some other form of distraction must suffice. Others take the more rational escape route by literally getting out, like yours truly.

If it were really that bad, why in the world would anybody want to continue doing it? Why does a heroin user keep shooting up? He's addicted. Most journalists are transfixed in the same way, only their drug is public exposure. The rush that comes with seeing your work sent over the public airwaves or put into print can be briefly euphoric. Any journalist who denies this hard-and-fast fact needs to stop self-medicating. In the movie *Broadcast News*, Albert Brooks returns to the editing room to watch his story on the Vietnam veteran one more time. He's delighted that the network anchor, played by Jack Nicholson, actually smiled after watching the report. Like any addict, Brooks was desperate to make his latest fix last as long as possible.

As any junkie knows, with every hit the highs are not as high and the lows get lower. Before long, the drug ceases to be a pleasure and becomes a need. So the addict increases the dosage and eventually goes looking for bigger and better drugs. For the journalist, this means a job in a bigger market or maybe a promotion. But even in fast-paced Newsland, such increases in ego juice don't happen often enough. Not to worry though, the addict's supplier, the Beast, regularly doles out designer smack. The clinical term for this special fix is "journalistic recognition."

To call a newsperson an "award-winning journalist" is about like praising a lifeguard for being "well tanned." The only news people who aren't "award winning" are either brand new to the business or they're folks who should be considering a career change. Winning one of the Beast's awards is about like popping a balloon at the county fair. A five-year-old can do it and walk away with his genuine plastic toy made in India. Yippee! Please forgive my sarcasm, but anyone who's been through the annual awards banquet scene knows what I'm talking about.

It's not enough just to give out one award for each category of news coverage (of which there are many). There's usually a first-, second-, and third-place award, and maybe even an honorable mention. Those same prizes are given to multiple segments of the news community—one set for small, medium, and large market broadcasters or publishers. The proliferation of self-congratulation has gotten so out of control that the news business hands out more awards than even public relations and advertising firms do. In fact, journalists give themselves more awards than any other profession on the planet! Even the prestige of the Pulitzer Prize has been diluted. In 1917, the inaugural year of the Pulitzer, there were three categories of awards for journalistic achievement. Today there are fourteen.

I think it's safe to say that in general journalists are pretty needy in the Ego department. They wouldn't have been attracted to the profession if they weren't. This is not necessarily a bad thing. It takes a strong sense of self to be an effective newsperson. A milquetoast personality does not a good reporter make. But what does all this have to do with you, the publicity seeker? Plenty. Knowing what buttons to push—and not to push—is key to getting the positive, free exposure *your* ego desires.

Real Compliments Require Detail

You might think that the best way to deal with journalists is to treat them like you would any true member of the club. Isn't that what they want? Isn't praise and recognition the drug that makes up for the lumps handed out back in the newsroom? One might think so, but one would be wrong.

The affection journalists receive in the outside world is often shallow and unsatisfying. People honor them simply because they work for the Beast. Or they feign respect out of fear and/or greed. No rational human being wants to be treated special just because he/she is capable of doling out gifts or lashings. And yet, that's what happens most of the time. Journalists want what all creative people want—recognition for their work. But the praise must be sincere. Telling a newsperson that, "I respect what you do," "You're good at what you do," or the perfunctory "I know who you are" doesn't cut it. Reporters, photographers, editors, writers, and producers don't want generic accolades. They want you to tell them their work is good and *why* it is good. Otherwise, you're just another hack who wants a handout. Who needs it?

Therefore, successfully using the Rule of Ego requires that you do your homework. Don't just watch, read, or listen to the news. Analyze it. Pay attention to who is doing what. Decide what reporters do the best work. These are the people you're going to want to target anyway (Rule of Resource). Of course, you can't keep track of everybody or even every medium. Just decide which people and organizations are your best targets and watch them closely. When the opportunity arises to pass out a compliment, you'll deliver one that truly makes an impact.

You would be surprised what little recognition news people get from their readers, listeners, and viewers. Most of the sincere stuff that does pop up is the verbal kind, which is nice, but its impact fades quickly. If you really want to make an impression on a journalist, take the time to put your praise on paper. Believe me, it makes a difference. Every time I received a letter from someone who thought I produced an exceptional story, I would read it twice and drop it into a fan-mail file. If I ever heard from that person again, I would remember him. That's saying a lot for someone with newsheimers (a common condition among journalists where places, names, stories, and even cities tend to run together).

If a reporter or photographer does a good job on your story, send her a letter of thanks, and while you're at it, send a courtesy copy to her managing editor or news director. If you happen to notice an exceptionally well-done story, send a letter praising the good work. Don't do this too often, no more than twice a year to any single person. Like any self-respecting club member, journalists are suspicious of those who are too generous with their compliments. E-mail is okay for informal communication with news people you know, but when it comes to the important stuff, go to the extra effort and do it with pen and ink.

The warped world of the journalist makes him especially vulnerable to those who take the time sincerely to appreciate a job well done. God knows there's precious little appreciation being passed around the newsroom. The catch is, you can't cash in on this opportunity without taking the time to do it. Remember, "Busy blows it."

If you are successful in winning the favor of a news gatherer, cultivate that relationship and never abuse it. Don't forget that he's got a crazy, rich uncle.

Ego? Me? . . . Really?

For most of us, worrying about the Beast's Ego is not time well spent. If you're ignorant enough to insult a newsperson, she will snub your advances—or worse. But I trust that you're a lot smarter than that. Reasonable, considerate people who abide by the Media Rules need not fear the wrath of the Beast. Journalists are not in the business of attacking victims at random. However, they do enjoy feasting on people who, because of their massive egos, do and say really stupid things.

I can see the videotape in my mind's eye. "I did not have sexual relations with that woman, Ms. Lewinski." You might say President Clinton got a little cocky. After five years starring as Teflon Man, he began to underestimate the power of the press. The gaffe proved to be politically fatal—almost. Amazingly, Clinton did not repent after his near-death experience. In the final hours of his presidency, "Slick Willy" pardoned billionaire fugitive Marc Rich and a whole passel of other criminals. The news media were not amused, nor were the American people. Even Clinton's fiercest defenders had to admit that this was a blunder of egomaniacal proportions. But that's the queer thing about ego, isn't it? Those who are most afflicted are those who are least aware of it.

But Bill Clinton didn't invent the presidential ego bomb. When William Jefferson was but a mere war protestor at Oxford, Richard Nixon was concocting the worst White House implosion in United

States history. Ego told Nixon he could use the FBI and the CIA for his own political purposes. Unrestrained self esteem led Nixon to put wiretaps on the phones of White House aides and reporters. And it was ego that convinced Nixon he could cover up his misdeeds by breaking into the Democratic National Committee Headquarters at the Watergate Hotel. As "Tricky Dick" found out, the greatest thrill in any reporter's life is exposing anyone who has done something wrong and then had the audacity to lie about it. The Beast takes such deception personally. We'll examine this particular issue in the next chapter.

... that's the queer thing about ego, isn't it? Those who are most afflicted are those who are least aware of it.

What Clinton and Nixon found out (the hard way) is that the Beast must always be treated with respect. But because familiarity breeds contempt, those who interact with the news media on a regular basis have a tendency to get sloppy. Their egos supersede a healthy wariness of media power, and that's when the trouble begins.

Former professional wrestler Jesse "The Body" Ventura expertly used the news media to win the governor's chair in Minnesota. Voters in the Land of 10,000 Lakes loved his no-nonsense approach to the political process and his snappy framing of blue-collar issues. To put it mildly, the man is a walking soundbite. With his gregarious style, the Reform Party candidate seduced the Beast and pulled off one of the most surprising upsets in recent memory. Ventura demonstrated an uncannily deft touch at using the press to his advantage. Then all the success went to his head.

Not long after moving into the governor's mansion, Ventura began referring to the press room in the capitol as the "rat-infested basement." He told the media that he was going to install heavy-duty shock absorbers on his Lincoln Navigator so it could run over reporters. Ventura even went so far as to ask a reporter to accompany him on a hunting trip, and then he graciously offered to give the reporter a 100-pace head start. *Newsweek* quoted one capitol reporter as saying, "If he thinks the questions are tough now, this is only the beginning." For Ventura, it was only the beginning. Seven months later The Body was featured in a *Playboy* magazine article. In it he called organized religion "a sham and a crutch for weak-minded people." He claimed President Kennedy was murdered by assassins hired by the "military-industrial complex" because Kennedy was planning to withdraw from Vietnam. Ventura insulted fat people claiming that they "can't push away from the table," and he rounded out the verbal assault by calling the infamous Tailhook scandal "much ado about nothing."

The mistakes made by Ventura, Nixon, and Clinton should make one thing abundantly clear: As soon as you start thinking that you're intelligent enough to get away with insulting the media's intelligence, you're ready for a fall. That goes for the heavy hitters as well as the little guy.

Public Leaders and Control Freaks

It's easy to see why leaders are so prone to violating the Rule of Ego. It's a control issue. Leaders are used to being in charge. They tell other people what to do, and for the most part the underlings do as they are told. So it's difficult to change gears and behave differently in a situation where controlling someone is inappropriate. (How many leaders have lost their families and friends because they are unable to stop being in charge once they've left the office at the end of the day?) Although this problem plagues leaders of all stripes, those who work in government are the most afflicted. Let's take a look at a few real world examples. Names will be withheld to protect the guilty.

I once covered a story in which a county treasurer's competence had been called into question. A newspaper reporter had uncovered some unethical, if not criminal, misconduct within the treasurer's office. The county official responded by calling a press conference to address the accusations. After the treasurer had read an opening statement, he invited the dozen or so reporters in attendance to ask questions. The newspaperman who had broken the story immediately fired the first shot. The treasurer refused to answer the question and announced that he would not acknowledge the newspaper reporter because he had misrepresented the facts in his original story. What was this guy thinking? Did he really believe that all the other reporters would just go along with what he said because *he* was the public official and this was *his* news conference? The treasurer's arrogance made his problem much worse and our stories much better. I immediately jumped out of my chair and asked the public official the same question. He hesitated for a moment, which prompted a third reporter to yell, "Just answer the question." What followed was probably the most humbling half-hour of this man's life. With great excitement we pummeled his every remark. And after he was beaten into a pitiful pulp, we all raced back to our stations and newspapers to convince our producers and editors to elevate the scandal to "lead story" status. What great fun we had.

Then there was the public official who was arrested for speeding and drunken driving while trying to chase down his girlfriend. (His wife apparently wasn't interested in a late-night joy ride.) Several days later the official tried to introduce an ordinance that would have prohibited any business from even applying for a liquor license in his district. Clearly, this man was trying to muddy the water by attempting to attach his name to a second, presumably positive, alcohol issue. But his plan began to unravel when the president of the governing body said that the measure had not been submitted on time and, therefore, would not be considered until the next meeting. Enraged, the philandering official with multiple drunken-driving arrests held court with reporters outside the meeting. After allowing him to vent his frustrations, I asked the official about the suspicious timing of his anti-alcohol efforts. I thought the guy's eyes were going to pop out of his head. He screamed his answer back at me—and our camera—and suggested that the next liquor license granted would be to a bar in my neighborhood. He couldn't have made me happier. We suddenly had a new lead story. I especially liked showing our audience that it was my question that provoked the public official's conniption.

I recently saw a similar violation of the Rule of Ego when a TV reporter pursued another civic leader on an ethics issue. The powerful lawmaker had a consulting contract with a large organization that did tens of millions of dollars in business with the state. The leader claimed that he only consulted on projects outside the state, so there was no conflict of interest. What? Did he really expect reporters to just say "okay" and not question at least the appearance of impropriety? In spite of the legislator's persistent denials that he was doing anything wrong, the reporter kept pressing the issue. Finally, the leader lost his cool. He told the reporter that no matter how many times he asked, the answer would be the same. Red faced and breathless, he angrily told the reporter's camera "There is no conflict! There is no conflict! There is no conflict!" Oh, the sweet smell of success. The lawmaker's outburst was the first thing viewers saw and heard on that night's newscast. Before long the legislator had no choice but to give up his lucrative contract. His fellow lawmakers later voted him out of his long-held leadership position.

Try to put a collar on the Beast, and he will surely bite you. Reporters have a natural aversion to being controlled, and they enjoy nothing more than smacking down those who egotistically try to strong-arm their way through the news process. This is true for both negative *and* positive stories. Ask any reporter if he or she has encountered a public leader who has been too aggressive in trying to control a positive story. You're likely to get a snarl and a list of names. Whenever I encountered a political or government official who worked too hard at using me to get his name and face more recognition, I worked just as hard to deny him the satisfaction. Help a journalist, and he will like you. Get pushy, and he will push you back.

Lip Service Can Lead to a Fat Lip

For those in the private sector, control isn't so much of a problem as neglect. Corporate leaders and their hires tend to be so overwhelmed by all the tasks in front of them that they don't take the time to work through a media strategy for each potential story. Unfortunately, a lot of these people wouldn't take the time even if it were a gift. That's right, they would leave it sitting on the desk while their egos reassure them that they don't need it. It's a big mistake that I hope this book will keep you from making.

CEOs are the worst. It's a rare corporate leader who fully appreciates the power of the press. I'm not talking about what they *say* about the Beast. No executive worth his stock options would dare tell anyone that the company's image as portrayed by the news media isn't a high priority. Such heresy would likely lead to a contract buyout. But what CEOs *say* about dealing with press coverage and what they *do* about it are often two very different things.

The CEO's lack of preparation for media issues is centralized in three areas. First, he believes that, for the most part, media coverage is not his job. That's why he employs public relations and marketing people. Second, he believes that if he needs to get involved with a press issue, his staff will be able to get him up to speed in a quick briefing. And, third, he only has time to deal with this stuff on an "as needed" basis. He's an important guy who has a lot of other pressing issues to deal with. Besides, he's done lots of interviews before, and he's done okay. For these three common CEO beliefs, I have three one-word responses: wrong, wrong, and . . . wrong.

A good CEO is the leader of a company's image team. The marketing and/or PR staff is there to carry the load behind the scenes and to handle mid- to bottom-level press inquiries. The higher-level stuff is (or should be) the responsibility of top-tier management. To anyone who disagrees with this structure I have one question: Other than making critical management decisions, what could be more important to a CEO than protecting or enhancing the company's reputation? A lot of corporate leaders will agree, but only a small percentage will actually take the time to do the work. That work consists of study, training, and ongoing participation.

As you have seen throughout this book, dealing with the news media is unlike any other endeavor you will encounter in life. The Beast has a unique set of handicaps and motivations that require you to use a specific set of rules in order to be successful. Many of these rules are counter-intuitive. That's why so many people violate them and wind up getting burned by journalists who meant no harm.

A reporter has questions, and you have answers—lots of answers. That violates the Rule of Simplicity. A reporter calls up and asks for an interview, so you give him one—right then and there. That breaks the Rule of Preparation. During the interview, you give the reporter detailed, factual answers. Without knowing it, you ignore the Rules of Emotion, Simplicity, Difference, Easy, and Repetition. The story appears, and you scream with frustration at the incompetence of the Beast, not realizing it is *you* who has failed.

Ego tells the CEO—and anyone else who will listen—that intelligence, charisma, and experience are all that are required to win the

Beast's affections and duck his punches. Ego is a liar. Intelligence and charisma are inadequate tools when wrestling with the Beast. And, contrary to the egomaniacal among us, *experience does not equal skill.*

Who? Me?. . . I Already Know this Stuff

The Rule of Ego was a primary reason I took the time to write this book. (My own ego was of course a factor as well, but right now *you're* on the shrink's couch, not me.) As I have conducted Media Rules conferences over the past several years, I have been most frustrated by one recurring problem: Those who most need the help are those who are least willing to accept it. Reading a book is a nonthreatening way of getting help without letting on that you need it.

When I host "open-call" conferences, to which anyone with the motivation and the cash is invited, few CEO's or other top-level people will come. As an established leader, they either think they know how to deal with the press or they are afraid to admit even partial ignorance. Private conferences for individual organizations work the same way. The big boss is too busy to attend—she's called away at the last minute on more important matters or she pops in and out throughout the session. Then there are those who hire me for individual training. While these folks demonstrate a much higher level of commitment to learning the Media Rules, most of them occasionally cancel or reschedule appointments because of "more important matters." Does this hurt my feelings? No. But it does increase the chance that they will feel the sharp pain that quickly follows when the Rule of Ego is violated. Remember Richard Nixon.

There is another group of people who let their egos get in the way of learning more about how to effectively deal with the news media. They are public relations and marketing specialists. If you are one of these people, I can empathize with your fear. Who wants to admit to the boss that he or she needs specialized training in an area within his or her expertise? I wouldn't, especially because the boss is likely to take a dim view of my lack of knowledge. She may grumble, "Don't you know this stuff already?"

The truth is, public relations is a generic job description that encompasses an incredibly broad range of duties from writing, to event staging, to internal communications, to dealing directly with reporters, to a hundred other jobs in between. And because of PR's catchall nature, only a small percentage of its practitioners are truly skilled in the sub-category of media relations. As we noted in chapter 8, the Rule of Resource, a chief complaint of reporters and editors is that many PR people frustrate them to no end. Countless people who work as public relations specialists have little or no formal education in the field, and fewer still log any miles working for the Beast before coming to PR, not that experience working in the news industry makes one an expert at dealing with the press.

Even though journalistic know-how can be quite helpful in the PR industry, it can also be a great handicap. You may think that you can jump the fence from news to PR, but you may fall flat on your face. When you are a journalist, people come to you looking for high-value exposure. They treat you with deference and respect. You can be pushy and abrasive and not only get away with it but be praised for boldness by colleagues. If you make a mistake in reporting, it's typically no skin off your nose. Now, switch places with the PR people who practically *groveled at your feet*, and you'll find that the transition is not so easy. Habits must be unlearned, and new skills (like humility) must be acquired. It's kind of like believing that because you've been a customer, you will be an expert retailer. Those who've slipped behind the counter have the bumps and bruises to know otherwise—myself included.

Cowboy-Up

To properly abide by the Rule of Ego, take a lesson from the cowboy. Acquire confidence through diligent and careful preparation. Never assume anything about the Beast you plan to ride. Always show the animal the utmost respect. Keep your own ego stuffed way down in your pocket. Take these precautions, and the Beast will either award you with a prize or show mercy when you hit the ground. Get cocky, and you will surely be stepped on, kicked, or even gored.

For many of us, the first ten Media Rules are all we need to have a positive, productive, and safe relationship with the Beast. We're not into bull riding or saddle-bronc competitions; we're just trying to ride a good horse that will only buck in highly unusual circumstances. The Beast has little or no motivation to attack us . . . unless we do something really stupid. However, that isn't the case for everyone.

The Beast is pre-disposed to attacking certain groups, while going out of its way to defend others. In the following chapter, you will see that the Beast does his work with a weighted scale.

◆ ◆ ◆

CHAPTER 12

The Rule of Balance

~the beast has two left feet ~

One of the basic tenets of journalism is a commitment to objectivity. Journalists are called to report the news without bias. No matter their political, cultural, or sociological philosophy, they are supposed to report the news straight up. It's a wonderful ideal. It's also a crock.

The mainstream press leans to the left. It does so for four reasons, two of them fundamental and two of them practical. On the fundamental side, it's highly unrealistic to expect any human being not to be influenced by his or her own biases. It's simply not possible. While "objectivity" is a worthy goal, it is not attainable. Additionally, as we discussed in chapter one, the vast majority of people who work in news have a more liberal view of the world. Because of their liberal pre-disposition, the stories they choose to cover and the manner in which they report them reflect a liberal bias. You might say that *the Beast has two left feet.* (More explanation on this in a moment.)

Practically speaking, the goal of objectivity often stands in direct conflict with another highly-valued principle, the mission to "comfort the afflicted and to afflict the comfortable." The media are obsessed with the notion of protecting "victims." As I will demonstrate, in the Beast's attempt to protect the downtrodden, it has created an entire class of "poor me" monsters. Finally, and perhaps most importantly, the liberal agenda is very friendly to the Media Rules. Those who whine, complain, and attack have a distinct advantage in that they can easily find Difference, Emotion, and Simplicity. Conversely, those perceived to be "comfortable," have the unenviable task of defending their territory—which tends to have a lot less DES.

Prepare to understand the news media's unique sense of balance. It stands on a hill that slopes to his left. And the Beast has a big rock in its left pocket. That rock is called Manhattan.

The Heart (and Mind) of the Beast

If Washington, D.C., is the political center of the planet, then Manhattan is at the core of all that we call media. Ten thousand journalists work on this little rock that in geographic terms is infinitesimal by comparison to the rest of the United States—let alone the world. But in its ability to shape the views of a planet through journalistic endeavor, Manhattan is king. Los Angeles, Miami, Mexico City, Tokyo, London, Paris, and Sydney are all paupers. Manhattan is home to what is generically known as the "media elite," an expression that originates from a 1986 book of the same name. All the major networks are here along with Fox News, Time Inc., the Associated Press, McGraw/Hill Business Week, the *New Yorker*, the *Wall Street Journal*, and, of course, the *New York Times*. And those are just some of the biggies.

My Left Foot

When terrorists attacked America on September 11, 2001, they chose Manhattan. The move wasn't so much brilliant as it was obvious. What better place to strike fear in the heart of the free world than in the center of the media universe? When follow-up terrorist attacks came in the form of Anthrax, major news organizations in Manhattan were at the top of the terrorist's mailing list. The Beast's fear became our fear, and in a big way.

A month after the first Anthrax case was discovered, only four people had died and just a handful of others had actually been infected. And most of those people had contracted the highly treatable skin form of the disease. In spite of the extremely small number of casualties, the Anthrax scare had generated more national stories than the war in Afghanistan, where as many American soldiers had lost their lives in the same time period. News on the clean up and recovery operation at "ground zero" was relegated to the back burner.

The major networks were especially indignant at being targeted. NBC's Tom Brokaw said that his outrage was so great that he couldn't convey his feelings in socially acceptable words. ABC's Peter Jennings expressed his anger in similar terms. The interesting thing was that at that time not one person at the networks had even gotten sick, and yet Brokaw and Jennings overflowed with more anger than when the World Trade Center collapsed, killing thousands.

Unquestionably, the Anthrax story (and other bio-warfare concerns) was an important, compelling one. However, it was nowhere near as important as the 9/11 attacks or the war on terrorism. The point is that news people are human beings. They report most intensely on those stories that are nearest to them—physically, and, yes, philosophically.

The problem with having such a concentration of media power in one place is that journalists write about the world as they see it. They come to the job—and the city—with a certain set of values and beliefs. That mindset is then altered and/or reinforced by a New York–centric viewpoint, which is on the far left side of the conservative/liberal scale. It not only means that reporter bias is slanted to the liberal point of view, but also that stories important to the elite get more attention—such as gay rights, race relations, affirmative action, abortion rights, etc.

One case that demonstrates this bias more than any other in recent memory is that of 13-year-old Jesse Dirkhising. In September 1999, the boy was bound, drugged, raped, tortured, and murdered by two gay men. What was interesting about the Dirkhising killing is that it was so similar to the murder of University of Wyoming student Matthew Shepard—except that the roles were reversed: the killers were gay and the victim was not. The national news coverage was also reversed. While the story about the gay murder victim received massive coverage, the story about the gay murderers was almost completely ignored. But then the *Washington Times* held a mirror to the face of the media elite in a front-page article contrasting the difference in coverage between the two. Then Brent Bozell of the Media Research Center appeared on Fox's "The O'Reilly Factor." The consensus was that the elite media were exposing their liberal stripes. The glaring contradiction became big news on the Internet and on talk radio, but for more than a year the major networks, CNN, and the *New York Times* still refused to pick up on it. Finally, a story by prominent gay writer Andrew Sullivan of the *New Republic* broke the silence.

In April 2001, ABC ran two lengthy stories on the Dirkhising case, the first on the murder, the second on the charges of bias. In the bias story, Sullivan told ABC, "I think that there is clearly evidence that many in the media decided that, well, we're not going to go there because we know that it will feed anti-gay prejudice." Aaron Brown, now an anchor with CNN, concluded his report by noting that the Dirkhising murder did not generate interest because it was not connected to the large issues of gay rights or hate law legislation. Brown said, "That may seem cold, but countless murders —gay and straight—go unreported for exactly the same reason, which is part of what is so remarkable about the debate, that it centers on a news decision that for most of the national media was easy and logical and routine." Brown nailed the problem apparently without even knowing it. The liberal viewpoint of the elite is so ingrained that the conservative perspective may not even be recognized, let alone given thoughtful consideration.

A similar bias can be seen on other issues that polarize the right and the left, with religion being tops on the list. According to a Pew Research Center study in the mid-1990s, nearly 60 percent of the public believes that the personal values of journalists make it difficult for them to understand and report on such things as family values and religion. A companion study found that 40 percent of journalists agree with this criticism. A survey by the Public Agenda Foundation found that nearly half the American public believes that the media's coverage of religion is worse than its reporting of other issues. In that same survey, people were asked if they thought that journalists had a built-in bias against religion. Fifty-six percent said yes, and 46 percent of journalists who were polled agreed.

Perhaps the most obvious reason that the media don't cover religion well—or enough—is that they don't employ people who truly understand it. There is no way to quickly get up to speed on the doctrine of Christians, Jews, Muslims, Buddhists and others. To make matters more difficult, a lot of what people think they know about other faiths—or even their own—is inaccurate. It takes expert knowledge to responsibly cover religion—something most news providers don't have. For example, not one of the major networks has a regular religion correspondent. (Peggy Wehmeyer used to cover religion for ABC, but the network did not renew her contract in October 2001). And since the networks are unprepared to cover faith-based stories, they rarely do. Studies conducted by the Media Research Center have revealed that less than 1 percent of network news time is devoted to overtly religious activities.

While the national news media heavily skew their coverage in favor of what is important to Manhattanites, the slant is not always to the left. Most of the time, however, it is. On the issue of the death penalty, national reporters focus their attention on the murderers who will be executed. The families of the victims, meanwhile, are virtually ignored. (The Timothy McVeigh case is a notable exception because of the heinousness of his crime.) The elite concentrate their coverage of the gun control debate on restricting Americans' access to firearms. The opposing view that allowing people to carry concealed weapons to deter crime is not discussed or roundly ridiculed as a terrible idea. The same kind of liberal bias is apparent in news coverage about abortion, the environment, and race relations.

Political Persuasion in the Press

The evidence of a significant liberal bias among the media elite is voluminous. It is most evident in the political process—the venue where a liberal viewpoint can have an impact on the shaping of public policy. We don't need to get into the minutiae of it all, but in the interest of thoroughness, please indulge me while I roll out some statistical and anecdotal evidence.

At the top of the list is CBS news anchor Dan Rather, who, in spite of great effort, cannot conceal his liberal persuasion. In the spring of 2001, Rather appeared as a guest speaker at a Democratic Party fundraiser in Austin, Texas. After conservative members of the media lambasted Rather, he conceded, "I made an embarrassing and regrettable error in judgment by going to this event." During an interview with Bill O'Reilly on "The O'Reilly Factor," Rather was asked about the honesty of Bill Clinton. The CBS anchor told O'Reilly, "I think at the core, he's an honest person. . . . I think you can be an honest person and lie about any number of things."

Dan Rather, who has openly admired Hillary Clinton's "political lightning" and her talents as a "crowd pleaser," is just one of many CBS journalists who has a tough time feigning objectivity. CBS "Early Show" anchor Bryant Gumbel is another. After interviewing a member of the conservative Family Research Council, CBS cameras unintentionally caught Gumbel saying, "What a _____ing idiot!" On another occasion, Gumbel's co-anchor, Jane Clayson, showed her own liberal mindset (or at least that of her producer) while interviewing Republican Representative J. C. Watts of Oklahoma. Clayson asked, "As an African-American, do you have any difficulty supporting (Dick Cheney), who voted against releasing Nelson Mandela from prison?" This was a highly misleading question because Cheney's vote—as well as that of many Democrats—was against the Communist-run African National Congress, not against Mandela's release. If you crave more information on the left-leaning tilt in network news, pick up Bernard Goldberg's illuminating book *Bias: A CBS Insider Exposes How the Media Distort the News.* Much to the chagrin of his former co-workers, Goldberg, a 28-year veteran of CBS, airs one massive load of dirty laundry.

I could go on and on with revealing comments made by the elite from all networks, but is that really necessary? In case you need more convincing consider the results of a 1992 Roper poll of Washington reporters and bureau chiefs. Eighty-nine percent voted for Bill Clinton, while only 7 percent voted for George Bush Sr. Eight years later, the Beast's preference for the Democratic Party was just as pronounced. *Editor & Publisher* magazine, which reports on the newspaper industry, found that "almost two-thirds of those who perceive bias feel that the candidate who has been 'favored' is: Al Gore" (2000). Even Democratic political specialist Charles Cook couldn't deny the pro-Gore slant. The writer for *National Journal* magazine and publisher of the *Cook Political Report* declared: "When Gore took off in the polls, it seemed like a firehouse bell going off, with reporters larding their stories with their own ideological biases. It was not a pretty sight."

One issue that always draws out elite media bias is the subject of tax reduction. Listen to what some of the elite had to say about President George W. Bush's tax cut proposal, which the National Taxpayers Union found to be much smaller than the Ronald Reagan and JFK tax cuts. *Newsweek*'s Jonathan Alter (2001) called George W.'s plan "one of the most irresponsible pieces of legislation to come down the pike in a long time." Alter claimed that "every economist" knew a tax cut would be totally irresponsible. In fact, many conservative economists favored Bush's plan. *Time*'s Margaret Carlson called the tax cut idea just plain stupid: "The only thing that could explain this love of tax cuts is a lowered IQ." The major networks were equally as biased. The Media Research Center analyzed every ABC, NBC, and CBS evening news story on the tax cut from January 20 to March 31, 2001. The study found that the liberal position (the tax cut was "massive" or "huge") was quoted five times more often than the conservative position (the tax cut is extremely small in contrast to the overall budget). The survey also showed that the network anchors (led by Dan Rather) expressed their personal opinions that the tax cut was "big" or "very big" 30 times. The MRC reported that not once did a broadcaster call the tax cut modest or small. Nor did they mention that the top five percent of wage earners carry more than half of the tax burden.

The spectrum of the media elite is not entirely left-leaning. The conservatives, for the most part, own talk radio. The king of all conservative talk is, of course, Rush Limbaugh. "El Rushbo's" broadcasts are syndicated on nearly 600 radio stations for three hours daily across all 50 states and Guam. When Limbaugh steps away from the microphone (which could be soon because of a sudden and dramatic loss of hearing in the summer of 2001) another staunch conservative will be found to fill the void. Rush's female, family-friendly counterpart is Dr. Laura Schlessinger. Dr. Laura is a dominating force on radio, but, like Rush, her attempt to spread her message to a television audience failed. I'll explain why in the following chapter, the Rule of Ambush. Many stations carry both Limbaugh and Schlessinger and fill the balance of their time with local conservatives or other right-leaning syndicated talkers. The liberals aren't totally shut out on the radio dial. They have National Public Radio, universally known as NPR.

In spite of all the evidence of media bias to a liberal worldview, the elite continue to shrug it off. You might be tempted to ignore it as well. After all, the elite are dealing with national issues, and all you care about is the local stuff. Your local news organizations don't lean to the left. Or do they?

Local and Unconsciously Liberal

I can say with absolute conviction that the number of local reporters who want to foist their liberal views on the public is relatively small. And those who are on a crusade don't get that many opportunities to carry their torch. News people in cities across the USA spend most of their time covering stories that are happening close to home— many of which have no strong ideological basis. Additionally, there exists a media elite backlash in many news organizations. They pay attention to what the national press is doing, but all the while they shake their heads.

This anti-elite feeling—especially among newspaper editors— came out loud and clear in the March 2001 edition of the *Columbia Journalism Review*, which dedicated almost the entire issue to the subject of "How the Manhattan Mindset Shapes the Nation's News." Out of the dozens of journalistic contributors to the issue, there was a virtual consensus that the New York–based media have a moderately to severely warped view of the world. Sandra Mims Row, editor of the *Oregonian*, wrote, "[M]uch as we read, rely on, and revere the New York–based media kings, they are occasionally so culturally out of touch with the rest of the United States that it's fine sport for us to skewer them." *San Francisco Chronicle* editor Phil Bronstein told *CJR*, "Frankly, most of those *Time* and *Newsweek* cover stories about life-style 'trends' are months and even years behind the rest of the country." Jim Squires, former editor of the *Chicago Tribune*: "By the time something new and important becomes the grist of luncheon conversation and cocktail talk in the Big Apple, it has already made news somewhere else."

In spite of a general feeling among journalists outside New York City that they are more "in touch" with their audience, studies prove otherwise. You may recall the Peter Brown research that I discussed in chapter 1. Brown, an editor for the *Orlando Sentinel*, hired a polling company to see if there were any significant social and/or cultural differences between journalists and the people who live in the communities they serve. The study focused on medium-sized cities and one large metro area—Dallas Ft. Worth. Brown's data revealed a sizable disconnect between the two groups. Among the findings, journalists are more likely to live in upscale neighborhoods and trade stocks, while they are less likely to do volunteer work, put down roots in a community, or go to church. In short, the journalist in Tulsa, Roanoke, or Dayton tends to have a worldview more in line with the media elite in Manhattan than the residents in his hometown.

As I said before, I believe that much of the liberal bias among news people is unrecognized. Most reporters, producers, and editors don't consciously act on a liberal agenda. Instead, they make decisions about what stories to cover and how to cover them based on how they view the world. There is no conscious attempt to favor one side or the other. Journalists, for the most part, are so busy trying to get the job done that it never occurs to them how their own personal biases are affecting their work.

However, that is still only part of the picture—and probably the least important part. The primary reason that news coverage tends to lean to the left is that the news media are duty-bound to comfort the afflicted and to afflict the comfortable.

Comforting the Afflicted

It might be the most important mission of the press: Protect the weak. You don't need a study to prove that journalists strongly identify with society's victims. For the most part, that's a good thing because it's the press that keeps a society's big bullies from squashing the little guy. Without a free press, the strong—including the government—have a much easier time victimizing the weak. Just ask the freethinker who lives in Cuba or China or Iraq.

Besides, who wouldn't want to comfort a victim? Don't all socially well-adjusted people believe that they would stop along the roadside to help someone who had been beaten? Yes. Thank God there is a strong desire in many of us to be a Good Samaritan. The responsibility of protecting victims is perhaps the most honorable calling in the journalism profession. In fact, one of the most gratifying moments of my news career was receiving an award from a victim's assistance organization. That honor meant more to me than any plaque for exceptional reporting. I believe most journalists feel the same way about being a protector for those who need it.

If whoever established the Beast's creed to "comfort the afflicted" had stopped right there, it would have worked pretty well. Or, maybe, it could have continued, "comfort the afflicted and hold bullies accountable." But that kind of credo lacks the zippiness that the Beast loves. So, for the sake of parallelism, journalists are called to "comfort the afflicted *and* to afflict the comfortable." Unfortunately, this mantra raises all sorts of open questions that it does not answer. For starters, who, exactly, are the comfortable? And if an organization qualifies as comfortable, does that mean it should be the target of affliction? Who qualifies as a victim? And which "victims" need comforting?

The Jesse Dirkhising/Matthew Shepard contrast illustrates this point. The news media obsessed over the murder of Shepard because he was a member of an "afflicted" class of people—homosexuals. The Dirkhising murder was largely ignored because the heterosexual boy did not come from a "victim" category. And, as gay writer Andrew Sullivan noted, the elite chose not cover the Dirkhising murder for so long because it was assumed that the victim class (homosexuals) would be victimized further by press coverage.

The same brand of comforting and afflicting can be seen on a regular basis in issues involving race. Jesse Jackson is recognized as a champion of issues involving blacks in America. So, when Jackson fathers an illegitimate child the mainstream press aren't too interested (with the exception of Fox's "The O'Reilly Factor," that aggressively pursued the story). When it's revealed that Jackson paid his mistress, Karin Stanford, $120,000 a year out of the tax exempt Citizens Education Fund, the media yawned. The media elite didn't even care Stanford's "salary" didn't appear on the

CEF's original tax returns for 1998, which were prepared before the scandal broke. Jackson's lawyers called it "an oversight." Most of the press called it something to "overlook."

When blacks rioted in Cincinnati after a young African-American man was killed by a police officer, the press rushed to comfort those who had long suffered under the persecution of a rogue police department. At least that's what one would believe after watching and reading press coverage of the event. Reporters constantly repeated the fact that the Cincinnati police department had killed 15 people in six years—all of them black men. Sounds pretty bad, doesn't it? Now, consider a broader view.

When the *Cincinnati Enquirer* produced a crime series in 1999, it discovered that in the previous five years Cincinnati police shootings were extremely low for the surrounding region. In that time period, officers in Columbus, Cleveland, and Indianapolis had fired on civilians more than twice as often as cops in Cincinnati. The *Enquirer* also found that proportionally black policemen in Cincinnati shot suspects at the same rate as white. Yet you got the feeling from much of the media coverage that the riots were *necessary* in order to draw attention to a racist situation. The *Los Angeles Times* said, "While no one wants to say that the riots were good, there was on Friday an undeniable sense of relief that the mayhem . . . had laid bare Cincinnati's fissures. Now, perhaps, there could be progress." Perhaps the *Times* should take a look at the heavily black police departments in Detroit and Washington, D.C., that each kill about 10 civilians every year—four times that of Cincinnati.

There is no conspiracy here. The press is not out intentionally to pit blacks against whites, heterosexuals against homosexuals, men against women. Reporters are simply following the credo of protecting the "victims" of society. It's just that sometimes the victims are not so innocent and the "oppressors" are not so nasty.

Michael Kelly nailed the problem when he wrote in the

Washington Post, "for survival's sake, most journalists learn to see the world through a set of standard templates into which they plug each day's events." Conservative syndicated columnist John Leo agrees: "One of these templates is that newsworthy violence is the kind perpetrated by the strong against the weak (gays, women, and minorities). This is why reporters feel comfortable tapping out stories that fit the template but uneasy about reporting things like black-on-white crime or the rate of female violence against their male partners." Leo concludes, "It's about underdog status, the do-good newsroom ethic, and those darned templates."

Okay, so you get the idea that the news media has a liberal bent and that journalists want to be the champions of people perceived to be victims. So? What does all of this have to do with you, the publicity seeker? Why do you need to know this? Because in all likelihood you are on the list of those targeted for afflicting.

Afflicting the Comfortable

So who are the "comfortable"? It's a strange mix of people and organizations, many of which have very little in common other than the press perception that they wield power over a weaker class. The comfortable include any large public or private organization. It could be a government agency or a corporation. The comfortable are perceived to have wealth or power, though the perception is much more important than the reality. For example, anyone who owns a small business is typically going to be thought of as a member of the privileged class. The fact that you work 80 hours a week, rarely take a vacation, and sometimes struggle to make payroll is irrelevant. If you work hard at your job, own a home, and pay taxes, you are in the privileged majority. Anyone who doesn't fit these parameters is afflicted. This is a good starting place, but there is another element that often has more to do with news coverage than strong versus weak. It's called DES—the rules of Difference, Emotion, and Simplicity.

The truth of the matter is the news media don't just rush to the aid of "victims" because they are trying to do the right thing. Sometimes their true motivation is justice and fairness. However, much of the incentive is simply that it's more fun, more profitable, and a whole lot easier to listen to someone who is screaming. These are the kinds of stories that sell newspapers and bring viewers to the TV set. In the Rule of Balance, it's the complainer who has the power to do the afflicting.

. . . in all likelihood you are on the list of those targeted for afflicting.

When 34 governments came together to discuss free trade at the Summit of the Americas, protesters came and so did the news media. Activists—presumably speaking for the poor—threw rocks, sticks, bottles, and other items at the police who were trying to keep them from disrupting the conference. Protesters were especially upset that Quebec community leaders decided to put up a security fence two blocks from the summit site. They dubbed the fence the "Wall of Shame" and likened it to the Berlin Wall, a symbol of oppression and division. One protestor told the Associated Press, "The provocation started with that darned wall. There's a level of anger out there that responds to that sort of provocation. From where I'm standing, the provocation feels like 99.99 percent on the other side." Let me get this straight. Quebec puts up a fence to protect summit attendees from bottle and rock throwing protesters, and it's the summit leaders who are doing the attacking? Journalists don't cover events like this because they believe the protestors are being oppressed. They come (and report more on the protest than the summit) because it's an exciting, visual, and easy story to cover.

It's not any real or perceived oppression that journalists are most interested in. It's the screaming, yelling, name-calling, and hyperventilating that journalists like so much.

In New Mexico, a small but highly vocal activist group badgered Intel Corporation into reducing the emissions from a plant in Sandoval County. They complained loudly that the plant put out noxious fumes. Even after Intel spent millions of dollars trying to appease the group, its members still complained. These protesters, who lived many miles from the Intel plant, must have had pretty sensitive noses. I lived directly below the plant for four years and never smelled a thing. Nonetheless, every time the Intel harassers called, the news media was there to "protect" them.

Don't misunderstand me. I'm not standing on top of holy ground pointing a self-righteous finger. I know how irresistible it is to "protect" the less fortunate.

One day while driving down the highway in central California as a young reporter, I noticed a big bulldozer in a field. It seemed odd to me, so I investigated. What I found were a few shacks inhabited by a half-dozen vagrants that the city was about to demolish. I raced to get my cameraman, and we put together one heck of a tearjerking story. I was so excited to show everyone how those mean old city workers were taking away the ramshackle homes of the homeless. How dare they! The fact that these folks were illegal squatters was not the point. The big mess they had made of the city's property was not my concern either. I also wasn't too interested in the services that the city supplied to homeless people. The comfortable needed afflicting. Besides, the crash of the shacks as they hit the ground was awesome video.

You've seen some of these stories in your own community. A woman is told that she cannot breast-feed her baby inside a coffee shop because it makes the other customers uncomfortable. So guess what? She tells a breast feeding advocacy group that spreads the word and stages a "nurse-in." The news media are called and two-dozen women show up to breast-feed their babies. As one protester put it, "If anyone is uncomfortable with it, that's not my problem. They should learn to deal with it." So who is being afflicted here? Is it the in-your-face breast-feeder or the coffee shop owner who is losing business because the sight of baby having lunch suppresses the appetites of others? The reporter knows the "victims'" claims are exaggerated, but who can pass up such a titillating (sorry) story?

In the following chapter I'll talk more about those who use their "victim" status to attack others—namely you—and what can be done to minimize the damage. But now let's move on to one last potentially dangerous aspect of the Rule of Balance.

He Said, She Said

The very nature of the news business is pre-disposed to an "us versus them" structure. In almost any story, there will be disagreement. He sees it this way; she sees it that way. For better or worse, that friction is what drives most news reporting, and it's also what makes a story interesting. The reporter's quandary is that one person may speak for a few dozen people, while another speaks for hundreds, thousands, or even millions. In an ideal world, the journalist would be able to weigh the interests of the larger group against the smaller. She would have time to ask a few key questions. Is the minority truly being oppressed? Is the larger group behaving badly or acting irresponsibly? Are anyone's rights being trampled? Are the charges legitimate and reasonable? Is someone trying to manipulate the power of the press for his or her own political agenda?

But this is the real world. Reporters and editors don't have time to ponder such philosophical questions. All they know is that somebody is screaming that they have been wronged. So the reporter sets out to be fair and tell "both sides" of the story (even though there may be multiple sides). The idea is to present the facts, and let the viewers or the readers decide who is right. The problem with this approach is that it favors the complainers.

For starters, the activist wants the publicity. The person or organization being attacked for its alleged bad behavior does not. Simply covering the story lends credibility to the protester's point of view, while it tarnishes the reputation of the organization being attacked. Therefore, even if the activist's agenda is weak and the group targeted has a strong defense, the activist still wins.

Another problem is that protesters are free to do and say what they want, even if their claims are exaggerated or even untrue. Who is going to hold them accountable for making false or misleading statements? The press won't. That would mean afflicting the afflicted. I can remember the mother of a drunken driver who wept for the cameras on the steps of a courthouse. The elderly Indian cried and protested that her son was a good man. She, and others, suggested that her son was being persecuted because of his race. Such a claim was ridiculous. The truth of the matter was that her son got drunk at a strip club on Christmas Eve and sped down the highway in the wrong direction while police tried to get him to stop. The drunk crashed head-on into a car killing three little girls and their mother (and critically wounding the husband) who were returning home after a church service. In spite of these inconvenient facts, no reporter was bold enough to challenge the poor, afflicted, distraught mother.

Now let's say that you are the spokesperson of a large corporation. If you try to mislead or lie to the press, a horde of people will make you pay. Whistleblowers, disgruntled employees, and activists will feed the news media information. Government officials will want to know if any laws were broken. Stockholders, employees, and customers will demand answers. There is a huge penalty to be paid by the "comfortable" when they say and do wrong things. For activists, however, there is no one to hold them accountable.

The activist's position is highly emotional and simple to explain, while the organization being attacked must exist in a much more complicated world. A group of people that lives next to an airport screams and yells because the planes make too much noise. They hire sound experts who present a slice of the overall data, which suggests that the level of noise is "above an acceptable tolerance." While the complainers lob stink bombs, airport management tries to present a complicated picture of increased air traffic, runway construction, public funding shortfalls, and their own data which shows that noise levels fall within an acceptable range. The manager of the airport must weigh the interests of the flying public, the airlines, the community at large, the city council, the mayor, the FAA, and who knows how many other regulatory agencies. The protesters, who purchased their homes knowing that an airport was nearby, are free to pound away at one piece of a larger picture.

That brings us to my final point on this issue. Because a protester is free to complain about one specific issue, her message is highly focused. A tight, emotional quote or soundbite is exactly what the reporter wants for his story. Therefore, the activist gets her message across loud and clear. The "comfortable" organization being attacked has no such luxury. The spokesperson feels compelled to give the reporter the full context of the story. Even a summation of the most salient points is extremely difficult, if not impossible, to fit into ten seconds or ten words. Nonetheless, the reporter gives each side "equal time," and his conscience is clear.

This is what the Beast calls Balance.

Slightly Shifting Sand

There is a bright spot in this dark picture I have painted. In recent years, the Beast has shifted its weight slightly to the right. There are three reasons for this unprecedented and long overdue move. First, the public's dissatisfaction with the networks' liberal bias has caused people to tune out in record numbers. Second, the Internet is emerging as a powerful force for the exchange of ideas. And, third, the proliferation of new news sources on cable TV and on the Internet has given moderate and conservative voices a wider audience. Consequently, some "old media" have responded in a small, but noticeable manner.

According to a June 2000 report by the Pew Research Center for the People and the Press, only 30 percent of American adults say they watch national news on a regular basis. That's a 50 percent drop from 1993 to 2000. And it gets worse. Pew reports that only one-third of adults say they believe most of what they see on ABC, CBS, and NBC. Media analyst Michael Kelly writes, "With their chronic sensationalism and their chronic ideological bias, the network news divisions have forfeited trust." That frustration with network bias and a quick-hit story format has opened up opportunities for cable programs such as Fox's top-rated, "The O'Reilly Factor," a show that takes an in-depth look at only a handful of issues, often choosing stories that the networks ignore.

The networks have lost a significant portion of their audience to the Internet. The Pew study found that in 1998 35 percent of Internet users said they regularly watch a nightly network broadcast. Two years later that number had plummeted to 26 percent. Recently there has been an Internet shakeout that has caused many news providers (including the networks) to cut back on resources devoted to their web sites. However, once the Internet community figures out a way to make money from content other than using annoying and ineffective banner ads, its influence will continue to grow.

Finally, cable news and the Internet have forced the networks and other media elite to see how out of touch they are with the rest of the nation. Murder coverage of the Jesse Dirkhising case is a classic example. Without the influence of the Internet, talk radio, and cable TV, ABC and other members of the elite may never have considered the reality of their own bias.

Everything I've just mentioned is good news, even if it is just a faint cry in the crowd.

The Balancing Act

It serves no purpose to complain about the Beast's strange sense of balance. It may be shifting slightly, but significant change is not going to happen. To varying degrees local news coverage will always favor the liberal viewpoint. The media elite will continue to push the liberal agenda, either subtly or obnoxiously. Reporters will always be trained in left-leaning universities. Like it or not, it is what it is.

This does not mean, however, that there is no hope for the beleaguered "comfortable." To the contrary, there is a lot you can do to protect yourself. The key is to keep yourself and your organization out of the defensive position. Effectively dealing with the Beast's warped sense of balance requires that you actively use the Media Rules before the storm clouds are upon you. It also requires some delicate handling of those who would use the Beast to punish you—whether you deserve it or not. This is where the Rule of Ambush comes into play.

◆ ◆ ◆

CHAPTER 13

The Rule of Ambush

~ happy dogs don't bite ~

In the summer of 1975, I was a teenager visiting my grandmother in Long Beach, California. On one hot July day, my friends wanted to get off the sweltering sand and go for a swim in the Pacific. I went, but I was absolutely terrified. With the pulse of a scared rabbit, I constantly scanned the water looking for the horrific . . . the unthinkable . . . a dorsal fin! The night before my grandmother had taken me to see the movie *Jaws*.

Twenty-six years later my wife and I took our children to a Gulf coast beach. As we played with Waverly and Weston in the surf, I continually scanned the water for a fin. Just a few weeks earlier, a shark had attacked 8-year-old Jesse Arbogast, biting off the boy's right arm. His uncle heroically dragged the 7-foot shark to shore and retrieved the limb from the animal's gullet. Of course, the heartbreaking story received an enormous amount of news coverage, as did the fact that unusually high numbers of sharks were spotted feeding off Florida beaches. I knew that the Arbogast attack was extremely rare. I also knew that *my* 8-year-old boy had a greater chance of being killed by a falling airplane part than by a monster of the deep. And yet, I scanned the water for a dorsal fin. That is the incredible power of fear. Those who successfully engage the News Beast learn how to face this irrational trepidation and dive in anyway.

Any paranoia you have about being ambushed by a reporter on your way to the office is a product of the hype generated by "20/20," "Dateline," "60 Minutes," and your local TV station. No doubt you've also seen dozens of movies that show a pack of reporters rushing up to throw hostile questions at some poor soul. Or maybe you've taken a media-training course. The typical scenario involves an instructor who jams a microphone in your face and then peppers you with questions. My message to you: Forgetaboutit. It's all hype. The odds of you getting ambushed by a reporter are about the same as you becoming a Great White's lunch during your Florida vacation. There is a lot to be concerned about in the press, but a reporter jumping out of the bushes isn't one of them.

For our purposes, there are two categories of events that fall into the definition of "Ambush." In the first one, the Beast stalks you because of a wrong that has been committed. People who find themselves in this situation are typically corrupt and/or arrogant, or so scared that their fear overrides their common sense.

In the second type of Ambush—called "attack dog"—the Beast is not the instigator but a willing accomplice to someone who wants to hurt you. Don't waste your time worrying about the classic Ambush ruining your life, but always keep a watchful eye on the attack dog. He's the one that will jump out of the bushes to bite you if you're not paying attention.

If scenario one is akin to getting eaten by a shark, then scenario two is comparable to suffering a nasty sunburn while napping on the beach. We'll spend the latter part of our time in this chapter talking about the importance of proactively applying sunscreen (the Media Rules). But first, let's go for a little swim.

Hang 'Em High!

A classic reporter Ambush—the kind you've seen on newsmagazine shows—always follows the same pattern. Like any Hollywood flick, the Ambush has a three-act structure. In act one, a person or an organization does something wrong. In act two, the offending party denies the wrongdoing or tries to cover it up. The deception is then followed by the conscious avoidance of reporters. The climax of the story comes in act three when the reporter and photographer move in for the kill, camera rolling. The result is a sensational story that might as well flash big red letters that say . . . guilty! And you know what I say to that? Good job reporter! Hang 'em high! Every lying, cheating, and philandering scoundrel out there should get the same treatment.

This is where the misnamed "afflict the comfortable" really works. We should all want journalists publicly to humiliate the strong who abuse the weak or the powerful who think that the rules don't apply to them. When federal judges go on junkets paid for by lobbyists, let the cameras roll. Hurray for the journalist who sticks a microphone in the face of the corrupt Wall Street analyst. Kudos to the reporter who tracks down the fugitive who has raped, murdered, or pillaged. Hang 'em high!

This kind of Ambush is not your problem. It is a penalty reserved for those who thumb their noses at a watchdog press. That's what billionaire Marc Rich did when he fled the country to avoid paying tens of millions of dollars in taxes. ABC's Brian Ross hunted him down in the Swiss Alps to ask him about his bad behavior. The videotape rolled while Rich (Can you believe this guy is actually named "Rich"?) nervously waited in line to get on the ski lift. ABC also shot video of Rich driving away in his limousine. The slow-motion picture screams, guilty! Rich may have gotten away with his greedy scheme by way of a Bill Clinton pardon, but he has forever been branded as an exiled scoundrel.

Presidents can't be ambushed in the traditional sense, but when reporters sniff out buried corruption, the end result is still the same. President Nixon is probably the most famous "victim" of a reporter Ambush. Exposing the Watergate break in and the subsequent cover-up was one of journalism's greatest moments. It was also an event that led to a lot more Ambush journalism—which, for the most part, is a good thing. Twenty years after the Nixon fiasco, President Clinton wagged his finger at America and lied, "I did not have sexual relations with that woman, Miss Lewinski. I never told anybody to lie, not a single time. Never. These allegations are false, and I need to go back to work for the American people." Clinton briskly walked out of the room amid enthusiastic applause. The Ambush came later.

In each of these cases, the common denominators are dishonesty, arrogance, and, some would argue, stupidity. But more important than these is deception. There's nothing that arouses blood lust in the Beast more than tracking someone who has left the scene of the crime. And there's nothing the Beast enjoys more than solving a good whodunit mystery.

'Fess-up Already

Only in rare cases do people get ambushed as a result of evil intent or deliberate deception. In many more instances it's simply a matter of fear taking over after something bad has happened. It's the "If I just ignore the problem, maybe it will go away" philosophy. That kind of wishful thinking is what ruins careers, corporations, and confidence in public institutions.

It was just about a century ago that John D. Rockefeller Sr. found out—the hard way—that you shouldn't ignore a reporter once she has latched onto something deliciously scandalous. Rockefeller's nemesis was Ida Tarbell, a reporter for *McClure's* magazine. Tarbell had a pretty good idea that Rockefeller had used unfair and unethical practices to create and sustain the Standard Oil dynasty. She took it upon herself to use the story of Standard Oil to illustrate the widespread problem of lawlessness in business and politics. Tarbell ultimately studied and investigated Rockefeller and his company for five years. The result was a 19-part series called "The History of the Standard Oil Company." Tarbell's work rocked the corporation and greatly damaged its reputation. To his death, Rockefeller Sr. ignored this reporter, and for that she made him pay a much higher price than if he had simply come clean. The federal government ultimately broke Standard Oil into several pieces.

Unfortunately, there aren't many reporters like Ida Tarbell around anymore. But what the news business lacks in investigative doggedness is made up for by intense media saturation. If something begins to stink, it may take a while before the newshounds pick up the scent. But once they do, Forgetaboutit.

Most of us had never heard the term "tread-separation" until the summer of 2000. That's when *USA Today* "broke" the story about the deadly problem that was occurring in the Bridgestone/Firestone ATX tire. As we all found out, there was a pattern of ATX tires losing their tread at higher speeds, usually a highway, which would cause the driver of the vehicle to lose control. The typical case was a rollover involving a Ford SUV. The death toll for such accidents exceeded 100. Following *USA Today*'s story on August 1, 2000, tread-separation became a huge national story. Firestone executives were pummeled with questions and accusations. There was no escaping the onslaught. Eight days later, the company was forced to recall more than 6 million tires. A congressional inquiry would follow, as would the resignation of Ford CEO, Jack Nassar.

The interesting—and horrifying—aspect of this story is that Bridgestone/Firestone knew about the problem as early as 1996. At that time, the corporation was already dealing with lawsuits from accidents involving tread-separation. One of those lawsuits came from Jan Gauvain, the widow of a reporter from Houston, Texas, station KTRK. Stephen Gauvain died when the tread came off the left rear tire of the Ford Explorer he was riding in. Four months after the accident, another Houston station, KPRC, ran a story on the problem of tread-separation. According to a report in *Content Magazine*, three other local television stations aired similar stories over the next four years.

It's hard to imagine what Firestone executives were thinking. Did they really believe that the problem was going to go away? Didn't they notice that their big secret had killed a *news reporter*? Did they not understand that at some point the national news media was going to wake up and lower the boom? Charges of corporate arrogance may be in order, but fear of what a recall might do to the company is more than likely what led Firestone to play such a high-stakes gamble. Even though today's news media can be slow on the uptake, playing it for a sucker is a bad idea.

It's not just big shots that let fear get in the way of better judgment. Lots of little people are forever learning the lesson that it's better to give (unflattering information) than to receive (punishment for withholding it). If a mistake has been made or a wrong has been committed, go ahead and own up to it. Confession on your own terms is a whole lot better than having it beaten out of you on the evening news or in the morning newspaper. By the way, anything short of a full confession is a bad idea.

I can recall a story from my reporting days where a school district had over-promised and then over-spent. Because of some bad accounting and a great desire to please the voters, the school board had spent on paper millions of dollars more than it had in its account. So when budget time came, several schools found out that improvements such as new playgrounds, new buildings, and new roofs would have to be put on indefinite hold. More than a few people got a little upset, and the board hastily called a news conference. During that meeting the superintendent went through a jargon-filled tap dance in which he said a lot but confessed nothing. I made two attempts to get a coherent answer, but the superintendent was determined to get ambushed. So I obliged.

I told my unwitting victim that the people wanted to know who was at fault and that if he gave me more administrative-speak I would stop him. He started babbling again and, as promised, I yelled "whoa!" It was at that point that the school district's public relations specialist (the person to blame most for such a huge mistake) stood up and yelled at me to let him finish. Of course, all that did was get me revved up—camera rolling. I explained to all the mortified board members that I was asking a simple question, and I expected a simple answer. "Who is responsible for this blunder?" Finally, the school board president spoke up and took the fall. What a mess. My boss couldn't have been more pleased. The school board president chose not to run for reelection, and the superintendent did not have his contract renewed.

When something bad happens and the press needs to know, put your fear aside and take your medicine. If you don't, be prepared to suffer much more than might be necessary.

You Just Shot Yourself in the Foot . . . Officer

Being paralyzed by fear of the Beast is understandable. There is a tendency in all of us to just sit back and hope our problems will somehow go away. However, ignoring a reporter when he is politely asking for a little of your time is a dumb mistake born of arrogance. Unfortunately, it's much more common than it should be.

The moment you think you are too busy to talk to a reporter is the instant that you should smack yourself in the head with the telephone, or whatever else is consuming all of your time. Maybe the sudden trauma will bring you back to your senses. A bruise on the forehead will smart a little, but it's a lot better than getting hammered by the Beast for no good reason.

It's a sad reality, but reputations are damaged in the press daily because self-important people (Rule of Ego) won't take a few minutes to talk to a reporter. At a minimum these folks deny themselves the opportunity to present their side of the story. They run the foolish risk of angering the reporter. Or, at worst, the busy person forces the journalist to publicly chastise them when he otherwise would not. Public servants are the most common offenders, and the most notorious among these are cops.

One beautiful California morning, I was given an assignment that involved a small town police chief. The story did not involve any wrongdoing on the part of the chief or anyone in his department. I had a good relationship with the top cop and, therefore, expected no resistance to getting an interview. But he was apparently a really busy guy that day. After waiting hours to get an appointment, I decided to go to the police department in person.

I explained to the chief's secretary that my deadline was approaching and that, if the chief did not speak to me, I would be forced to tell our viewers that he wouldn't talk to us. My producer had given me two minutes to fill, with or without an on-camera comment from the chief. To my amazement, he could not be pulled away from his important business, not even for five minutes. Now I was unhappy. So on the 6:00 P.M. news, I stood in front of the police department and said, "We tried all day long to get an interview with the police chief on this issue, but he refused to talk to us."

The chief apparently took a lot of heat for his mistake. I heard through sources that he "hated" me. Too bad, I liked him and did not want to hurt him. He, however, gave me no choice.

Many years later in another state, I encountered the same type of situation with yet another police chief. This time the issue was the "Blue Flu." A massive number of officers were planning to call in sick the next day in protest of unsatisfactory contract negotiations. The story had nothing to do with the chief himself, but it did involve his men. After trying all day to get an interview with the chief, I told his public information officer exactly what I would say on my 6:00 o'clock live report if I didn't hear from him. I even gave the PIO the phone number to the live truck in case the chief wanted to place a last-second call. He didn't, and I told more than 100,000 people that the city's top law enforcement officer "just didn't have the time."

This chief was even more perturbed than the last. When another reporter from our TV station showed up the next day to follow-up on the story, he gave my colleague a long, profane tongue-lashing and subtly implied that someday I would pay for what I had done. Once the report of the chief's outburst hit the newsroom, we all had a good belly laugh.

I had no interest in damaging the reputations of either of these men. And, in truth, I wasn't the one who did it. They chose to ignore a reporter who was doing his job.

Hit Me with Your Best Shot

You've probably seen it in a half-dozen movies. It's the scene where one guy sticks out his chin and bravely tells the other guy, "Go ahead . . . take your best shot." If you ever find yourself in trouble with the press, pretend you're the one who is asking to get punched—only replace the machismo with humility.

It seems counter-intuitive, but the best way to deal with a disaster in the press is to step up and take the hardest punch the Beast can deliver. Don't flinch, don't dodge, don't do anything but stand there and take it. You could get bloodied something awful, but it's a lot better than the alternative—getting pummeled over and over again.

The strategy here is to stop your negative story from "growing legs." This is the dark side of the Rule of Repetition. When you delay owning up to a mistake or wrongdoing, the Beast has a chance to punch you in the face repeatedly until the confession comes. With every story, your name and your organization's image are degraded. If you lie or hold back important information, then the story sprouts legs, because it *will* come out. The Beast's blood lust is aroused, and now you're in real trouble. The story spreads to additional media, the frequency of reports increases, and you become an unwilling punching bag. It's not a pretty sight.

> the best way to deal with a disaster in the press is to step up and take the hardest punch the Beast can deliver.

That's what happened to Bill Clinton during the Monica Lewinski affair. After the story broke, Clinton went into full denial mode. He adamantly professed his innocence, but his power play only served to make reporters hungrier for the full story. Every so often a new detail would emerge and that was enough to keep the story moving—for months. The Beast hammered away in every newspaper and magazine, on TV, and on the Internet. With each new hit Clinton's integrity diminished. The D.C. beltway hadn't seen a story with legs this strong since Nixon got into the recording business. It was as if Slick Willy thought he could become Rocky Balboa—somehow receiving more strength and resolve with every punch from Apollo Creed. It didn't work—unless, that is, he wanted to look like a post-fight Rocky.

It's my firm belief that if Bill Clinton had immediately confessed his sin and sincerely apologized to the nation that the Lewinski matter would have been just a pothole instead of a chasm. There would have been no impeachment. Without the constant beat of controversy in the press, Congress would have lacked the will to punish the president. People have an amazing capacity to forgive those who are truly remorseful, but unless the truth is forthcoming, people are happy to watch the Beast draw blood.

Lawyers Should Stick to Practicing Law

Perhaps Bill Clinton got some bad advice from a fellow lawyer. It wouldn't surprise me. When people find themselves in trouble, they tend to stick common sense in their pockets and put all their faith in the best legal minds they can afford. Unfortunately, well-meaning lawyers muck up many more public image problems than they ever solve. The reason is simple. Attorneys look at any situation from a legal standpoint. While that's exactly what you want in a murder trial, it can be a killer in the court of public opinion.

Gary Condit spent most of August 22, 2001, huddled with his lawyers and advisors. He was mapping out his strategy for an interview with ABC's Connie Chung for the following day. It would be one of the worst interviews in television news history. Chung peppered him with questions about his relationship with missing congressional intern Chandra Levy. He danced. He dodged. He demurred. He showed no emotion and offered no apology for his bad behavior. So much for depending on the advice of lawyers and so-called "media experts." Apparently, these were the same people who had advised him to lie about his relationship with Levy, to stonewall the media, and to play games with the police. All the while the press beat him mercilessly. (And that creepy, pasted-on smile didn't help.) Did Condit learn nothing from Bill Clinton? Had Condit immediately confessed, apologized, and emoted, the Beast (and the public) would have shown him mercy.

I once had the opportunity to advise an all-star athlete who had been arrested for drunken driving. Too bad for him—he also had a lawyer. The attorney was certain that he could get the charge dismissed because the police had supposedly made some technical mistakes during the arrest. While that may have been true, the lawyer failed to understand that getting his client off on a technicality would have been the worst possible outcome in the case. The public is fed up with "privileged" people escaping punishment because they have the means to manipulate the system. Sidestepping justice would have forever tainted him in the eyes of most fans.

Unfortunately for the athlete, I was unable to convince his lawyer that in the public's eye beating the rap was as bad a crime as drunken driving. The ballplayer pleaded innocent. As the case proceeded through the courts, his name and picture were continually plastered onto the public consciousness next to the letters "DWI." Thankfully, at the last minute, sharper minds prevailed. The athlete changed his plea and spent a few days in jail. Then came time for the public apology. His well-meaning attorney wrote out a convoluted confession for the young man to read. *That* would have come across as sincere—NOT! To my great relief, I was able to persuade the young man, his parents, and his coaches that this was a bad idea. We worked for about a half hour structuring and then practicing his heartfelt apology (which it was), and then he delivered it to a room full of reporters and cameras. With one hard punch, that story dropped dead in its tracks. It was replaced with an outpouring of forgiveness and support. Too bad his lawyer had him get worked over by the Beast for a few rounds before yelling "uncle."

Honesty Really is the Best Policy

You've seen what not to do. Now let's take a look at a couple of cases that prove there is a much better way to go. It's called honesty without delay.

Professional golfer Notah Begay, a rising star on the PGA tour, made a big mistake in the winter of 2000. Like the previous athlete, he chose to get behind the wheel of a car after he had been drinking. When Begay went before the judge, he did something extremely uncommon in today's culture, and unheard of in professional sports: He immediately admitted his guilt and *volunteered* to the judge that he had a five-year-old DWI conviction in Phoenix, Arizona. By admitting that this was his second offense, Begay knew that he was turning a slap on the wrist (probably probation) into a week in jail, a fine, and community service. That straight-ahead shot was better than any swing he will ever take on the links.

If Begay had tried to avoid punishment through legal maneuverings or simply "forgotten to mention" his previous conviction, it might have ruined his career. Sooner or later, the truth would have emerged. Some reporter would have approached him on the golf course, in a parking lot, or in some other embarrassing location and nailed him with the truth. Begay would have been tagged as a two-time loser. But because of his full and speedy confession, sports reporters and others praised him as a role model.

Bob Ryan of the *Boston Globe* wrote a memorable article that came with an equally notable headline: "Looking for a hero? Notah 'I take responsibility' Begay's your man." Ryan asked, "How many contemporary jocks would call down the napalm on themselves, as it were?" The news media praised Begay for humbly and graciously accepting the consequences of his crime. Ryan spoke for a lot of people when he said, "You get the feeling that Begay is a man of such good sense and unquestioned integrity that he would emerge in a heroic manner under any circumstance." If Begay had tried to wiggle out of his problem, like so many other celebrities, the same reporters who praised him might have written articles telling him to get off the tour and clean up his act.

Of course, many bad news stories don't even have the potential of ending so well. For example, if Begay had gotten into an accident and killed someone, no amount of voluntary accountability would have cleared his name. However, even in the worst of situations a remorseful confession is still the best course of action.

On May 4, 2000, the National Park Service in Bandelier National Monument decided to conduct a "controlled burn." The fire wound up being anything but tame. Dry conditions and hot winds quickly overwhelmed the fire crew that had started the blaze. By the time the flames had been completely extinguished, 43,000 acres had been burned along with 400 Los Alamos, New Mexico, residences. Los Alamos National Laboratory had to be shut down for two weeks. A moment of poor judgment by several individuals turned into an absolute disaster. Were the people—even those not directly affected—just a little upset? I'd say so. But then an amazing thing happened. The Park Service learned the meaning of Proverbs 15:1: "A soft answer turns away wrath."

Karen Wade, regional director of the National Park Service, spoke to news cameras in a most uncommon manner. It was obvious to anyone watching that she and her colleagues were in deep agony over the agency's mistake. Wade accepted complete responsibility on behalf of the Park Service. She stood still and took the hardest shot the Beast could muster—which wasn't all that bad. Journalists and the public were still angry about the disaster, but most of the bitterness that had been building immediately evaporated when Wade softly said, "We are responsible for what has occurred . . . and the buck stops with us. My heart hurts for everyone tonight that has suffered a significant loss, and I wish we could turn back the clock, but we can't." The anger turned into a feeling of compassion for members of the Park Service, who were suffering right along with everyone else.

If Wade had chosen to make excuses—or to let even one hint of denial be verbalized—journalists and the public would have lowered the boom, and rightfully so. The lesson here is that the human race is capable of more forgiveness and compassion than our fear will let us believe. When things go wrong, just 'fess up and take the beating you deserve. And don't be surprised if hard-edged reporters pull their punches a little. They're human too, you know.

"Victims" Who Victimize

As I mentioned at the outset of this chapter, most of us will never come close to being ambushed by the Beast. No reporter is ever going to hunt you down if she doesn't have good reason to do so. However, every day journalists allow themselves to be used as someone's attack dog in the name of justice. Sometimes the harassment is warranted. Often times it's not.

In the previous chapter, the Rule of Balance, I demonstrated that it is the "comfortable" who are most likely to be damaged by bad publicity. That means you! Small business owners, large corporations, non-profit organizations, conservative political groups, school districts, universities, police departments—you're all considered comfortable in the eyes of the Beast. Those who have power or are perceived to have power are open to the attack of anyone who wants to come along and scream, "I'm a victim!"

The most dangerous activist is the professional victim. Los Angeles talk show host and columnist Larry Elder calls them "victicrats." These are people and organizations that have a political agenda. Their central mission is to use the news media continually to spread and reinforce their message.

Jesse Jackson is a victicrat. His goal of advancing the interests of black Americans is entirely honorable. However, his primary tool for winning the battle is not. Jackson and others in his organizations play on the news media's instinct to "comfort the afflicted." As we saw in the Rule of Balance, this strategy works well. It is much more seductive to the Beast than the opposing view that constantly trumpeting your victimization does more harm than good. Authors Thomas Sowell, Walter Williams, John McWhorter, and Larry Elder (all men of color) have published compelling evidence that Jesse Jackson and others like him are hurting the cause of black Americans much more than they are helping it. These four men, however, exist in relative obscurity because the media elite, for the most part, ignore them. Elder's book, *The Ten Things You Can't Say in America*, is a best seller, but you wouldn't know it from all the non-existent book reviews.

Beware of Dog

There's an 800-pound gorilla in the victicrat game, but it doesn't look like King Kong. Instead, picture the scene from the *Planet of the Apes* when Charleton Heston and his companions are captured in nets. The marauding apes represent the dozens of environmentalist groups that ceaselessly attract media attention.

The leader of the pack is Greenpeace, a group that long ago began employing Difference, Emotion, and Simplicity in its attempts to raise public awareness about the environment. President George W. Bush got a taste of what Greenpeace is all about not long after being elected. The group didn't like Bush's proposal to open the Arctic National Wildlife Refuge to oil drilling nor his opposition to an international global warming treaty. So a Greenpeace contingent went to the tiny town of Crawford, Texas, to harass the president. Three of the group's members climbed a water tower near W's ranch and unraveled a huge banner. It read: "Bush the Toxic Texan – Don't Mess with the Earth." While dozens of reporters gathered for the made-for-TV event, another Greenpeace protester distributed press kits to reporters. About two hours after the "protest," the Greenpeace crew ditched the banner and climbed down to be immediately arrested for trespassing. It was a small price to pay considering the media attack dogs went back to their newsrooms and turned the event into a national story.

The media success of those who scream racism or environmental sabotage has helped create a whole new class of professional victim groups. One of the powerful new players is the homosexual lobby led by GLAAD, the Gay and Lesbian Alliance Against Defamation. When popular radio show host Dr. Laura Schlessinger expressed her opinion that the homosexual lifestyle was "deviant," GLAAD took it personally. The group launched an aggressive attack against Schlessinger, winning mountains of free publicity along the way. Dr. Laura apologized for her comments, but GLAAD would have none of that. The attack continued and still does to this day.

GLAAD's crowning achievement was the cancellation of Schlessinger's TV show in March 2001. The angry homosexual group successfully used the news media to scare off sponsors, and it ultimately forced Paramount to stick the show in a late-night time slot. In 130 shows, Schlessinger never discussed homosexuality. Nonetheless, GLAAD kept yanking on the attack dog's chain.

Jesse Jackson, Greenpeace, and GLAAD have a lot of competition these days, and not just from the Sierra Club and the American Civil Liberties Union. The Ruckus Society is one of a few organizations that has taken the craft of victim-hood to an entirely new level. Ruckus is in the business of training professional victims how to protest against anyone who is saying or doing something they don't approve of. It's kind of like a school for would-be owners of attack dogs. These groups typically target high-profile people, organizations and events (World Trade Organization meetings, political conventions, etc.), which may not be a direct threat to you. However, there is a large and growing indirect problem that has the potential to impact all of us.

The dramatic increase in the number of professional protesters has correspondingly translated into an escalation of attack-dog reporting. The inevitable result is that people with a victicrat mentality have a lot of role models to emulate. These days it's easier than ever to do or say something that might unintentionally provoke a protest. It's gotten so bad that it's impossible for many organizations to avoid being bitten.

Appease the Bully . . . to a Point

The favorite targets of professional and amateur protesters are the centralized. The reason is simple. Big organizations are easy targets that are scared to death of bad publicity. They tend to move slowly and can be boxed-in politically because they are accountable to various groups that typically have different objectives (chapter 12, Rule of Balance). When the "victim" cries foul and the attack dogs come to the rescue, the "offending" institution feels powerless to do anything about it. Returning fire is usually not considered an option because there's a good chance of coming across as a bully—exactly what the protester wants. So what's a "victim's" victim to do? Just treat them like you would any other bully.

When I was in junior high, I made the mistake of offending another boy's girlfriend. He announced to me on the playground that he was going to "kick my butt." I told him I was sorry for what I had said, that I had no interest in fighting him, and then I walked away. He followed me into the boy's bathroom, where he pushed me. I tried to reason with him some more, but he wasn't interested. When a janitor walked in, I escaped. A few moments later he pushed me again in a hallway. I faced him and said I didn't want to fight. He called me a few names and threatened me. So I punched him as hard as I could in the nose and kicked him just as hard in the groin. He staggered away with a bloody nose and never bothered me again.

What I did in the eighth grade is the exact formula for the proper handling of a protester. First, do everything you can to appease them. The last thing you want is a fight. If an apology is in order, do it and be sincere. Make compensation efforts if necessary —they'll usually cost you a lot less than the bad publicity hit. Second, always be reasonable. Even when protesters call you names and falsely accuse you, keep your cool. Look for every opportunity to resolve the issue, even if the attacker has already stung you with some negative press. Third, stand your ground. It's not worth compromising your integrity just to avoid some bad publicity. Besides, standing up to a bully is an excellent way to get him to back down. Finally, if all else has failed, and the bully is intent on relentlessly stalking you, let him have it. Fight fair, but hit hard. (You might want to skip the kick to the groin). In my opinion, far too many organizations just stand there and let activists pound them mercilessly—usually on the advice of their lawyers.

Here's a classic case of what *not* to do when a "victim" uses the Beast as an attack dog. A high school senior severely beat his female teacher, sending her to the hospital. The 17-year-old boy pleaded guilty and spent six months in a residential treatment center. As the boy was about to be released from the center, his mother staged a "protest" to support the return of her son to school. The beaten teacher sought a restraining order to keep the criminal out of school, but a judge denied her request. So not only was the ex-con allowed to return to class, he was welcomed back with media-assisted support from protesters. In one article, a friend of the boy said, "He's so kind. He's kindhearted toward everybody." Really?

And what was the school district's response? The superintendent said, "We are committed to having a safe and healthy environment for all our students and staff, but we also have to make certain that we protect his (the assaulter's) rights." Yeah, right.

This ridiculousness provides us with an illustration of how completely terrified many large organizations are of people who use journalists as their attack dogs. The school district didn't even stand up for its own teacher! With this one instance of cowardice, the district completely compromised its integrity and demoralized a significant number of teachers, students, and parents. The worst part is that the school system made this mistake because of misplaced fear.

Yes, reporters want to comfort and afflict, but that doesn't make them stupid. The news people who reported this story knew that the kid was the bad guy and that the teacher was the *true* victim. But what's a reporter to do when the school district doesn't even bother to put up a fight? The press can't tell the other side of the story if nobody is willing to present it. If school administrators had stood up to the pressure, supported the teacher, and told the kid to take a hike, they would have been rewarded. Yes, there would have been more press attention—perhaps a lot more. But the community would have rallied behind the district, and the media would have had a chance to tell the other side of the story. By assuming that controversy in the press is always bad, the school district never gave the press a chance to do the right thing.

When you're wrong, admit the mistake, apologize, be reasonable, and bend over backwards to make it right. If someone uses the Beast as an attack dog, remain calm and reasonable, and speak softly. But if a "victim" demands that you compromise your integrity, forget your fear and stand your ground. If necessary, punch the protester in the nose as hard as you can. Would you respect someone who won't stand up for what is right? I wouldn't. Nor would any decent reporter.

Whipping the Whiners

I'm going to let you in on a little newsroom secret. While the Beast loves victicrats, journalists loathe them. It sounds like a contradiction, but it's not. The news machine adores whiners and complainers and protesters because they bring simple, emotional, sensational—and best of all—easy to cover stories. However, the people who have to deal with professional and amateur victims quickly grow to despise them.

Think about it. On the one side, you have people who are shrill, obnoxious, and demanding. They oversimplify problems and insist upon impractical solutions. They don't care what has to be done so long as they get their way. On the other side, you have mostly reasonable folks who are trying to do the best they can in a complex world. Who would you like better?

Every community has its victicrats. A handful of them—because of their persistence—become publicity regulars. Reporters have to talk to them because they are *told* to, not because they *want* to. Mention the name of a local activist group in any newsroom, and you'll hear a collective groan. Victicrats are the Cruella De Vils of the news business. Nobody likes them, but they're a necessary evil in order to tell a good story.

This one piece of inside information is the foundation of your strongest defense against the protester. The best part is you don't have to learn anything new. All you have to do is diligently follow the rules of Resource, Easy, and Ego.

Because centralized organizations deal with the news media on a fairly regular basis, they have lots of opportunities to establish good relationships with journalists. Following the Rule of Resource means that you make it your job to help out reporters at every opportunity. Tip them off to stories, whenever possible, and generally make yourself useful. The Rule of Easy dictates that you go to great lengths to reduce a reporter's pain. Whenever they need an interview or information, you're there to handle it quickly. And through it all, you are extremely nice and complimentary—the Rule of Ego.

Now here comes the victicrat to complain against you and your awful organization. How do you think the reporter is going to respond? If the protester has a weak case, there's a chance the story doesn't even get covered. But even if it does, your relationship with the reporter and/or news organization is going to have a positive impact on how the facts are told. Conversely, if you have no rapport with the reporter or, worse yet, a bad one, your chances of getting slammed are pretty high.

I once consulted with a group of progressive community leaders that had big plans for their town. But they had one sizable pain in their necks: a group of retired citizens that wanted to kill all projects that would change the city in any way. We called them the CAVE people—Citizens Against Virtually Everything. Because the group's members were highly vocal and had a lot of time to stir up trouble, they got a lot of press. There was no way to stop their whining, and we didn't try. Instead, we concentrated on building strong, cooperative relationships with members of the news media. The CAVE people still screamed, but their power was minimized. They eventually began complaining against the "biased" press— poetic justice for us. In the end, the community's leaders got what they wanted in spite of the murmuring in the background.

In my news career, I covered hundreds of stories that involved "victims" and the organizations they wanted to abuse. When I had a positive relationship with the group being attacked, it made a big difference in how I handled the story. In some cases, I think the activists groaned when they saw me coming.

Having an established relationship with journalists is the ideal situation, but it's simply not possible for many organizations that are de-centralized. However, the Media Rules are still in play. Cooperative and reasonable behavior will always be your best defense. Do everything you can to stay on the good side of media K-9s and their canines because *happy dogs don't bite.*

One client of mine was attacked after her organization raffled off an expensive car in a fundraiser. The "victim" in this case complained because she couldn't afford to pay the taxes on her shiny new prize. My client wouldn't give the complainer what she wanted (a big check to pay for the taxes), so she called a TV news consumer reporter. When the journalist called, my client cheerfully invited him to come to her office at his convenience. Upon his arrival, she calmly explained her side of the story and gave the reporter and his photographer a tour of the facility. Completely disarmed by her pleasant and reasonable attitude, the reporter decided to drop the story. If my client had been defensive and non-cooperative, the attack dog would have gotten angry.

The protester will always have the advantage in getting the Beast's attention. However, the victicrat's strength (shrill whining) is also his weakness. Use it against him by applying the Media Rules.

Bring the Sunscreen and the Surfboard

The lesson of this chapter can be summed up by considering two successful Hollywood flicks—*Jaws* and *10.* First, don't waste your time worrying about being swallowed up by the great white Beast. That spooky music you hear is just a bunch of hype. Second, don't let irrational fear keep you from getting in the water. Publicity is the most powerful form of marketing in existence—and it's free. Get in the game and take your share. But don't be like Bo Derek's husband in the movie *10,* who was so blissfully clueless that he got scorched by the sun. Slather on the Media Rules like you would high-grade sun-block. The victicrats are always lurking about to see whom they can burn. No one—least of all the centralized—is safe. Protecting yourself through proactive measures will minimize the damage when and if it happens.

The Hazards (Balance, Ego, Ambush) teach us that the Beast is not nearly so dangerous as it seems. Yes, the news media love to defend "victims." But that's okay. It's the news media's job to make sure the strong don't abuse the weak. The danger of the victicrat and other whiners is just a part of the game that we all have to deal with. Journalistic egos, too, are an inescapable mountain in the landscape. But to the skilled publicity seeker, that's no handicap—it's an advantage. The real danger lies in our own reluctance to be humble.

Fear Not!

Ralph Waldo Emerson said, "Fear always springs from ignorance." That is why so many people are scared of the Beast—they don't understand him. You, however, are no longer part of that group. You know the Rules that lie beneath all the commotion on the surface.

There are the four big problems that can make the Beast dangerous: He is Handicapped, Hungry, Harried, and Human. But you know that these four "problems" are actually the fountain of opportunity from which we all may drink. Without a clear understanding of these simple concepts, there would be no way to quickly, easily, and predictably position yourself to cash in on the publicity prize. And how easy that is . . . now that you are tuned into the fundamental truth that was in your head long before you picked up this book.

Why is the reporter interested or not interested in a particular story? Ask the Seducers. Does the news item have the critical elements of Difference, Emotion, and Simplicity? Good or bad, these factors should always be measured to see if they can be enhanced or even downplayed, depending on the situation.

Want to put the Seducers to work for you? No problem, simply consult the Enablers—Preparation, Easy, and Repetition. And don't forget the extra juice that the Aggressors can provide—Resource, Invention, and Timing. When problems pop up, you know right where to go. Your understanding of Ego, Balance, and Ambush will minimize the damage, if not stop it completely.

That's it. The process for creating winning publicity is no more complicated than the simple Rules described in this book. Anyone who makes working with the Beast more complex than this systematic approach is not someone you should trust. But you already knew that, even though you didn't read it in a headline.

EPILOGUE

At the beginning of this book I aroused your publicity palette with images of TV-bone steak, baby-back of the front-page ribs, tossed magazine salad, and rhubarb radio pie. I talked about the Beast liking meat and potatoes, while hating mayonnaise and cooked spinach. But as you now realize, feeding the Media Beast is never so cut and dried. If it were, anybody could do it, and you wouldn't need this book. I hope you'll forgive me for this slight deception, but I had to utilize the Rules of Difference, Emotion, and Simplicity to drawn you in.

In truth, the Beast only eats one kind of food—stew. That's because no news story ever contains just one Media Rule. As a matter of fact, you'd be hard pressed to find any news item that has fewer than half of the Rules. And this is why so many people are so frustrated in their dealings with the press. All they see is this confused mixture of ingredients that don't appear to make a whole lot of sense. But they want to cash in on the power of free media exposure, so they strap on an apron and turn on the stove. With less than adequate skills our would-be publicity chefs whip up some grub for the Beast. Predictably, the result is usually somewhere between bland and vile. They skimp on the meat, forget the spices, and ignorantly chunk in a few rocks and sticks. Then they're shocked when the Beast turns up his nose—or worse, takes a bite and spits the foul concoction back in their face.

You, however, are no longer one of these unfortunate souls. You don't look at the Beast's stew and see a confusing mess. Instead, you spot the key ingredients that comprise the soup that the Beast loves. Difference is the meat. Emotion is the spice. Simplicity is the broth. Then there are all the vegetables—Preparation/green beans, Easy/carrots, Repetition/corn, etc. The Media Rules are, quite simply, the recipe for publicity success. The system works because there is no confusion about how and why the media behave in the way they do. Let's digest a few dishes to see why the Beast feasted, or why he didn't.

In chapter 2, the Rule of Difference, I told you about Chicago photographer Steven Gross. As you recall, Gross has carved out a lucrative niche for himself as a wedding photographer by shooting non-posed pictures on black and white film. His work is clearly different from that of the mass of other photographers who churn out predictable, antiseptic, boring wedding albums. Gross is a poster boy for the Rule of Difference. However, I could have just as easily used him as an example for the Rules of Emotion and Simplicity. When done well, candid black and white photos are especially dramatic. Also, the idea of stripping away color from a wedding (a highly emotive occasion) is almost shocking. The first question a bride is asked about her wedding is, "What are your colors?" Gross's concept is extremely simple—no color, no staging of photos. This is the kind of story that a journalist has no problem grasping—immediately. There are other Rules at play here as well. It fits the Seducers so well that the black and white wedding photographer story has been told over and over again from "Good Morning America" to *Esquire* magazine to syndicated newspaper coverage —Repetition. It's an Easy and fun feature story. The concept also uses Invention (though other photographers have jumped on the bandwagon in recent years). Gross, as you might imagine, gets more press in the spring and summer wedding season—Timing.

In chapter 3, the Rule of Emotion, I told you about a report prepared by the United States Commission on National Security/21st Century. This very important report, which could possibly have helped authorities avert the September 11, 2001 terrorist attacks, received little attention in the national press. Why? It violated the Rule of Emotion. It is a heavy piece of bureaucratic work that failed to inspire editors and producers. But there were other problems that led to the commission's lack of publicity success. Members of the national press said the report looked like so many other warnings of terrorist threats prepared by Washington policy wonks in the past twenty years. But had the report preparers been sensitive to the Rule of Difference, their report would have convinced the media that the terrorist threat had escalated. And, of course, national security is a highly complex subject, something to put off even the most dedicated journalist—a violation of Simplicity and Easy.

If commission members understood the Media Rules, they could have approached this publicity opportunity in a completely different way. For starters, they could have paid a lot more attention to the seducers: discussed the terrorist threat in stark, dramatic terms; dumped the extraneous details to send a clear message; and emphasized the one or two issues that separated this document from past reports. Next, they could have staged an event making use of props and pictures (damaged U.S.S. Cole, World Trade Center bombing in 1993, etc.), anything to make the event visually appealing—Preparation, Invention, and Easy. The event could have been staged on December 7, 2000. Connecting the Japanese sneak attack on Pearl Harbor to the potential for a terrorist attack now would have been a natural for the media—Timing. Does this sound like Monday morning quarterbacking? I don't think so. The commission plainly stated that it expected an attack on United States soil in the near future that might kill Americans "in large numbers."

How about the Gary Condit case from chapter 13, the Rule of Ambush? The California congressman is also a natural fit for the Rule of Ego. Indeed, it was his self-assuredness that led him to believe he could control press coverage of his connection to missing intern Chandra Levy. If Condit had put his ego in check and understood the power of Emotion, he might have confessed everything right away and saved his political career. Instead, he found himself on the wrong side of Repetition—for months. And how about that interview with Connie Chung? He memorized a bunch of canned phrases (not how Preparation should be used), and stuck his heart in his back pocket. Not showing any remorse or sadness or concern in a tragic and highly controversial story is an blatant violation of the Rule of Emotion. Condit listened to his lawyers and bad media consultants and put himself through much more pain than was necessary. (I warned you about well-meaning lawyers in the Rule of Ambush.) Need I mention that the Condit case was also Different, Simple, and Easy to cover?

So what? Who cares? Having the ability to look at any news item and pick out the Media Rules is not valuable unless you put this talent to use for your own publicity needs. That means applying the system in a proactive way, *before* the Beast is engaged. You know the process. It is straightforward, practical, and clear. The system works the same for any publicity situation—positive story or negative story, hard-nosed interview, or softball interview, planned exposure, or unexpected exposure. It doesn't matter what the situation is—the Media Rules are there to help you make the most of it.

All publicity is grounded in the three Seducers. Find them in your story and play to that strength. Use the Enablers to simmer your material into something the Beast will want to devour. That includes the story itself as well as what you say in your interview. Constantly work the Aggressors so you can create publicity where none existed or spot opportunities that previous to your Media Rules knowledge would have gone unnoticed. Beware of the Hazards, even on a good news story.

If suddenly you find yourself in a bad publicity situation, don't panic. Stop what you are doing, separate yourself physically and emotionally from the problem, and work the system before you do anything else. Ask yourself some questions. How are the Seducers being used to hurt me? How can I use these same Rules to blunt the trauma or even turn them to my advantage? Which Rules have I violated? What is my message? Prepare the best response that works (even if it hurts), and constantly refer to the Rules as the story progresses. They will minimize the existing damage and keep you from creating any new problems.

As you have learned throughout this book, those who actively use the Media Rules are far less likely to get burned by the press. For most of us, worrying about negative exposure is a poor use of our time. Working the Rules to get more and more of the good stuff is where the publicity game is won. But, deep down inside, you already knew that. Now you know that you know it. The next step is up to you. Get busy Feeding the Media Beast . . . and enjoy great publicity success.